THE ILLUSTRATED ENCYCLOPEDIA OF

SMALL ARMS

FROM HAND CANNONS TO AUTOMATIC WEAPONS

THE ILLUSTRATED ENCYCLOPEDIA OF

SMALL ARMS

FROM HAND CANNONS TO AUTOMATIC WEAPONS

THUNDER BAY
P·R·E·S·S
San Diego, California

RUPERT MATTHEWS

IN ASSOCIATION WITH THE BERMAN MUSEUM OF WORLD HISTORY

Thunder Bay Press
An imprint of the Baker & Taylor Publishing Group
10350 Barnes Canyon Road, San Diego, CA 92121
www.thunderbaybooks.com

Publisher: Peter Norton

Moseley Road Inc.
129 Main Street, Suite B, Irvington, New York 10533
www.moseleyroad.com

Moseley Road
President: Sean Moore
General Manager: Karen Prince
Art Director: Tina Vaughan
Production Director: Adam Moore

Design: Andy Crisp, Heather McCarry
Editorial: Phil Hunt, Lesley Malkin
Assistant Editors: Finn Moore, Charles Robertson
Index: Finn Moore

Photography
Jonathan Conklin, Sean Moore
Additional photography by Richard McCaffrey

Additional Picture Research
Jo Walton

Chinese signal gun (see page 53)

Knife pistol (see page 67)

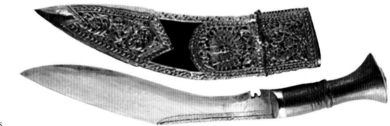

Kukri (see page 41)

Miniature key-pistol (see page 69)

Library of Congress Cataloging-in-Publication Data

Matthews, Rupert.
The illustrated encyclopedia of small arms / Rupert Matthews. -- First
edition.
     pages cm
Includes bibliographical references and index.
ISBN 978-1-62686-089-6 (hbk. : alk. paper) -- ISBN 1-62686-089-0 (hbk.
: alk. paper)
1. Firearms--Encyclopedias. I. Title.
TS532.15.M38 2014
683.4003--dc23
                              2014015823

Harmonica gun (see page 176)

Printed in China
1 2 3 4 5 18 17 16 15 14

Duckfoot pistol (see page 71)

CONTENTS

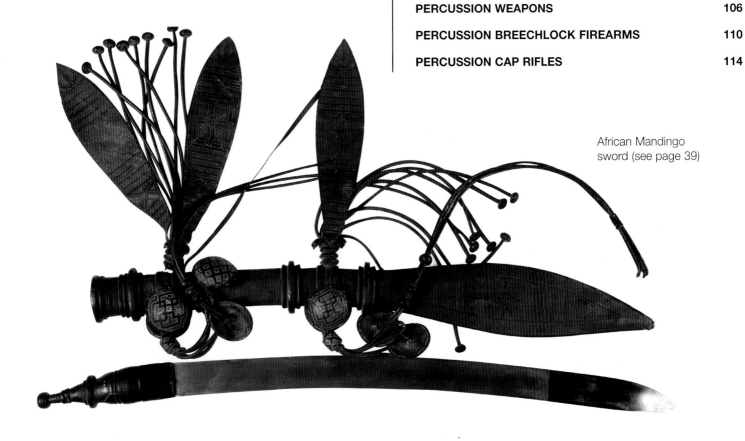

African Mandingo
sword (see page 39)

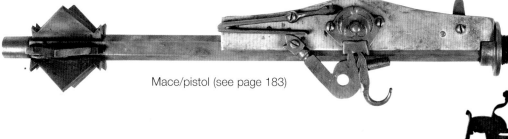

Yanyue dao polearm (see page 25)

Partisan (see page 22)

Mace/pistol (see page 183)

German wheel lock rifle (see page 62)

Flute gun (see page 249)

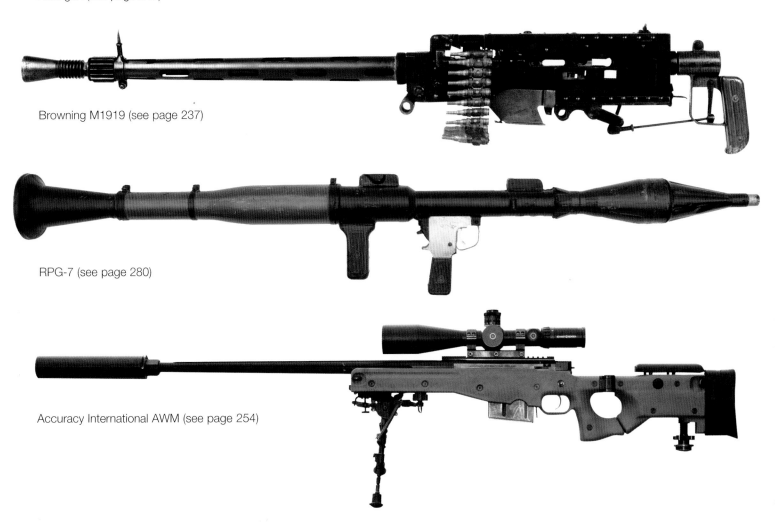

Browning M1919 (see page 237)

RPG-7 (see page 280)

Accuracy International AWM (see page 254)

Post-WWII Weapons 1945 – Present 252

Resources 310

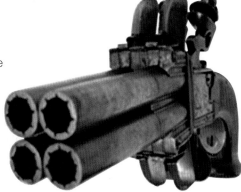

Four-barrel pepperbox (see page 71)

INTRODUCTION

FROM STONE AGE AX TO HIGH-TECH ANTI-MATERIEL SNIPER
RIFLES, THE IMPERATIVE OF THE WEAPONS DESIGNER HAS
ALWAYS BEEN TO PRODUCE A WEAPON THAT IS FASTER,
DEADLIER, AND MORE EFFECTIVE THAN THE WEAPON IN
THE HANDS OF THE OPPONENT. THIS BOOK TRACES THE
DEVELOPMENT OF SMALL ARMS FROM PREHISTORY TO THE
BATTLEFIELDS OF THE TWENTY-FIRST CENTURY.

Small arms have been used throughout history by humans, whether
they are hunting for food or protecting their homes and families from
enemy attack. They are weapons that can be picked up and carried by
a single person—though some require a second person to carry
ammunition and accessories.

Going back in time, this class of weaponry included swords, spears, clubs,
axes, maces, javelins, bows, polearms, and other weapons wielded by a single
warrior. More recent examples include revolvers, pistols, rifles, carbines,
submachine guns, light machine guns, grenade launchers, anti-tank systems,
anti-materiel rifles, sniper rifles, and a host of other portable weaponry.

Heavier weaponry includes artillery, heavy morters, missiles, naval guns, and
all other weapons that cannot be moved by one person. These weapons are
almost exclusively held by the military or paramilitary bodies, and only in
the very rarest circumstances fall into the hands of private individuals.

For millennia the only weapons humans had were small arms—the spears,
axes, and clubs that could be made from organic materials such as stone and
wood. Bows and arrows were developed in the late Stone Age, but for
thousands of years thereafter, there was very little evolution in small arms.

Once humans progressed to living in permanent farming
communities, they were able to have more in the way of personal
possessions and had more need to protect possessions that remained
in one place. Learning how to use metals resulted in an arms race

between offense and defense that became increasingly dramatic and fast-moving. As armor was developed to protect against one type of sword, a new blade was developed that rendered the armor obsolete. Weapon manufacturers were constantly challenged to to come up with new defensive products.

The ingenuity of smiths and armorers led to the development of a wide range of small arms weaponry. The swordsmiths of Japan produced exceptionally fine blades for their samurai warriors, and in Europe the business of killing created an equally effective range of combat weapons.

The invention of gunpowder led to a revolution in small arms. The earliest firearms were primitive metal tubes with gunpowder packed down the barrel, topped by a stone or metal slug, and set off by the application of a red-hot coal

DEATH OF KING HAROLD
The Battle of Hastings in 1066 featured infantry and cavalry, both of which carried small arms such as swords and axes.

from a nearby brazier. It was not only the weapons that were primitive—so, too, was the gunpowder. The chemistry was not clearly understood, so the powder varied enormously in its power, effectiveness, and the amount of smoke it produced.

By the sixteenth century, the search was on for more effective ways to discharge a gun. The matchlock came first and lasted for generations, though the complex wheel lock was a more reliable alternative for those wealthy enough to afford it. The first relatively cheap and effective way to fire a gun was the flintlock mechanism, which combined a pan and cover to keep the powder dry with a flint-on-steel ignition system that functioned even in damp weather. By the later seventeenth century, when the flintlock became widespread, new ways of manufacturing gunpowder also helped make guns more reliable.

THE MODERN BATTLEFIELD
Today, troops are armed with sniper rifles, heavy machine guns, and other weapons capable of taking out personnel, vehicles, and buildings.

Even so, soldiers went into battle carrying swords, knives, or bayonets because wet weather could still render firearms useless. Rain dampened the powder and made the sparks from the flintlocks incapable of setting it off. The smoke from a discharge could also give away the shooter's location in battle.

The development of smokeless powder and the integrated metal cartridge made firearms weatherproof for the first time. The new cartridge also opened the way for automatic and semiautomatic weaponry, so the battlefield came to be dominated by machine guns, submachine guns, and assault rifles. Allied to innovations in tactics and heavy weaponry, the new small arms first produced the stalemate of the trenches in World War I, then the fast moving blitzkrieg in World War II, and finally the shapeless anti-insurgency warfare that has become common in Afghanistan, Iraq, and Syria.

When the counter-insurgency fighting in the Middle East moved into an urban environment, U.S. troops needed effective house-clearing weaponry—it saw them, for the first time, being supplied with large numbers of tactical shotguns. Longer range fighting in the mountains and deserts demanded sniper rifles, so weapons with increased long-range accuracy were developed with the aid of computerized sights. With each change in tactics or fighting style, weapons designers sought to give the fighting men and women an advantage over the enemy.

Asymmetric warfare between technologically advanced western forces and poorly equipped insurgent units with a strong ideological drive will not soon end. Small arms development may move in a divergent direction that reflects the need for a variety of specific weapons that enable soldiers to kill without being observed by a less-technologically equipped enemy. Production cost and field maintenance also play a vital role in successful armaments. As we move into the twenty-first century, the struggle for superiority will continue to push the invention of increasingly sophisticated weapons, and the ingenuity of those who wield them.

THE FIRST SMALL ARMS
Prehistory—1300

Humans began using small arms as soon as they learned how to make tools. Indeed, the very first tools ever made by prehistoric humans may have been small weapons used to hunt animals for food. These early weapons were made of stone, wood, or other organic materials. However, as technology improved, humans began using metals such as copper or bronze, and then iron and steel to make sidearms. These increasingly sophisticated weapons dominated warfare until the invention of gunpowder.

BHIMBETKA CAVE PAINTING
Paintings on the walls of the Bhimbetka rock shelters in India date back about 30,000 years and show hunters using a variety of weapons.

STICKS & STONES (THE FIRST AXES, WAR CLUBS, AND SPEARS)

The weapons of the Stone Age that survive to the present day were made primarily of stone, but other materials were also used. Flint and obsidian were split to produce cutting edges as sharp as the most modern steel, though they had a tendency to blunt easily. Other stones, such as jadeite or greenstone, were polished to produce more durable—if less sharp—cutting edges. Several of these stone weapons incorporate marks where they were attached to wooden hafts or handles. Bone, antler, and wood were also used to make sidearms, but being far softer materials than stone, these rarely survive.

PEBBLE TOOLS

These simple stone choppers, often termed pebble tools, were found in Olduvai Gorge in Tanzania, and date to about 2.6 million years ago. They are associated with a prehistoric form of human known as *Homo habilis*. It walked upright and stood about 51 inches tall as an adult. This may have been the first member of the human genus, though its brain size was considerably smaller than that of modern humans.

Cutting edge

Original pebble surface

Broken surface caused by heavy blow

EARLY HAND-AXES

The Acheulean culture of stone tool making is named after the French village of Saint-Acheul where these tools were first found, but the culture probably began in Africa about 1.7 million years ago. The characteristic tool is the pear-shaped "hand-ax" with elongated cutting edges along two sides tapering to a sharp point. These multipurpose tools were used by their *Homo erectus* makers for cutting, scraping, and chopping.

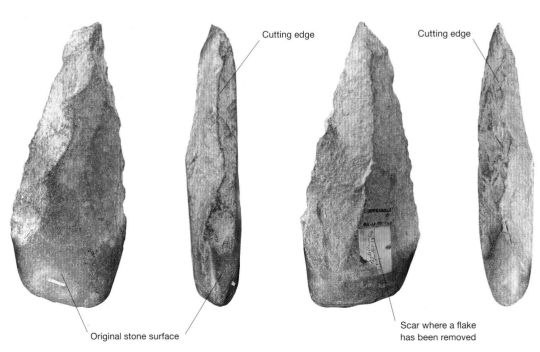

Cutting edge

Cutting edge

Original stone surface

Scar where a flake has been removed

CLOVIS POINTS

Named after the site in New Mexico where the tools were found, Clovis points are among the first weapons to be used by humans in the Americas. The blades are relatively thin, and have long, serrated cutting edges produced by applying pressure and carefully flaking off tiny shards of stone, not by striking as with earlier tools.

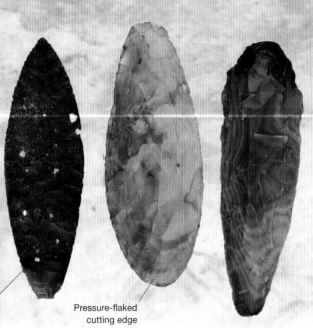

Symmetrical shape

Pressure-flaked cutting edge

Tang

SPEARHEADS

Some stone tools have a tang, or prong, projecting from the base of an otherwise triangular weapon. The tangs were pushed into a wooden shaft to produce a stone-tipped spear or javelin.

GREENSTONE AXES

By the time farming was introduced to northwestern Europe, there was a flourishing business manufacturing greenstone axes based in Britain's Lake District. The axes were exceptionally hard and durable, though not especially sharp. They were used primarily for cutting down trees and other heavy-duty tasks. They have been found hundreds of miles from where they were made, which illustrates that by 2500 BC there were widespread trading networks.

Cutting edge

Surface polished smooth with sand and water

Groove ground to hold leather securing strap

HAFTED AX

This greenstone ax from Britain dates from about 2000 BC. The groove shows where a wooden handle was held in place by leather straps.

Natural jadeite patterning

JADEITE AX

This ax is made of jadeite, a heavy mineral found in northern Italy. The attractive coloring and marking of jadeite may have meant these were for display as much as for practical use.

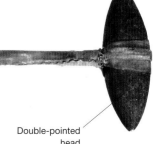

PLAINS WAR CLUB

This club dates to the nineteenth century and was produced by the Native Americans of the Great Plains. It has a double-pointed head and is attached to the handle by similar means to those of more ancient stone weapons.

Double-pointed head

CLUBS, MACES & FLAILS

Perhaps the most basic weapon of all is the club—a stick or stone that is used to beat an opponent into submission. Certainly, some of the very oldest stone tools recovered by archaeologists seem to have been used as clubs. The club, however, can be a much more sophisticated and subtle weapon than its simplicity would indicate. The shape of the weapon can be adapted to make it effective against different types of armor, a hinge or chain can enhance the force delivered, and the weapon allows scope for design and decoration for ceremonial purposes.

NORTHWEST INDIAN CLUBS

The dense forests of the Pacific Northwest gave the indigenous peoples plenty of wood to work with, so carpentry dominated their culture. These clubs show the highly decorated nature of weapons and tools from that area.

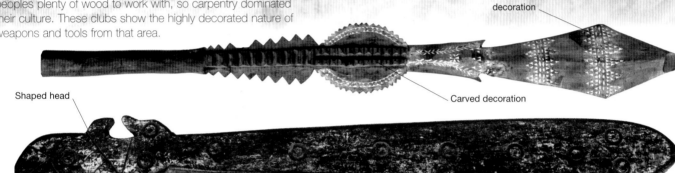

Painted decoration

Carved decoration

Shaped head

CEREMONIAL SIOUX CLUB

Beadwork is a traditional craft among the Plains tribes. On this ceremonial club beading has been used to decorate both the handle and what would be the destructive end in a war weapon.

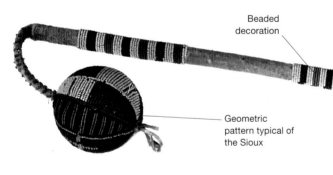

Beaded decoration

Geometric pattern typical of the Sioux

One piece construction

AFRICAN CLUB

This short club from Africa has a head shaped like the head of a cow. The delicate nature of the horns and ears indicates that this is a ceremonial weapon rather than a weapon of war. Cattle are a measure of wealth in traditional African cultures.

The design suggests this is a ceremonial piece

TOOTHED MAORI PATU

The patu used by the Maori of New Zealand was an interesting variation on the club. It was used to thrust violently under the ribs to wind and thus disable the enemy. The addition of shark teeth, as here, meant the weapon cut as well as bludgeoned.

Shark tooth

Handle

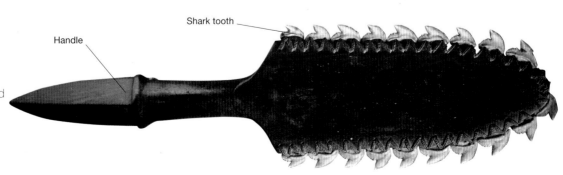

NUNCHAKU

Consisting of two wooden batons connected by a short chain or rope, the nunchaku is a traditional weapon from Okinawa, Japan. It probably began as a form of flail, but by the nineteenth century it was being used as a martial arts tool rather than as a weapon of war.

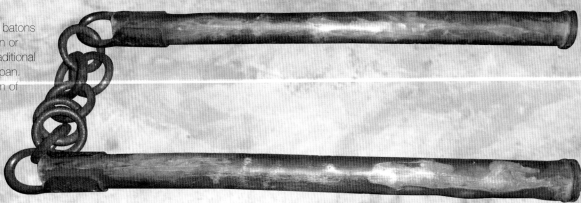

FIJIAN WAR CLUB

The short, broad war club was a popular weapon throughout the Polynesian islands. This example is from Fiji and is decorated with chevron carvings. It was used to deliver a horizontal thrust to the head of an enemy.

Decoration colored with natural pigments

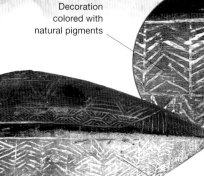

Handle

Decorative carving

FIJIAN CULACULA

The long paddle club, or culacula, probably originated in Tonga, though this example is from Fiji. It was used in a more conventional overhead swinging blow, unlike the thrusting motion of the patu.

Edge carved with tooth design

INDIAN WOODEN CLUB

The hardwoods of the forests of India were ideal for creating clubs. This example has a large, heavy head to increase the energy imparted by a swinging blow.

Flanged head

Carving on handle improves grip

Patterning natural to the greenstone

Hole for leather thong

MAORI PATU

This patu from the South Island of New Zealand is made from a greenstone known as pounamu. This stone was highly prized in Maori ritual, so this is almost certainly a ceremonial object rather than an actual weapon.

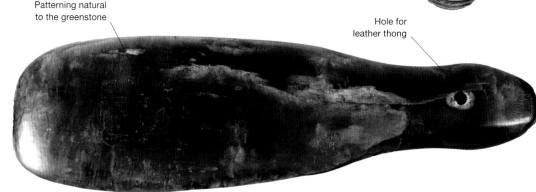

CLUBS, MACES & FLAILS

CEREMONIAL MACE

In later medieval Europe, the mace decorated with an engraved coat of arms became a symbol of authority carried by the officials of royal or noble households. These seventeenth-century artifacts are the Maces of the Rector Magnificus of the University of Santo Tomas in the Philippines, an example of European colonists bringing their traditions with them as they converted other peoples to Christianity.

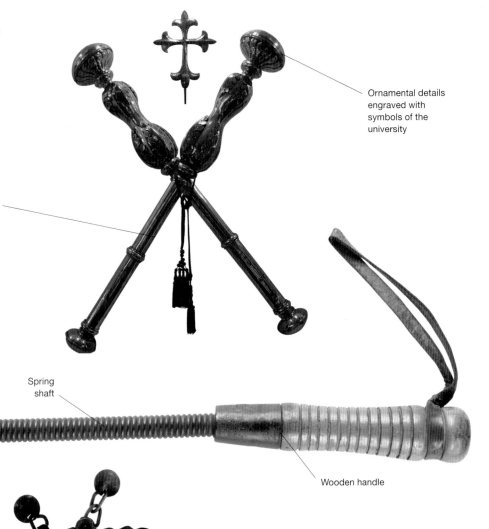

Ornamental details engraved with symbols of the university

Mace made from silver, which was unsuitable for use as a weapon

MORNING STAR MACE

The morning star design of mace had a heavy head that was attached to the shaft with a chain, which allowed the user to swing the head around to increase its momentum. This fifteenth century example from England has a shaft made from a strong spring to achieve the same effect.

Spring shaft

Wooden handle

TURKISH MACE

A mace is a club with a head, and sometimes shaft, made of metal. This Turkish example has a short (22-inch) shaft and a head adorned with metal knobs on short chains that would lacerate as well as bludgeon. The sharpened point shows that it could be used to thrust as well as swing.

Spearhead end

Short handle

RARE MACE

This ceremonial bulwa (Russian mace) is from the Caucasus Mountains. It is decorated with silver and turquoise mounts, and has a soapstone head. The symbol of command, the bulwa was carried by senior officers.

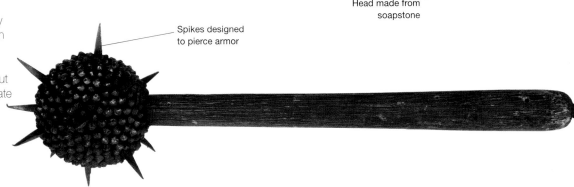

Head made from soapstone

Spikes designed to pierce armor

MORGENSTERN

Dating from sixteenth-century Germany, this mace is known as a morgenstern. It has a wooden shaft and a heavy metal head incorporating stout spikes. The spikes concentrate the force of the blow onto a small point and would thus pierce the plate armor of the time, while the impact of the head could break bones.

ENGLISH FLAILS

This weapon has a metal shaft, chain, and spiked head. It was made in England around 1470 and so may have seen action in the Wars of the Roses. The idea was that the chain allowed the ball to reach behind shields and inflict a blow to a part of the body hidden from a sword or spear thrust.

Iron shaft may have had a wooden grip

Spiked head

RUSSIAN FLAILS

Dating from the early eighteenth century, these flails are rudimentary weapons from Russia. They were intended for close-quarter combat, and may have been used as a weapon of last resort when a sword or spear had been lost.

Weighted head

Plaited leather

Twisted metal bar construction

SIX ISLAMIC AND MUGHAL MACES

Dating to the sixteenth and seventeenth centuries, these maces originate from northern India and Central Asia. The flanges and spikes on the heads are intended to concentrate the force of the blow onto as small an area as possible, greatly enhancing the destructive power of the weapon. The metal shafts may have had wooden or rope grips to prevent them slipping out of sweaty hands.

Flange

Spike

Metal shaft

Ax head

Metal shafts may have had a wooden grip

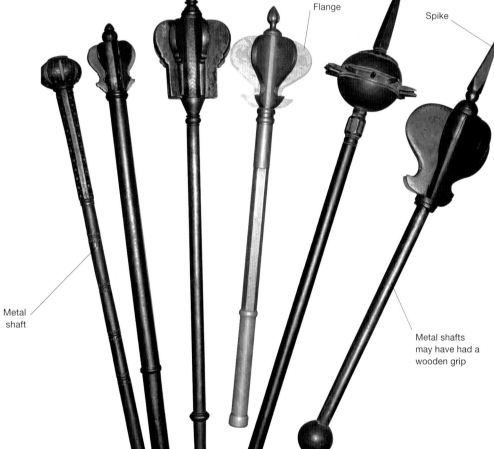

Steel head

BULJAWA

Known as a buljawa, this is a style of mace that was popular in Turkey, though this example may come from the Balkans. It has a heavy spherical head intended to crush its way through armor and inflict blunt force trauma on the flesh and bones beneath. The steel shaft gives the weapon added durability.

Leather grip

SPEARS & LANCES

Fitting a sharp point onto the end of a wooden pole to create a spear gave the user a much greater reach than could be achieved by holding a weapon in the hand. The earliest spears were made of wood sharpened to a tip, but soon stone heads were fitted. When metal was first smelted, the manufacture of spearheads was one of the first military uses of the new material. Spears come in three basic forms: the javelin is a light weapon designed to be thrown; the spear is a heavier weapon used by someone on foot to thrust at the enemy; and the lance is a longer implement employed by those on horseback.

OLDEST KNOWN WOODEN SPEAR

This wooden spear was excavated near Schöningen, Germany, in 1995 and is dated to about 400,000 years ago. It was found close to a large group of horse bones, so it was most likely used to hunt these animals.

Spear bent due to aging

GREEK SPEARHEADS

The Ancient Greeks used bronze-tipped spears to thrust at the enemy while standing in a densely packed formation known as a phalanx. A bronze butt was used to rest the weapon on the ground when it was not in use.

Butt

Spearhead

THE KEMPTEN PILUM

Roman legionaries used a javelin called the pilum. It had a wooden handle and a long head that was specially forged into a sharp, hard point. However, the shank was soft and, as in this example, bent on impact. This made it impossible for the enemy to hurl the pilum back.

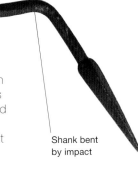

Shank bent by impact

ZULU SPEAR

This javelin, also known as an assegai, comes from the Zulus of southern Africa. They used these throwing assegais at longer range, then switched to the short, broad-bladed iklwa spear in hand-to-hand combat.

Lightweight construction

Small head

Wooden shaft

AMAZON SPEAR

The indigenous peoples of the Amazon have adopted metal tips for their spears since the Europeans brought metal to the Americas. This example from the Carajas is decorated with colorful feathers, and may have been created for ceremonial or ritual uses.

Macaw feathers

VIKING SOCKET SPEARHEAD
Vikings of the ninth to eleventh centuries fought in a formation dubbed the "shield wall," with men standing shoulder-to-shoulder and presenting a wall of shields to the enemy. To attack, heavy spears were used—the wooden shaft was fixed into the hollow socket at the rear of the spearhead.

Hollow socket

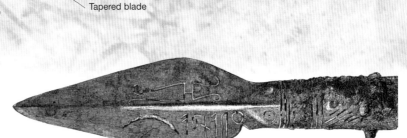

LONG VIKING SPEARHEAD
The shape and design of Viking spears varied considerably. This elongated, slender spearhead may be from a javelin designed to be thrown at the enemy as rival shield walls drew closer.

Tapered blade

SPEARHEAD OF DAHMSDORF-MÜNCHEBERG
This heavy, thrusting spearhead was made for a Goth warrior in the fourth or fifth century. It carries an inscription in runes that reads "ranja," which may translate as "router" or "way forward."

Runic inscription

CAROLINGIAN SPEARHEAD
Dating from the tenth century, this spearhead was designed for use by the armored infantry favored by the Germanic Frank tribe. The cross bar behind the blade was to stop the weapon penetrating too far into the body of a victim, which would have made it impossible to retrieve.

Cross bar

GREEK JAVELIN

The Ancient Greeks used the javelin as a weapon of war. While wealthier male citizens fought as heavy infantry with armor, round shields, helmets, and thrusting spears, the poorer citizens served as "peltasts." These men wore no armor except perhaps a helmet, carried a light wickerwork shield, and threw their javelins at the enemy. Cavalry fielded by city states of Thessaly threw javelins while riding at a gallop. Athletic competitions often included javelin throwing, though it was accuracy as much as distance that was prized.

PIKES & POLEARMS

By the later medieval period, the heavy thrusting spear had developed into a variety of pikes and polearms. While these varied in detail, they were all intended to make infantry effective against the armored cavalry that had dominated the battlefield for centuries. Infantry were trained to move in dense formations, with their long weapons held horizontally to present a bristling and impenetrable barrier of sharp points that horses would not attack. The infantry was highly flexible, being trained to adopt a number of different formations with speed. However, it should be stated that not all infantry were able to perform such complicated maneuvers on the field of battle with equal efficiency.

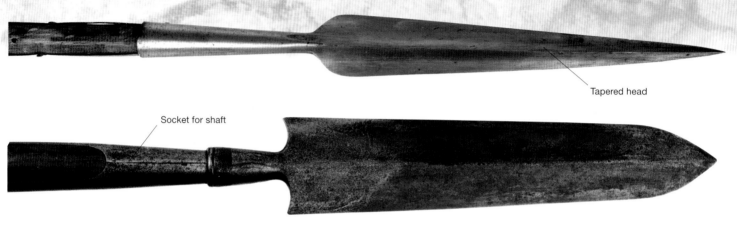

Tapered head

Socket for shaft

ENGLISH POLEARMS
The simplest polearm was the pike, a heavy weapon about 16 feet long, ending in a stout spearhead.

Hooks

ITALIAN POLEARM
The glaive had a cutting edge down one side of the spearhead. This example also has a pair of hooks intended to snag a rider and pull him from his horse.

Broad head sharpened on both sides

Metal studs to protect wooden shaft

PARTISAN
This eighteenth century weapon was designed as a cheap and easily stored weapon to be used by local militia that could be hastily pressed into service should the need arise. The term "partisan," meaning an informal militia, was coined in the eighteenth century by Hungarian army officer Mihaly Jeney.

Engraved design

SWISS POLEARM
Equipped with heavy pikes and superbly trained, the Swiss infantry became the most feared in Europe in the fifteenth century.

Socket for shaft

FRENCH POLEARM
This French pike head from the eighteenth century has been designed to resemble the fleur-de-lis, the traditional symbol of the French monarchy.

SAMURAI WITH NAGINATA

The naginata was a favored polearm of the samurai of medieval Japan. The wooden pole was about 6 feet long, and the steel blade added another 18 to 24 inches. The blade had a single cutting edge, and curved at the end to give a cutting tip as well. The naginata seems to have been developed in the mid-twelfth century to counter the increasing use of mounted troops. The weapon was later associated with the sohei, the warrior buddhist monks who rivaled the nobles for political power.

Curved blade widens toward the tip

NAGINATA
The Japanese naginata consisted of a curved-edge blade set on a pole up to 8 feet long. Modern martial arts contests use a naginata that has a bamboo blade in place of the steel original.

SLEEVE GRABBER
The Japanese sodegarami was used almost exclusively by police. The pronged head and spiked shaft was used to snag the traditional robes and stop a suspect from escaping.

Spiked shaft

PIKES & POLEARMS

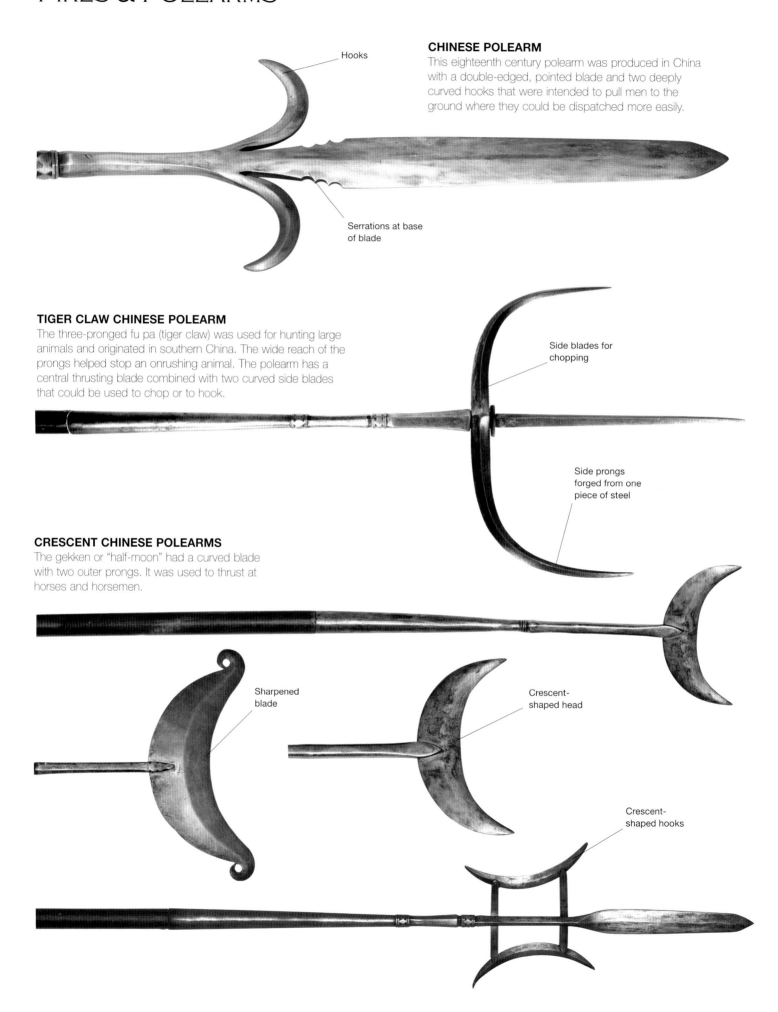

CHINESE POLEARM
This eighteenth century polearm was produced in China with a double-edged, pointed blade and two deeply curved hooks that were intended to pull men to the ground where they could be dispatched more easily.

Hooks

Serrations at base of blade

TIGER CLAW CHINESE POLEARM
The three-pronged fu pa (tiger claw) was used for hunting large animals and originated in southern China. The wide reach of the prongs helped stop an onrushing animal. The polearm has a central thrusting blade combined with two curved side blades that could be used to chop or to hook.

Side blades for chopping

Side prongs forged from one piece of steel

CRESCENT CHINESE POLEARMS
The gekken or "half-moon" had a curved blade with two outer prongs. It was used to thrust at horses and horsemen.

Sharpened blade

Crescent-shaped head

Crescent-shaped hooks

GUAN YU

The Chinese general Guan Yu is one of the great heroes of early China. He served the warlord Liu Bei and became famous for his loyalty as well as for his fighting talents. So many legends and anecdotes were told about him that it can be difficult to distinguish them from the facts of his life. It is known that for a few years he served another warlord, Cao Cao, but his long journey back to Liu Bei at the end of this service is largely fictional.

YANYUE DAO POLEARM

The yanyue dao consisted of a curved, single-edged blade mounted on a pole about 8 feet long. This example has a dragon's head, indicating it belonged to the Imperial Army.

Dragon's head motif

Blade edged with hooks and serrations

Ornate blade

INDO-PERSIAN LANCE HEAD

This two-pronged spearhead, or bident, dates to nineteenth-century Persia and is probably a hunting weapon.

Blades sharpened on the inside

Sharp spike

Hammerhead

INDO-PERSIAN CROWBILL

The crowbill was a popular weapon across Asia and Europe from about 1300. It consisted of a polearm with a spike—sometimes curved in the shape of a crow's bill—mounted at a right angle to the pole, and a blunt hammer facing the spike. The blunt end could be used to knock men off their feet, but the real purpose of the weapon was to drive the spike through mail or plate armor. This example is from India or Persia and dates to the early eighteenth century.

BATTLE-AXES

The ax began as a working tool, useful for felling trees, chopping wood, and a number of other domestic or agricultural tasks. It was not long, however, before the potential of the ax as a weapon was appreciated. The weapons tended to have wider blades and longer shafts than the tools. The trend reached its height with the massive double-handed ax of northern Europe in the tenth and eleventh centuries, with a shaft up to 6 feet long. At the other extreme small, light axes could be used as throwing weapons. Again this style reached a peak in northern Europe with the Franks.

Holes

Socketed head

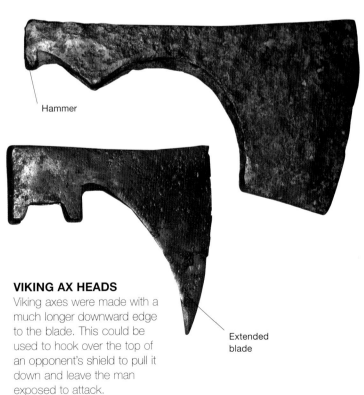

Chipped cutting edge

ANCIENT EGYPTIAN COPPER AX
This ax has a shape characteristic of the old kingdom of ancient Egypt. The curved blade is set onto a long hollow tube which held the wooden shaft. The two holes through the blade lightened the weapon without reducing its strength.

AX HEAD
A pair of copper ax heads from the Middle East. Copper was the first metal to be widely used to make tools, perhaps in the Balkans about 5500 BC, followed by bronze, a harder alloy of copper and tin around 3500 BC.

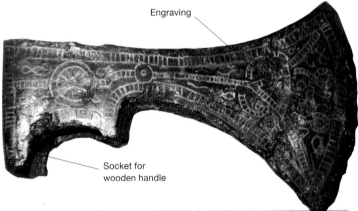

Engraving

Socket for wooden handle

MEROVINGIAN AX
The Merovingian dynasty ruled the Franks of northwestern Europe for three centuries until AD 752. This highly decorated ax head is typical of the quality weaponry produced by the Franks.

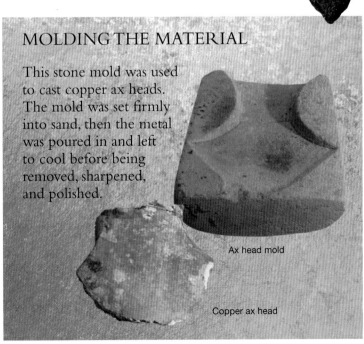

MOLDING THE MATERIAL

This stone mold was used to cast copper ax heads. The mold was set firmly into sand, then the metal was poured in and left to cool before being removed, sharpened, and polished.

Ax head mold

Copper ax head

Hammer

VIKING AX HEADS
Viking axes were made with a much longer downward edge to the blade. This could be used to hook over the top of an opponent's shield to pull it down and leave the man exposed to attack.

Extended blade

BRONZE AGE AX

Bronze was first developed about 3500 BC, perhaps in upper Mesopotamia. The metal is harder than its predecessor copper, and able to retain a sharper edge. This socketed ax head was cast in bronze about 2800 BC. The metal was originally smooth and polished, but has become pitted and dull due to centuries buried in the ground.

Bronze is dull and pitted after centuries buried in ground

Decorative lion motif

MIXTURE OF METALS

This ax head from Iran dates to about 900 BC. It has an iron blade set into a bronze mount that includes a lion decoration. At this date iron was still a rare and prestigious metal, with bronze being used for most everyday purposes.

Hole for wooden shaft

QI BATTLE-AX

This unusual ax comes from Yunnan in China and dates to about AD 500. The blade is almost circular, being sharpened around its rim. The wooden haft passed through the hole in the tang beside the cast animal, which may be a unit recognition device.

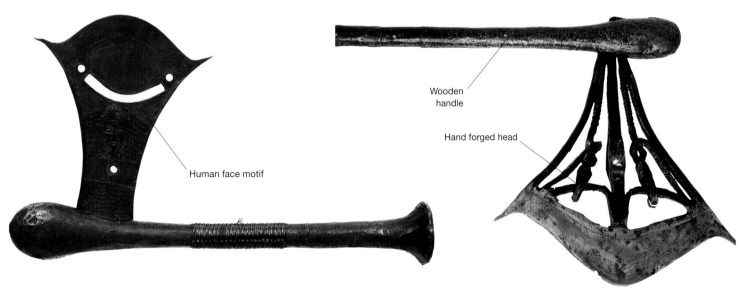

Human face motif

Wooden handle

Hand forged head

AFRICAN COPPER AX

Originating in western Africa, this copper ax is typical of local weapon design before the advent of European-style weapons into the region. The blade is pierced for lightness and elaborately engraved.

AFRICAN CEREMONIAL AXE

The Sonya people of the Congo are best known for their elaborate wood carving tradition, but they are also skilled metalworkers. This ax dates to perhaps the later nineteenth century. It has a hand-forged iron head fixed to a wooden shaft by copper pins.

BATTLE-AXES

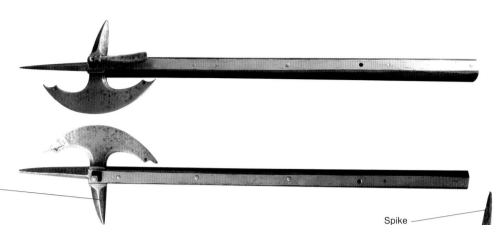

FIFTEENTH–CENTURY BATTLE-AX
This European weapon has metal prongs extending along the wooden handle from the ax head. These are to stop the ax head being taken off the handle by a blow from an enemy's weapon.

Metal prongs

Spike

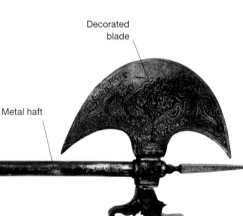

TURKISH BATTLE-AX
Made about 1550, but fitted with a modern handle, this battle-ax features a stout spike behind the blade. This was designed to punch through the plate armor of the time, inflicting a deep puncture wound on the victim.

GREEK LABRYS
The double-headed ax of ancient Greece, the labrys, originated as a simple forestry tool, but around 2000 BC was being used as a ritual weapon in the sacrifice of large animals, particularly bulls. By 1500 BC it was a symbol associated with priestesses and goddesses, though its precise meaning is now unclear.

Decorated blade

INDIAN BATTLE-AX
Manufactured in India in the early eighteenth century this battle ax has an elaborately etched blade that is typical of the decorative patterns applied to weaponry in India at this date.

Metal haft

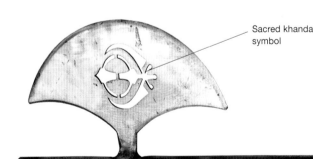

Sacred khanda symbol

SIKH SYMBOL HAND AX
This modern hand ax is cast from one piece of metal and the blade is pierced with the sacred khanda symbol of the Sikh faith. The symbol embodies the Sikh slogan "kettle and sword," which is usually rendered as "victory to charity and arms." It is unlikely this is anything other than a symbolic weapon.

Blade

EIGHTEENTH-CENTURY BATTLE-AX
The highly curved blade of this ax is typical of the more elaborate shapes adopted by weaponsmiths in India in the eighteenth century. It shows little sign of being used and may have been a display item.

Spear point

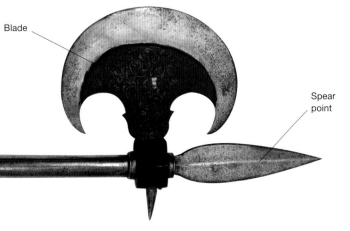

INDIAN AX

A more functional ax from India, again probably from the eighteenth century. The long, curved blade carries decorated etching, as does the metal handle. The spear point at the top is a simple spike of little use.

INDO-PERSIAN BATTLE-AX

This light weapon has a long, slender haft of iron and a highly curved blade that is thinner than most military axes. It was probably intended for use on horseback.

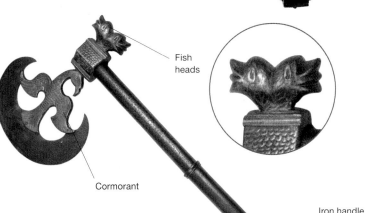

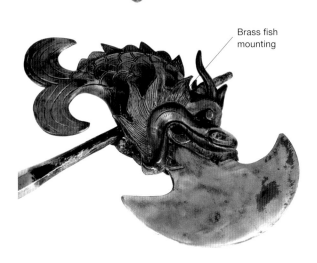

Brass fish mounting

Fish heads

Cormorant

Iron handle

CORMORANT MOTIF

This Chinese weapon has been elaborately designed so that the blade indicates a splash of water and is held to the haft by a brass mount depicting a diving cormorant, which is after the two fish on the other side of the haft.

CHINESE BATTLE-AX

An unusual Chinese weapon from Imperial times, this ax has a highly ornamental brass mounting in the shape of a fish that attaches the steel blade to the steel haft.

ROBERT THE BRUCE

In September 1314, the armies of Scotland and England faced each other at Bannockburn. As King Robert the Bruce of Scotland supervised his army getting into position, he strayed far from the nearest troops and was suddenly attacked by the English noble Henry Bohun. Bruce was at risk for he was not wearing armor, carried only an ax, and was mounted on a small riding horse, while Bohun was fully armored, mounted on his great warhorse, and was fully equipped with lance, sword, and shield. Bruce waited patiently for what seemed certain death, but at the last moment he dodged his horse to one side, avoided the lance, and brought his ax down so hard it split Bohun's helmet and sliced open his skull, causing his instant death. Bruce went on to win the battle.

SHORT SWORDS

Short swords have long been a favorite sidearm for military men and civilians alike. They are easy to carry, convenient to keep out of the way when slung from a belt, and relatively cheap to purchase. At the same time they can be highly effective in a confrontation of almost any kind, and when wielded with skill can be lethal. Over the centuries perhaps the main use of short swords has been as a secondary weapon to be used when the primary weapon breaks or is dropped, but some armies have made the short sword their main infantry weapon with dramatic and effective results.

EGYPTIAN CURVED BRONZE SWORD
This single-edged sword was used for slashing. The blade widens toward the tip to give increased weight, and to increase the momentum and power of a blow. The curved blade allows the user to drag the blade back as it makes contact, cutting deeper into the enemy.

Distinctive Egyptian "notch"

Stabbing point

BRONZE SWORD FROM PERSIA
This tapering, double-edged weapon was designed for stabbing. The ridge of thickened metal along the blade served to strengthen the blade, for bronze was notoriously prone to bending when it hit an obstruction, such as armor.

Leaf-shaped blade

Ridge of metal

BRONZE XIPHOS
Measuring about 23 inches long, the xiphos was a short stabbing sword carried by most Greek soldiers. The primary weapon of the Greek hoplite, or armored infantry, was the heavy thrusting spear. The xiphos would be used only if the spear broke.

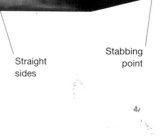

GLADIUS
The 31.5 inch-long gladius was the primary weapon of the Roman legionary for seven centuries until it was abandoned around AD 300. The stabbing blade forced the legionaries to fight at close quarters, where combat became more murderous and the victory all the greater when achieved.

Straight sides

Stabbing point

Shaped metal grip

BRONZE GALLO-ROMAN SWORD
The design of the Roman steel gladius was adapted from short, stabbing swords used by the Celts of northern Italy. This bronze example has a more slender blade than the later Roman version, but would have been used in the same way.

ROMAN ARMOR
The gravestone of Roman legionary Quintus Petilius Secundus was carved in about AD 65. It shows him wearing typical Roman armor of the period—made of strips of iron shaped to fit around his body—as well as a winter cloak and woolen tunic. In his right hand he holds a throwing spear, while a gladius is attached to his belt at the right hip.

EARLY BRONZE SWORD
This short sword has the distinctive shape of the Mycenaean Greeks, a culture that flourished for several centuries until it collapsed around 1200 BC.

Handle would have been
sheathed in wood

Handle

MODERN MAKHAIRA
The Mycenaean Greeks used a slashing sword known as the makhaira, which featured a single-edged blade with an elongated oval shape. Given its length of up to 35 inches, it was probably a weapon used by cavalry.

Cutting edge

ANCIENT INDIAN SWORD
This leaf-shaped short sword is typical of a design that was generic across much of Europe and Asia in Bronze Age times. The broad blade with a thickened center ridge served to strengthen the bronze, which might otherwise bend on impact.

Thick center ridge

ALEXANDER THE GREAT

The armies of Alexander the Great of Macedon achieved their stunning success by combining different types of soldier into a cohesive whole that was able to deal with anything an enemy could field. The solid core of the army was a phalanx of armored infantry equipped with long sarissa spears and short xiphos swords. While this solid mass of men engaged and held the enemy, lightly armed infantry would move about seeking to confuse the enemy. When a weak spot was identified, Alexander himself would charge into it at the head of his armored heavy cavalry to smash a hole in the enemy army through which his infantry could then advance.

LONG SWORDS

Generally used as a primary weapon rather than a back up, the long sword dominated infantry warfare for centuries. The long sword gave a greater reach to the wielder than did short swords, axes, or clubs, offering a distinct advantage. Most long swords have been dual purpose, designed to be used as either slashing or stabbing weapons. The skill needed to make a long, relatively thin blade that combined sharpness with rigidity, strength, and lightness represented a high point in the metalsmith's art. Long swords were therefore expensive items to purchase. In many pre-modern societies they were the exclusive weapons of the elite.

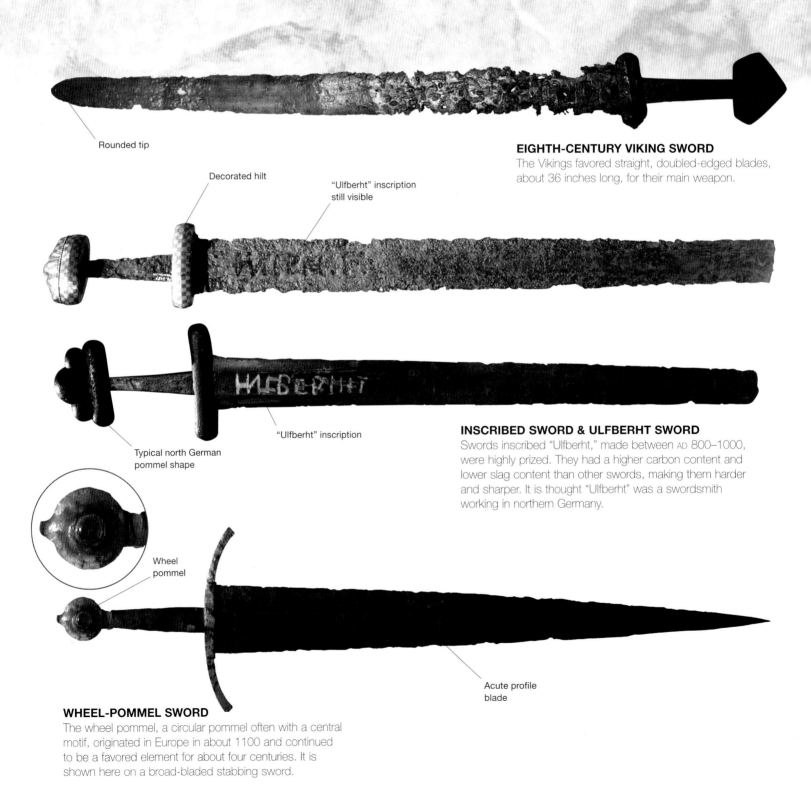

Rounded tip

EIGHTH-CENTURY VIKING SWORD
The Vikings favored straight, doubled-edged blades, about 36 inches long, for their main weapon.

Decorated hilt

"Ulfberht" inscription still visible

"Ulfberht" inscription

Typical north German pommel shape

INSCRIBED SWORD & ULFBERHT SWORD
Swords inscribed "Ulfberht," made between AD 800–1000, were highly prized. They had a higher carbon content and lower slag content than other swords, making them harder and sharper. It is thought "Ulfberht" was a swordsmith working in northern Germany.

Wheel pommel

Acute profile blade

WHEEL-POMMEL SWORD
The wheel pommel, a circular pommel often with a central motif, originated in Europe in about 1100 and continued to be a favored element for about four centuries. It is shown here on a broad-bladed stabbing sword.

LATER ARMING SWORD

The arming sword got its name as it was used by a knight in armor. The tapering blade was generally about 30 inches long, and was designed to be used in one hand. The other hand was kept busy holding the shield.

Tapered blade

LANDSKNECHT

The big, heavy double-handed swords used by late medieval landsknecht mercenaries could be up to six feet long. They were used to smash opponents' pole weapons and to bludgeon through armor.

Broad blade

Classic medieval wrapping over wooden sheath

Ornamental quillons

GREAT SWORD

The great sword became popular from about 1400 onward. It was a long but relatively light two-handed weapon that gave the user a greater reach than an arming sword, though at the expense of a two-handed grip, which meant the shield had to be dispensed with.

OFFICER'S SWORD

The final form of the long sword was worn by officers in European armies between 1740 and 1915. The weapon was not so much to fight the enemy as to show that the officer was also a gentleman, though it was also deemed useful in maintaining battlefield discipline among the troops.

KNIGHTS WITH SWORDS

This pair of fourteenth century knights are fighting with arming great swords. By this date, the plate armor made of steel was effective against lighter weapons, so many knights took up these heavier swords. The two-handed grip meant that the shield had to be discarded, which led to even more effective and all-covering armor being worn.

LONG SWORDS

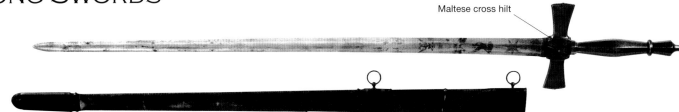

Maltese cross hilt

KNIGHTS OF MALTA SWORD
The 25-inch blade of this seventeenth-century sword is etched with Christian symbols and the hilt is in the form of a Maltese cross. It belonged to a Knight Hospitaller, an order of military monks who fought the Islamic Turks from their base on Malta.

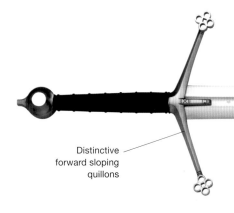

Distinctive forward sloping quillons

SCOTTISH CLAYMORE
This takes its name from the Gaelic *claidheamh mòr*, meaning "great sword." With a 42-inch blade and a weight of 5 pounds, these swords required two hands. They were used in the Highlands from around 1400 until 1689.

Basket hilt

SCOTTISH BROADSWORD
The Highland clansmen preferred the broadsword with its heavy, double-edged blade and basket hilt, which combined hitting power with protection for the hand and arm. The weapon continued in use with Scottish regiments into the early twentieth century, and is now retained for ceremonial purposes.

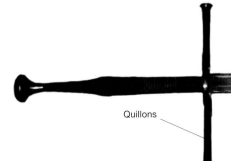

Quillons

SWISS LONG SWORD
Probably made in the sixteenth century, this double-handed Swiss sword has a longer handle than is usual, perhaps to allow for changes in the grip while the sword was whirled around.

KAMPILAN
The kampilan is a form of single-edged sword used in the Philippines from around the eighth century. The blade widens toward the tip, while the handle has a traditional forked design.

Wooden scabbard

FRENCH DRESS SWORD

This eighteenth-century sword is decorated with imitation diamonds and is typical of the sword-as-jewelry that was favored by nobles and courtiers at this time. Despite the ornamentation, the blade is a functional weapon.

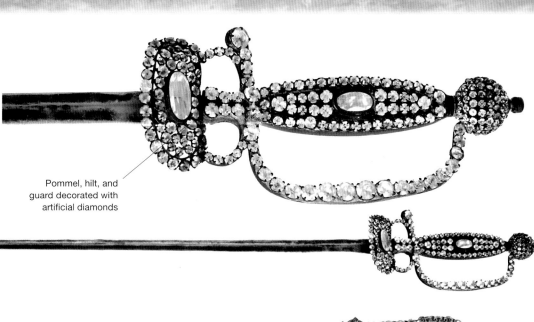

Rapier-style blade

Pommel, hilt, and guard decorated with artificial diamonds

Ivory grip

Finely decorated sheath

MASON'S SWORD

This sword, extensively decorated with freemasonry symbols, was made in the United States by Pettibone Brothers of Cincinnati for Charles Cornstock, the country's highest-ranking Freemason.

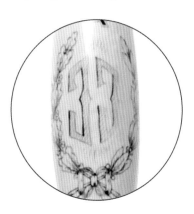

Masonic symbols

SWORD OF JUSTICE

In several countries the sword came to symbolize the punishment side of the justice system. In Britain the statue atop the Central Criminal Court carries a sword alongside the scales of judgment. At British coronations the sharp Sword of Justice and the blunted Sword of Mercy are carried in front of the monarch.

EASTERN SWORDS

While sword design in Europe produced a number of different sizes, shapes, and purposes, the designs in Asia tended to be variations on a single theme. These were single-edged, single-handed swords with an elegantly curved blade that were relatively light weight. The key to the weapon was the use of crucible steel—steel that is made molten at a very high temperature in a crucible before being used. This molten stage drives off impurities that would make the blade brittle, but allows the steel to absorb some carbon that makes it stronger and better able to take an edge. Blades made in this way have a distinctive wavy pattern in the metal.

FRENCH GUNNER SABER
Although single-edged, curved blades became fashionable in European armies in the course of the eighteenth century, many forms of saber were straighter than the Asian designs they copied. This allowed the European soldier to continue to thrust with the point.

Straight quillons

Greek classical badge

Wide, tapering blade

MOREAU'S SABER
Jean Moreau was a French General in the late eighteenth century who later moved to the United States. His saber, shown here, was a French-made weapon that copied the curved shape of Eastern swords. Many officers of this date adopted curved sabers as part of a fashionable obsession with Asian styles.

Sharply curved blade

Slightly curved blade

Sharp tip

CINQUEDEA
The cinquedea was a design that originated in Italy, but spread around the Mediterranean. This stabbing short sword was designed to be worn horizontally on the back of the belt at the waist.

KILIJ WITH NEPHRITE HILT
The kilij was a sword produced by the Turks and by the fifteenth century, it had become a national weapon. It had a curve that straightened toward the tip, which was often wider or thicker to give greater weight to a slashing blow.

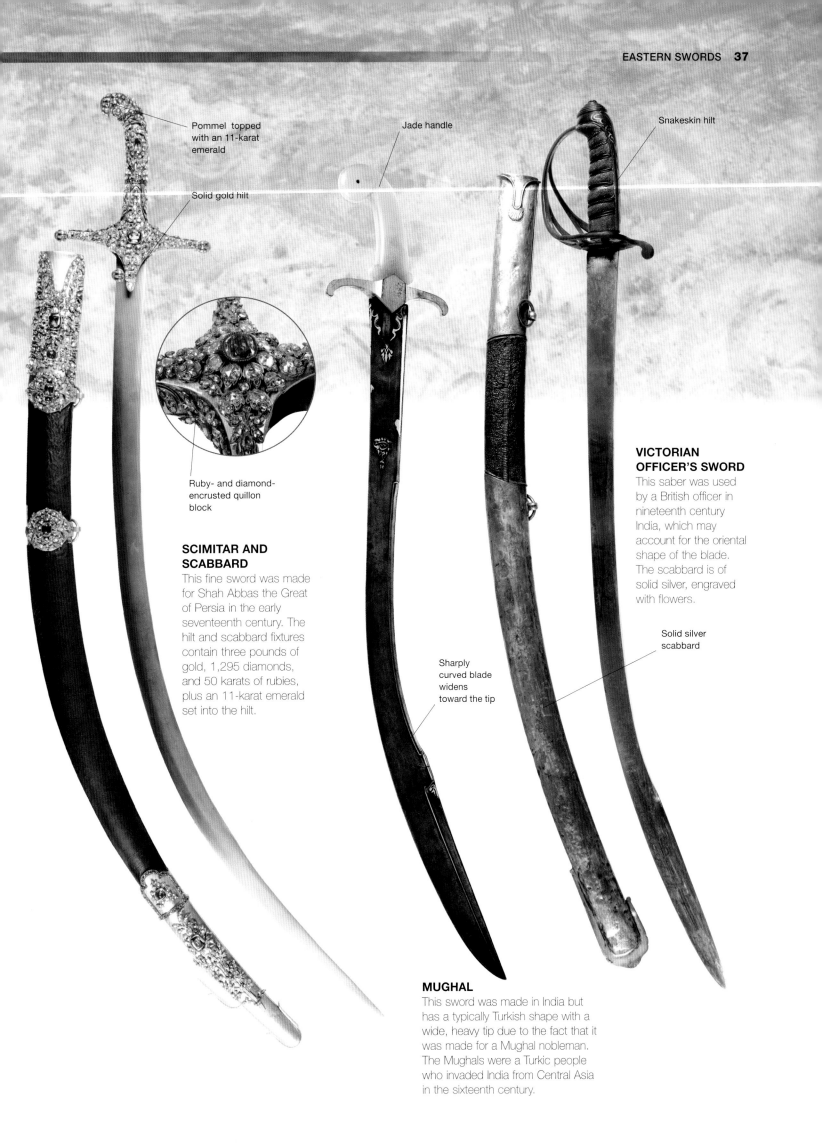

Pommel topped
with an 11-karat
emerald

Jade handle

Snakeskin hilt

Solid gold hilt

Ruby- and diamond-
encrusted quillon
block

SCIMITAR AND SCABBARD

This fine sword was made
for Shah Abbas the Great
of Persia in the early
seventeenth century. The
hilt and scabbard fixtures
contain three pounds of
gold, 1,295 diamonds,
and 50 karats of rubies,
plus an 11-karat emerald
set into the hilt.

Sharply
curved blade
widens
toward the tip

VICTORIAN OFFICER'S SWORD

This saber was used
by a British officer in
nineteenth century
India, which may
account for the oriental
shape of the blade.
The scabbard is of
solid silver, engraved
with flowers.

Solid silver
scabbard

MUGHAL

This sword was made in India but
has a typically Turkish shape with a
wide, heavy tip due to the fact that it
was made for a Mughal nobleman.
The Mughals were a Turkic people
who invaded India from Central Asia
in the sixteenth century.

EASTERN SWORDS

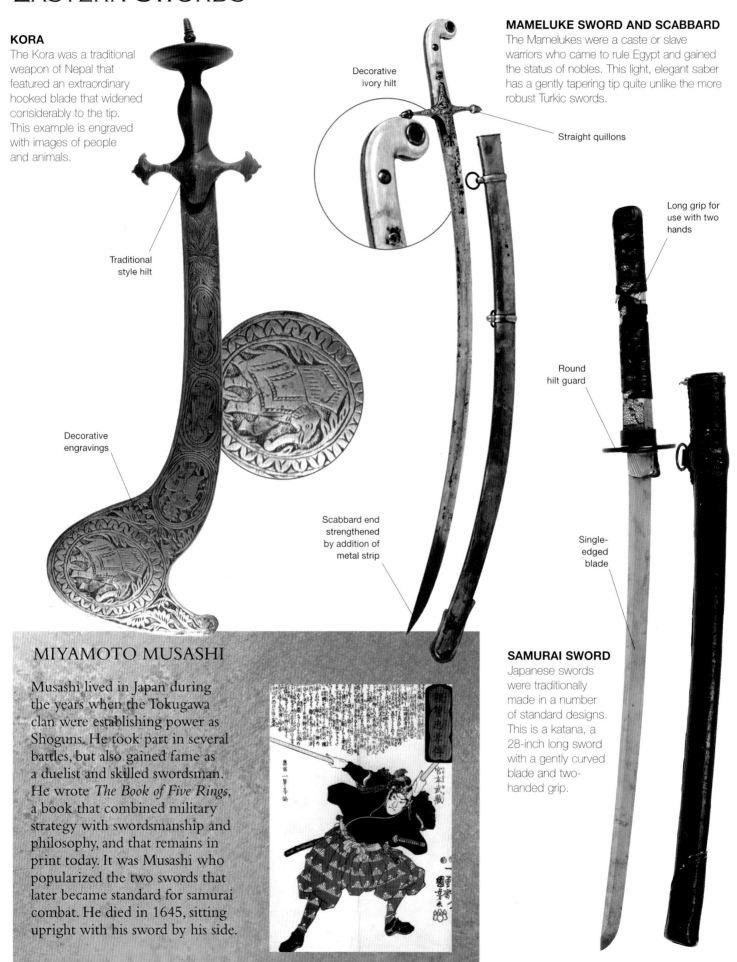

KORA

The Kora was a traditional weapon of Nepal that featured an extraordinary hooked blade that widened considerably to the tip. This example is engraved with images of people and animals.

Traditional style hilt

Decorative engravings

MAMELUKE SWORD AND SCABBARD

The Mamelukes were a caste or slave warriors who came to rule Egypt and gained the status of nobles. This light, elegant saber has a gently tapering tip quite unlike the more robust Turkic swords.

Decorative ivory hilt

Straight quillons

Scabbard end strengthened by addition of metal strip

Long grip for use with two hands

Round hilt guard

Single-edged blade

SAMURAI SWORD

Japanese swords were traditionally made in a number of standard designs. This is a katana, a 28-inch long sword with a gently curved blade and two-handed grip.

MIYAMOTO MUSASHI

Musashi lived in Japan during the years when the Tokugawa clan were establishing power as Shoguns. He took part in several battles, but also gained fame as a duelist and skilled swordsman. He wrote *The Book of Five Rings*, a book that combined military strategy with swordsmanship and philosophy, and that remains in print today. It was Musashi who popularized the two swords that later became standard for samurai combat. He died in 1645, sitting upright with his sword by his side.

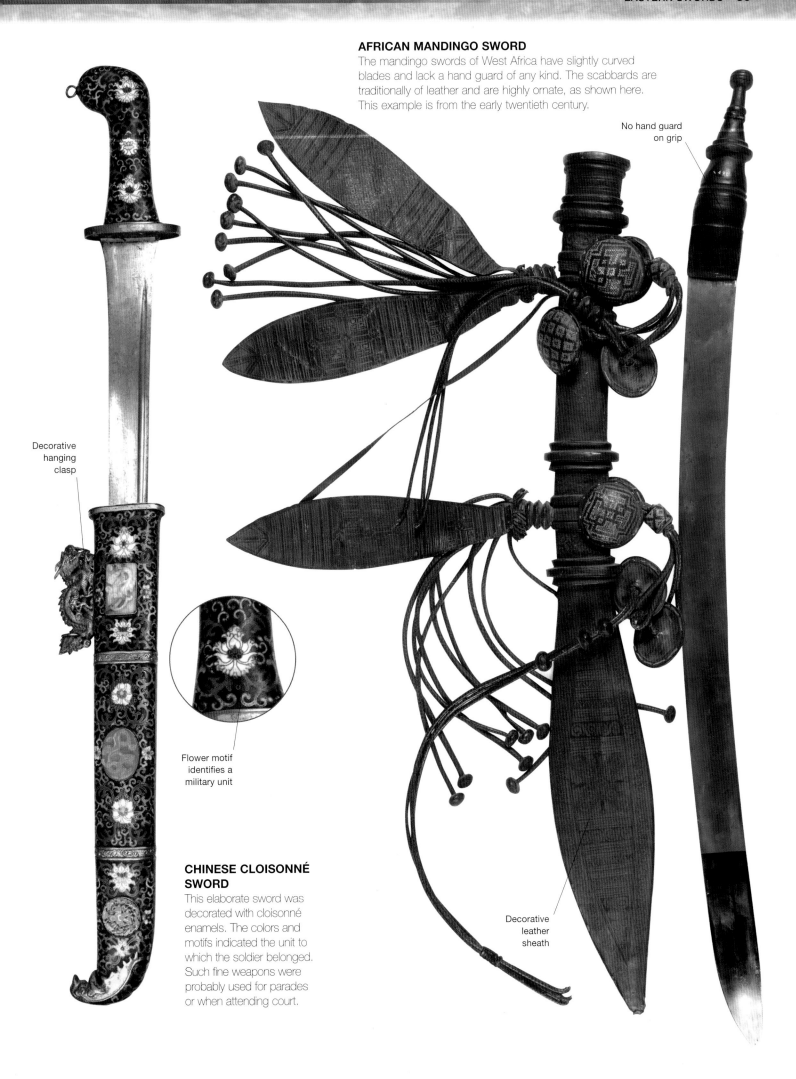

AFRICAN MANDINGO SWORD

The mandingo swords of West Africa have slightly curved blades and lack a hand guard of any kind. The scabbards are traditionally of leather and are highly ornate, as shown here. This example is from the early twentieth century.

No hand guard on grip

Decorative hanging clasp

Flower motif identifies a military unit

CHINESE CLOISONNÉ SWORD

This elaborate sword was decorated with cloisonné enamels. The colors and motifs indicated the unit to which the soldier belonged. Such fine weapons were probably used for parades or when attending court.

Decorative leather sheath

DAGGERS & COMBAT KNIVES

The distinguishing feature of the dagger is that it is designed primarily for stabbing an opponent, while a knife is primarily a cutting instrument. Of course many fighting knives combine a sharp point with a single- or double-edged blade, but the essential differences between the two weapons remain in the names they are given. Throughout most of history the dagger has had a reputation as a weapon of stealth. At a time when men habitually carried knives for a variety of everyday tasks, an assassin could carry a dagger toward a victim quite openly without arousing suspicion. In more recent times, the fighting knife has been used by elite forces when they wish to kill a sentry or other opponent as silently as possible.

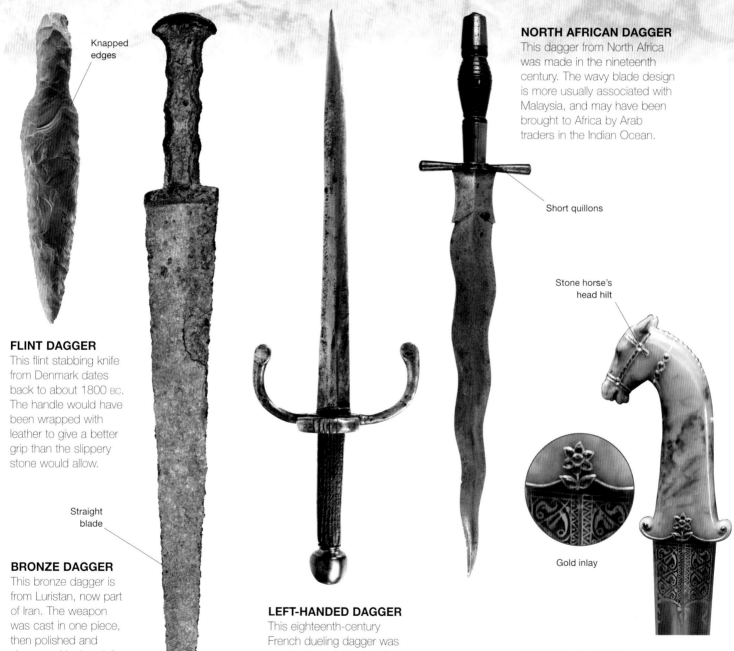

Knapped edges

FLINT DAGGER
This flint stabbing knife from Denmark dates back to about 1800 BC. The handle would have been wrapped with leather to give a better grip than the slippery stone would allow.

Straight blade

BRONZE DAGGER
This bronze dagger is from Luristan, now part of Iran. The weapon was cast in one piece, then polished and sharpened by hand. It is thought to date to around 5,000 BC.

LEFT-HANDED DAGGER
This eighteenth-century French dueling dagger was used in the left hand while the right hand held a sword. The sharply curved quillons were used to catch and trap the opponent's blade.

NORTH AFRICAN DAGGER
This dagger from North Africa was made in the nineteenth century. The wavy blade design is more usually associated with Malaysia, and may have been brought to Africa by Arab traders in the Indian Ocean.

Short quillons

Stone horse's head hilt

Gold inlay

MUGHAL DAGGER
This elegant dagger from northern India was made for a Mughal noble in the eighteenth century. The stone hilt has been carved into the shape of a horse's head.

Gilt decoration

Ivory handle

Kauda notch

INDIAN KHANJAR
The bent blade of the khanjar is sharpened on both sides. This style of knife is carried by men in Oman as a mark of their social status and it is considered a social taboo to draw it in public due to its past associations with feuds and revenge.

YATAGHAN
The yataghan of the Ottoman Turks had a slightly curved blade sharpened on the inside of the curve. It could be up to 30 inches long, but was carried and used as a knife rather than a sword.

KUKRI
Made in 1847, this Nepalese kukri has a sheath of felt and pierced metalwork. The heavy chopping blade is sharpened on the inside of the curve, and features the traditional kauda notch, which symbolizes the god Shiva.

CLOISONNÉ DAGGER
This short dagger was made in China where the handle and sheath were elaborately decorated in fired cloisonné enamel work.

BOWIE-STYLE KNIFE
The original bowie knife was created by smith James Black to a design by American frontiersman Jim Bowie in 1830. It was a 9-inch-long, heavy, single-bladed knife with a simple handle. The clip point was added to lighten the blade and soon became a distinctive feature of the bowie.

CLOAK AND DAGGER

During the sixteenth century a fighting method developed that used a dagger for offense, and a cloak to entangle the opponent's weapon and hide one's own weapon. It was widely regarded as a form of combat suitable for criminals and servants since gentlemen carried swords. The phrase "cloak and dagger" gradually shifted from implying a socially inferior method of combat to its modern sense of underhand or dishonest combat by the early nineteenth century.

EARLY PROJECTILE WEAPONS

Almost as soon as people began to use weapons they became aware of a problem with the axes, daggers, and other close-combat arms that they wielded. To get close enough to prey to use them, the wielder had to get within range of the horns, tusks, or teeth of the animal they were hunting. In combat with other humans the enemy's sword or ax was just as deadly. What was needed was a way of projecting the killing power of the weapon over a longer distance. Simply throwing an ax or javelin was an obvious move, but had its limitations. The answer came in the form of a variety of weapons that enabled the user to hurl a weapon much further and with greater force than was possible simply by picking up an object and chucking it. The projectile revolution in warfare was underway and continues into the twenty-first century.

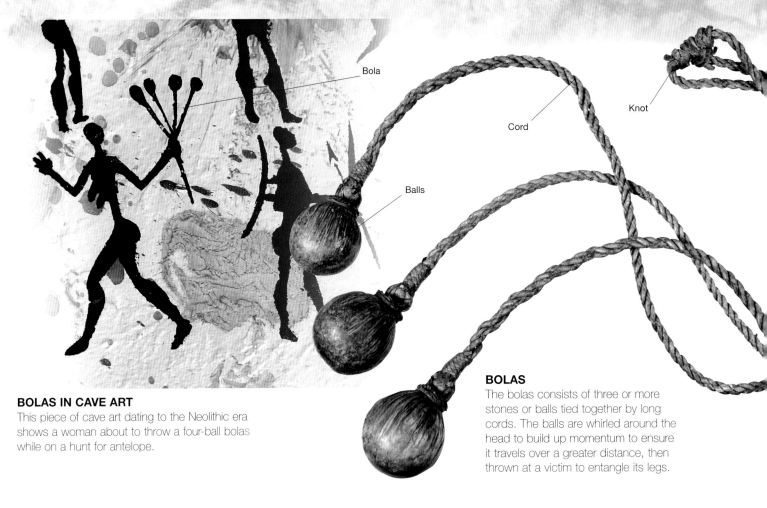

Bola

Cord

Knot

Balls

BOLAS IN CAVE ART
This piece of cave art dating to the Neolithic era shows a woman about to throw a four-ball bolas while on a hunt for antelope.

BOLAS
The bolas consists of three or more stones or balls tied together by long cords. The balls are whirled around the head to build up momentum to ensure it travels over a greater distance, then thrown at a victim to entangle its legs.

ATLATL
The spear thrower, or atlatl, was used to hurl a spear with greater force. The thrower acted as an extension of the arm to give greater speed to the spear. A refinement was the banner stone—a small weight to give greater resistance, resulting in a more forceful and accurate launch.

Spear placed
in groove

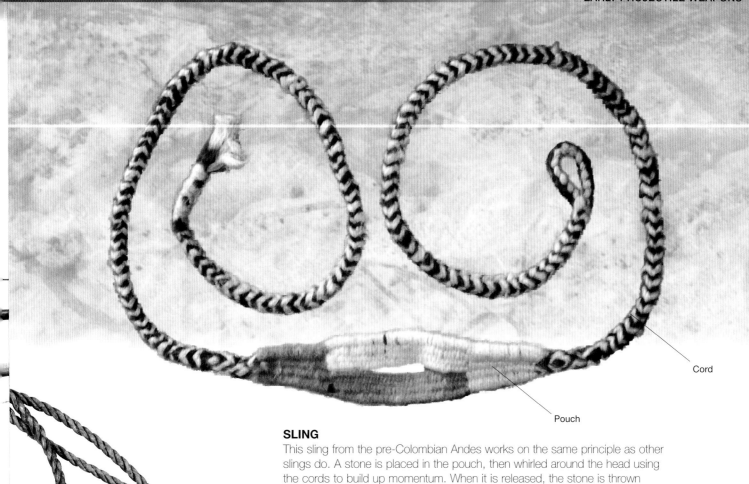

Cord

Pouch

SLING

This sling from the pre-Colombian Andes works on the same principle as other slings do. A stone is placed in the pouch, then whirled around the head using the cords to build up momentum. When it is released, the stone is thrown forward with great speed to travel a long distance.

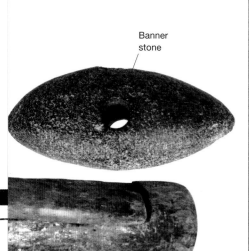

Banner stone

DAVID AND GOLIATH

The Biblical story of David and Goliath shows how projectile weapons technology can give a fighter an advantage. According to the Book of Samuel, David was a youthful shepherd when he carried supplies to King Saul and the Israelite army, which was in a standoff with the Philistine army. Because everyone else was too frightened, David chose to fight the gigantic Philistine champion, Goliath, who stood nearly seven feet tall, wore full armor, and was armed with spear and shield. David hurled a stone from his sling that struck Goliath on the forehead and killed him. The story shows David as a hero of the Israelites, but also symbolizes the triumph of God over paganism.

EARLY PROJECTILE WEAPONS

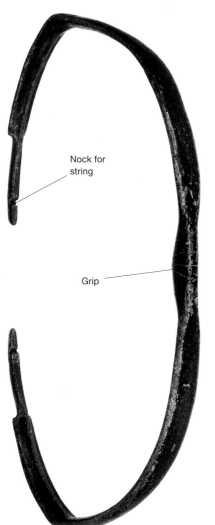

Nock for string

Grip

INDO-PERSIAN BOW

This complex composite bow is of a central Asian design, although this one comes from Persia. When strung, the bow is bent back so that the arms flex in the opposite direction from where they lie in the unstrung position (as shown). This gives enormous power to the bow when pulled only a short distance.

ENGLISH LONGBOW

The longbow is a relatively unsophisticated bow made from a single piece of yew or elm. Great care was taken in selecting the piece of wood to ensure it had the right mix of heartwood and sapwood before it was shaped and nocked. The weapon had a maximum range of 400 yards, but was generally effective at half that range.

Nock

Single-piece wooden construction

Bowstring

MONGOL BOW

From 1206, when they were united by Genghis Khan, to the fourteenth century, the Mongol tribes were unbeatable. This was largely due to their skilled archery from horseback. The Mongol bow was made up of several layers of different materials, including bamboo, horn, and sinew, layered so as to give the maximum tension from the shortest bow pull. This allowed them to shoot with power on a bow short enough to use on horseback.

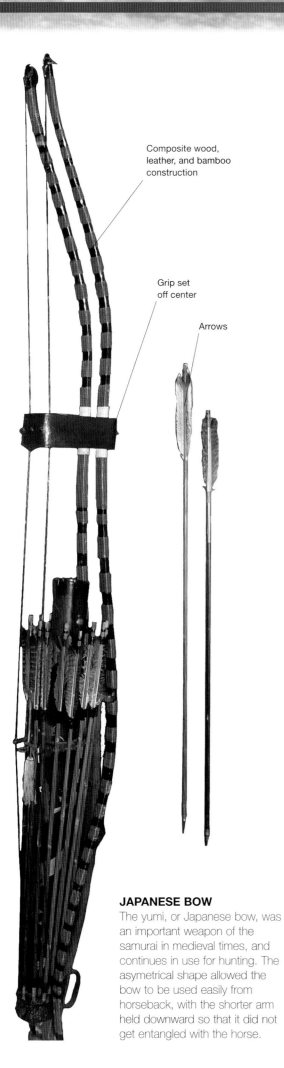

Composite wood,
leather, and bamboo
construction

Grip set
off center

Arrows

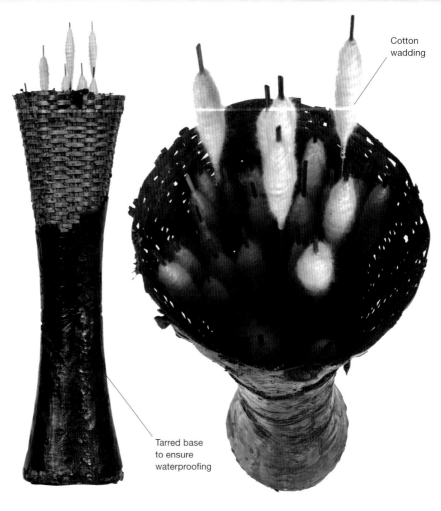

Cotton
wadding

Tarred base
to ensure
waterproofing

AFRICAN QUIVER

A selection of African blowdarts. The soft cotton wadding
around the end ensures a close fit within the blowpipe so
that a puff of air will propel the dart swiftly up the pipe.

JAPANESE BOW

The yumi, or Japanese bow, was
an important weapon of the
samurai in medieval times, and
continues in use for hunting. The
asymetrical shape allowed the
bow to be used easily from
horseback, with the shorter arm
held downward so that it did not
get entangled with the horse.

BLOWPIPE

The blowpipe (also
known as a blowgun)
has been used as a
hunting weapon by
various cultures, but is
most often associated
with the native peoples
of South America
and Southeast Asia.
The weapon shoots a
lightweight projectile
over relatively short
distances. Since the darts
lack hitting power they
are often coated with
poison to immobilize
the prey.

EARLY PROJECTILE WEAPONS

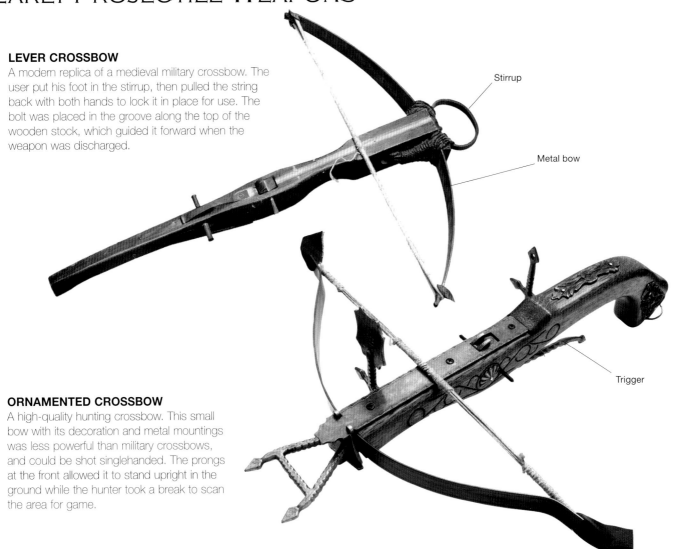

LEVER CROSSBOW

A modern replica of a medieval military crossbow. The user put his foot in the stirrup, then pulled the string back with both hands to lock it in place for use. The bolt was placed in the groove along the top of the wooden stock, which guided it forward when the weapon was discharged.

Stirrup

Metal bow

Trigger

ORNAMENTED CROSSBOW

A high-quality hunting crossbow. This small bow with its decoration and metal mountings was less powerful than military crossbows, and could be shot singlehanded. The prongs at the front allowed it to stand upright in the ground while the hunter took a break to scan the area for game.

BATTLE OF CRÉCY

Fought in August 1346, the Battle of Crécy marked the emergence of a devastating new weapon on the battlefields of Europe. For centuries war had been dominated by men on horseback wearing heavy armor and wielding the knightly combination of sword, shield, and lance.

At Crécy, infantry armed with the longbow slaughtered these knights wholesale. It was not that the longbow was a new weapon—it had been known for at least 200 years—it was the way in which it was used. Massed bodies of archers, each firing eight arrows per minute, deluged the French knights with tens of thousands of arrows, killing horses, punching through armor, and knocking men over by sheer force of impact. Medieval warfare had changed forever.

CROSSBOW

A nineteenth-century hunting bow. The wooden stock resembles that of a contemporary musket, as does the trigger mechanism and side plates made of brass. Many hunters preferred to use a crossbow as it neither made a loud bang nor gave off a large puff of smoke when fired, as did contemporary firearms.

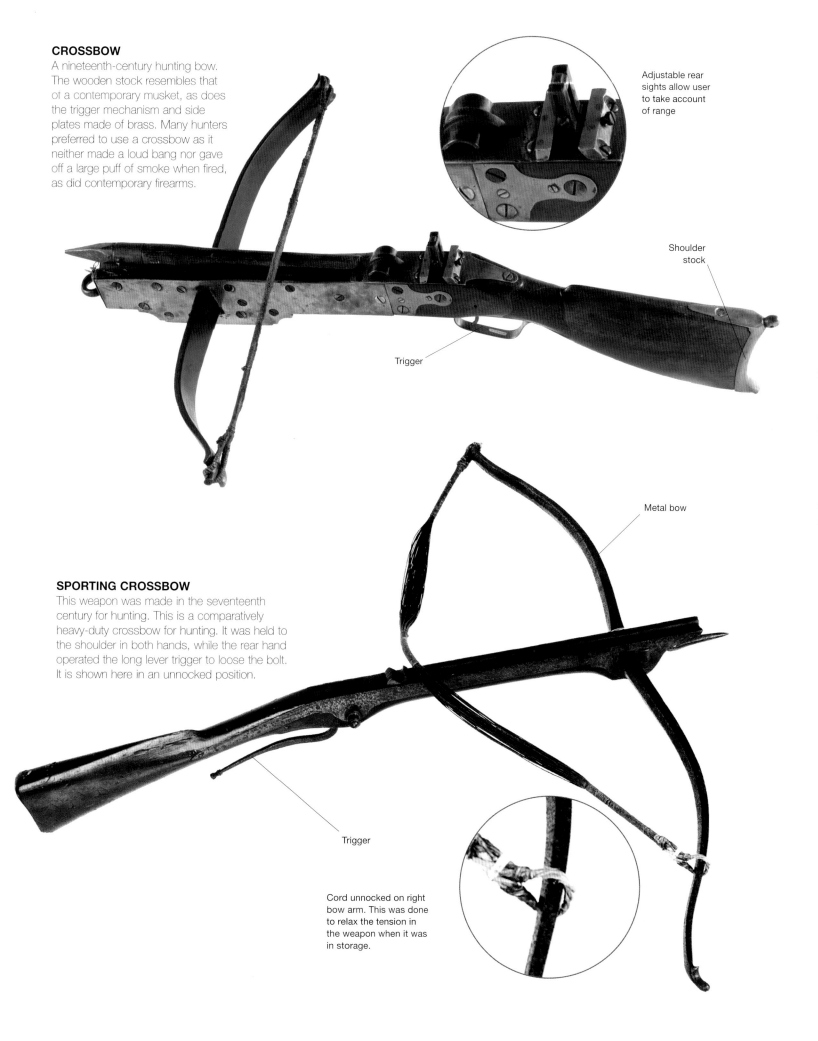

Adjustable rear sights allow user to take account of range

Shoulder stock

Trigger

SPORTING CROSSBOW

This weapon was made in the seventeenth century for hunting. This is a comparatively heavy-duty crossbow for hunting. It was held to the shoulder in both hands, while the rear hand operated the long lever trigger to loose the bolt. It is shown here in an unnocked position.

Metal bow

Trigger

Cord unnocked on right bow arm. This was done to relax the tension in the weapon when it was in storage.

THE FIRST FIREARMS 1300–1840

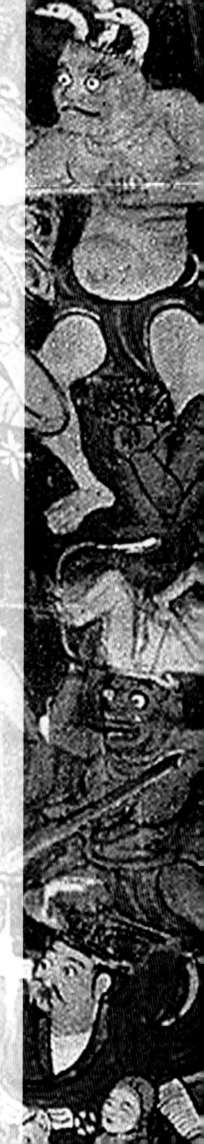

When the explosive mixture of charcoal, sulfur, and saltpeter was first discovered in China in the ninth century it was used to make fireworks and demolition charges. Its first use as a weapon seems to have been in the form of an exploding rocket around 950. It was not until about 1030 that someone had the idea of packing gunpowder into a tube and using it to hurl a projectile at the enemy. Early guns were inaccurate, unreliable, and often ineffective, but the potential was obvious. Within a few centuries improvements and refinements were made and the gun became the dominant weapon of war and hunting across Europe and Asia.

EARLY CHINESE WEAPONS
A Chinese illustration showing the temptation of Sakyamuni by demons. The demons below tempt him with women, those above assail him with a grenade and a fire lance.

THE INVENTION OF GUNPOWDER

The earliest forms of gunpowder were simple mixtures of the fuels sulfur and charcoal, and the oxidizer saltpeter. Because those making the mixture did not understand the chemistry behind the explosion, several centuries of experimentation resulted in a wide variety of powders able to deliver different powers and speeds of blast. All shared the fact that they were made up of the three components ground down to fine powder, and then mixed together. If shaken up, say by being moved on a cart, the three powders would tend to separate out, which made the powder less effective. The powder was also vulnerable to damp, either producing a less-powerful blast or failing to ignite at all. Despite these drawbacks, early gunpowder weapons proved to be fairly effective.

FIRE BOMBS
A Chinese illustration depicting a scene from the tenth century. One soldier is throwing a grenade or fire bomb, while another uses a fire lance, which fired a dart a distance of about 30 feet. It is unclear if this shows genuine tenth-century weapons or equipment that the artist thought might have then existed.

Fire lance

Grenade

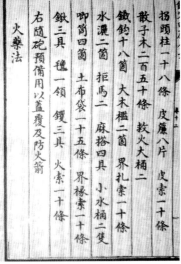

EARLIEST KNOWN FORMULA
This military manuscript was compiled in China in 1044 by scholars Zeng Gongliang, Ding Du, and Yang Weide. This page gives a recipe for making "huo yao fa," the "fire chemical." It is the earliest known instruction for making a form of gunpowder.

Chinese Rockets Repulse Mongols 1232

CHINESE REPULSE MONGOLS (1232)
In 1232, the Mongol armies invading China had overrun most of the north of the country and were laying siege to the capital city, Kaifeng. The defenders were heavily outnumbered, but fought back with a number of gunpowder weapons that caught the Mongols by surprise and inflicted heavy casualties. These weapons included rockets with powerful exploding warheads, and bombs that were dropped from the walls to explode and shower the attackers with shards of pottery. The city finally fell, through treachery.

CHINESE SIGNAL GUN

This small brass gun was made in China in the eighteenth century. The two blunt lugs were to fix the barrel into a wooden stock. This was not designed to be a weapon, but was instead a military signaling device. The sharp report of this gun could be heard over the din of battle, and the puff of smoke emerging from it would be seen by aides watching it and know the prearranged order it would convey.

Ornamental dragon

Lugs

BLACK POWDER FOR MUZZLELOADING WEAPONS

In about 1400, European gunpowder makers developed the process of wet mixing. This involved mixing the ingredients into a paste with urine. When the paste dried into a hard mass it was milled into a granular powder, each grain containing a stable mix of ingredients. This produced more reliable and effective gunpowder and massively boosted the use of the weapons.

Metal cartridge case

Evenly sized grains

BATTLE OF GUNTUR (1780)

In 1780 Haider Ali, ruler of Mysore in southern India, attacked the British colonies of Madras and Arcot in an effort to drive the British from southern India. At the Battle of Guntur, Haider Ali unleashed newly improved exploding rockets on the British infantry. The new weapons had a powerful warhead encased in cast iron that allowed the powder to be densely packed, which fragmented into sharp splinters on detonation. He also mounted his rockets on firing racks on carts, allowing more than twenty to be fired at once at a single target. The British broke and fled, leaving 3,000 prisoners in Haider Ali's hands. Haider Ali died two years later of cancer and the war against the British collapsed.

MATCHLOCK GUNS

The first guns were fired by the crude and relatively unreliable method of pushing something very hot into a touchhole at the breech end of the barrel. This should have ignited the gunpowder inside the barrel, but if the wire or coal was not hot enough, or was the wrong shape, the gun would not fire. An improvement in the form of the matchlock appeared around 1470. As well as being more reliable, the matchlock allowed the user to hold the weapon in both hands when firing it and to look toward the target, not the touchhole, both of which considerably improved accuracy.

THREE JAPANESE ARQUEBUSES
The first weapon to use the matchlock was the arquebus. This was a two-handed weapon that was tucked under the armpit or held to the shoulder to be fired. The arquebus was a smooth bore gun that was loaded from the muzzle with first the gunpowder, then the ball, and finally wadding to hold the rest in place. These examples were made in Japan around 1700.

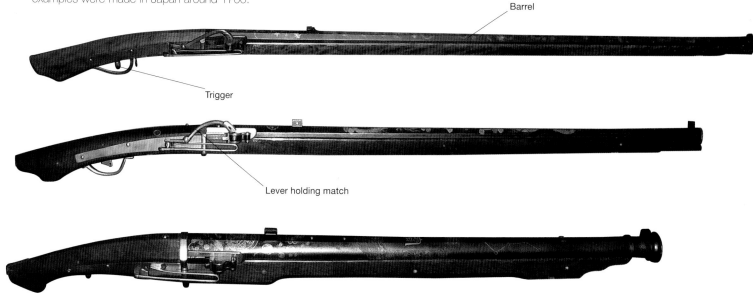

Barrel

Trigger

Lever holding match

JAPANESE ARQUEBUS

In 1543 the Japanese lord of Tanegashima Island bought two matchlock arquebuses from a Chinese ship that had been forced to take shelter from a storm. He gave the strange new weapons to a local swordsmith to see if he could copy them. Within ten years over 300,000 arquebus had been made in Japan. The government closed Japan to foreign contact soon afterward, so later improvements in gun technology did not reach the Japanese, who continued to manufacture and use arquebuses long after they went out of use elsewhere.

Arm to carry matchlock

Trigger

JAPANESE PISTOL

This pistol was produced in Japan in the eighteenth century and is essentially a smaller version of the arquebus made to be fired in one hand. By this date the Japanese government had severely restricted which members of society were allowed to own or carry firearms.

Trigger

Nut to remove mechanism from gun

INDIAN MATCHLOCK RIFLE

This early seventeenth century gun from India has very ornamental metalwork, but its mechanism is that of a basic matchlock. The barrel has been rifled, meaning it has twisting grooves inside to spin the bullet as it is fired to give greater accuracy. Rifling was developed in Germany around 1490, but the grooves quickly fouled with gunpowder soot when the weapon was fired.

Ramrod

Pricker to clean touchhole

INDIAN MATCHLOCK BLUNDERBUSS

The flared muzzle of this gun marks it as a blunderbuss. These guns did not fire a single bullet, but instead spewed forth a mass of smaller balls and projectiles that spread out rather like shot from a sawn-off shotgun.

Barrel lacks touchhole

Fake trigger

BALKAN DRESS PISTOL

By the later sixteenth century, a highly ornamented pistol was an essential part of everyday dress for any man in the Balkans with pretensions to be of the nobility. Rulers, for obvious reasons, did not want noblemen at court walking about with pistols in their belts. The answer was this fake pistol which has no working parts and is more a product of the jeweler's art than that of the gunsmith.

MATCHLOCK MECHANISM

Lever

The matchlock was a lever to the top of which was attached a burning "match," a type of fuse. When the bottom of the lever, the trigger, was pulled back, the match was thrust down into the touchhole, igniting the charge and firing the gun. The layout of trigger beneath the barrel and stock was retained by later guns which do not actually require this configuration.

Trigger

MATCHLOCK GUNS

INDIAN TORADOR
The torador was a form of Indian matchlock with a very long barrel that was intended to give the weapon greater accuracy. This example has a 46-inch barrel that ends in a brass muzzle chiseled to resemble a leopard's head.

Slender butt

INDIAN EIGHTEENTH-CENTURY TORADOR
This elaborately decorated torador has ivory inlay around the breech and stock. This is a relatively short weapon, having a barrel of only 17.5 inches, and lightweight construction. It is probably a hunting gun intended to be used by a woman or boy.

Ivory inlay

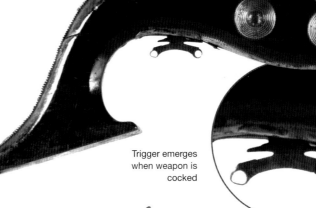

CORNAC-GUN COMBINATION
This peculiar looking weapon is a combination of a gun and a cornac, designed to be used by a mahout riding an elephant. The curved hook is the cornac, which was used to prod the elephant in the ear or mouth to give it instructions. The gun has a matchlock mechanism and was probably intended to be used if the elephant was attacked by the animal being hunted.

Trigger emerges when weapon is cocked

Butt designed to be tucked under the shoulder to be fired one-handed from horseback

Trigger

Match holder

EARLY MATCHLOCK CALIVER
The caliver was an improvement to the matchlock that was introduced to armies in the early sixteenth century. The key improvement was that they were all manufactured to have the same caliber. This meant that a soldier in action could use bullets from a central store, safe in the knowledge they would fit his gun. Previously each arquebus was individually made and came with its own bullet mold.

Trigger

CALIVER REPLICA
This modern replica of a sixteenth century caliver shows the improved firing mechanism. The lever holding the match is powered by a spring so that when the trigger is squeezed the match snaps down with force into the touchhole, increasing the chances of a successful firing.

Ramrod

Brass bands hold
barrel to stock

Ornamental scrollwork

Sharp point to
irritate elephant hide

KING JAMES I AND THE GUNPOWDER PLOT

In 1605 Robert Catesby and a group of Catholic gentry planned to murder King James I of England and most of the political elite by blowing up the House of Lords during the State Opening of Parliament on November 5th. On October 26th an anonymous letter warned Baron Monteagle not to attend the State Opening, and he passed the warning on to the government. A search of the Palace of Westminster found a mercenary named Guy Fawkes guarding thirty-six barrels of gunpowder in a cellar. He was arrested by King James's bodyguard, and under torture revealed the names of his fellow conspirators.

WHEEL LOCK WEAPONS

Although firearms were becoming increasingly effective by the end of the fifteenth century as gunpowder became more reliable and methods of casting barrels improved, the matchlock firing mechanism remained a problem. Matches were easily put out in damp weather or by careless handling, rendering the weapon useless. A partial answer to the issue was developed in Germany soon after the year 1500 when an unknown gunsmith developed the wheel lock, a clockwork device for firing a gun. The mechanism was expensive, so it tended to be used only on prestige weapons while the matchlock continued in use with the military for another 180 years.

RAMPART GUN
This bulky wheel lock weapon takes advantage of the fact that a wheel lock could be loaded and wound up in advance, being left for hours or days before being fired. Rampart guns were placed in parts of a fortification where a man could not fit, but which covered a blind spot. If an enemy reached the spot, a wire was pulled to fire the gun.

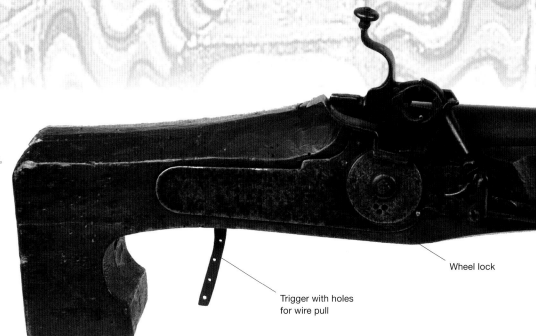

Wheel lock

Trigger with holes
for wire pull

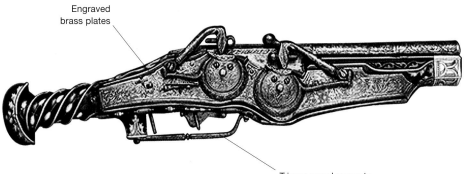

Engraved
brass plates

Trigger guard prevents
trigger being accidentally
pulled when in pocket

POCKET PISTOL
This tiny but highly ornamental sixteenth century wheel lock pistol is probably from Germany. The wheel lock meant that small pistols such as this could be secreted in pockets, impossible with a spluttering matchlock, then pulled out and fired in seconds. This made them a favored weapon of criminals and assassins. In 1517 Emperor Maximillian I banned wheel lock pistols in Austria, other than for himself, his bodyguards, and favored noblemen.

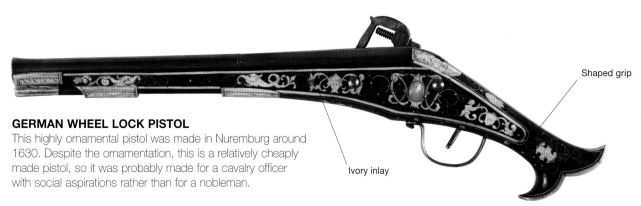

Shaped grip

GERMAN WHEEL LOCK PISTOL
This highly ornamental pistol was made in Nuremburg around 1630. Despite the ornamentation, this is a relatively cheaply made pistol, so it was probably made for a cavalry officer with social aspirations rather than for a nobleman.

Ivory inlay

Walnut
club

Bone inlay

WHEEL LOCK "PUFFER"

Made in Augsburg in 1580 this wheel lock belongs to a type of large-caliber pistols known as "puffers" due to the large cloud of smoke they emitted on firing. The stock is of walnut and the inlay is of bone. Note that the grip is angled downward. This means that some of the recoil is transferred into an upward jerk of the gun as it is fired, which reduces accuracy but is easier on the user's wrist.

WHEEL LOCK MECHANISM

The wheel lock worked by quickly rotating a notched steel wheel against a piece of iron pyrite. As the steel notches hit the pyrite they created a shower of sparks. The sparks then fell into a pan containing a quantity of gunpowder that, when ignited, flashed through the touchhole to ignite the main charge in the barrel.

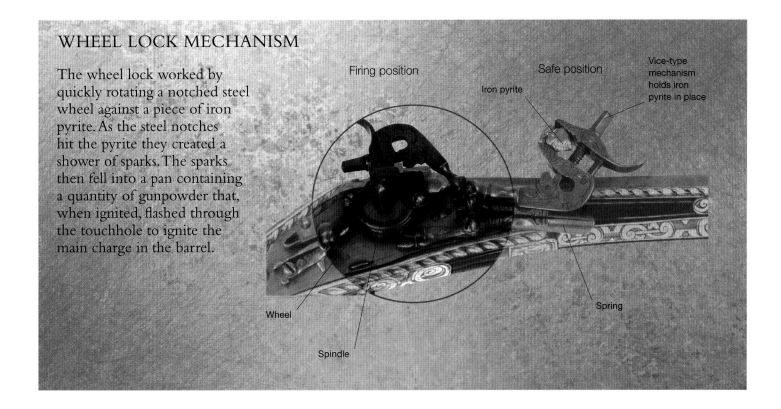

Firing position

Safe position

Iron pyrite

Vice-type
mechanism
holds iron
pyrite in place

Wheel

Spring

Spindle

WHEEL LOCK WEAPONS

WHEEL LOCK PISTOL

This unusual wheel lock pistol was made in Britain in the later sixteenth century. It has two firing mechanisms and two triggers, giving it an unusual appearance. The grip of these early pistols were almost in line with the barrel which made for a steadier aim when firing, but meant that the recoil pushed directly back on the user's wrist.

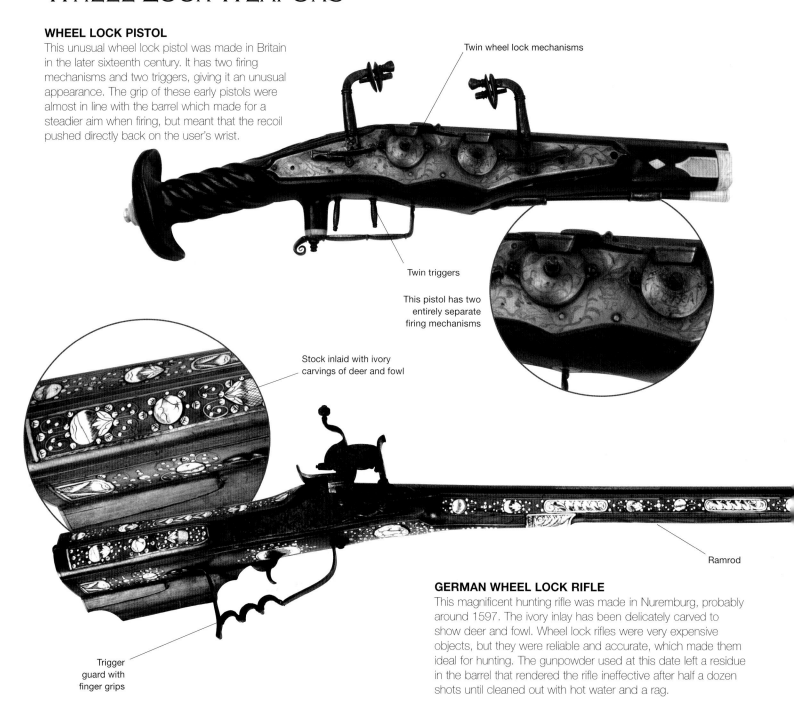

Twin wheel lock mechanisms

Twin triggers

This pistol has two entirely separate firing mechanisms

Stock inlaid with ivory carvings of deer and fowl

Ramrod

Trigger guard with finger grips

GERMAN WHEEL LOCK RIFLE

This magnificent hunting rifle was made in Nuremburg, probably around 1597. The ivory inlay has been delicately carved to show deer and fowl. Wheel lock rifles were very expensive objects, but they were reliable and accurate, which made them ideal for hunting. The gunpowder used at this date left a residue in the barrel that rendered the rifle ineffective after half a dozen shots until cleaned out with hot water and a rag.

SAXON-STYLE WHEEL LOCK PISTOL

This pistol is a highly elaborate example with delicate ivory inlay showing vine and leaf designs. The barrel is of the "cannon" type, so named as it resembled the barrels of contemporary cannons. The heavy wooden ball at the base of the grip could be used as a club once the pistol had been fired.

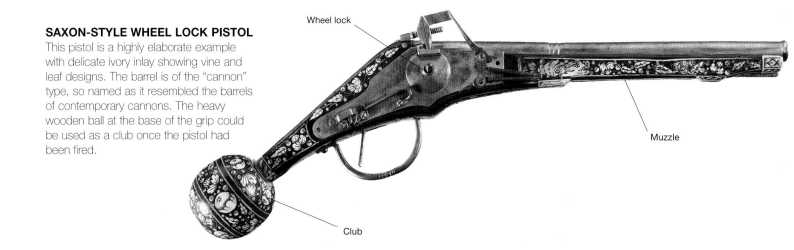

Wheel lock

Muzzle

Club

GERMAN WHEEL LOCK PISTOLS

These wheel lock pistols were made in Saxony around the year 1500. The elaborate decoration shows that these were intended for a rich customer. The pistols come with a matching cartridge box able to hold five balls and measured quantities of powder, each wrapped in paper. The key shown was used to wind up the spring that powered the wheel.

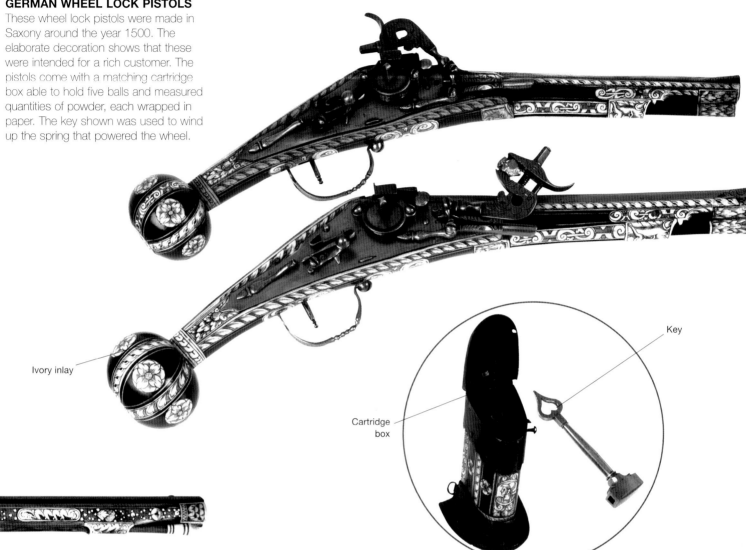

Ivory inlay

Cartridge box

Key

PISTOL OR MACE

Although effective at close range, all early pistols had the drawback that they were single-shot weapons. Once they had been fired, they were useless. It was for this reason that many were made with a heavy ball of solid wood or metal at the end of the grip. In a melee, a soldier could fire his pistol, then grip it by the muzzle and use it as a club.

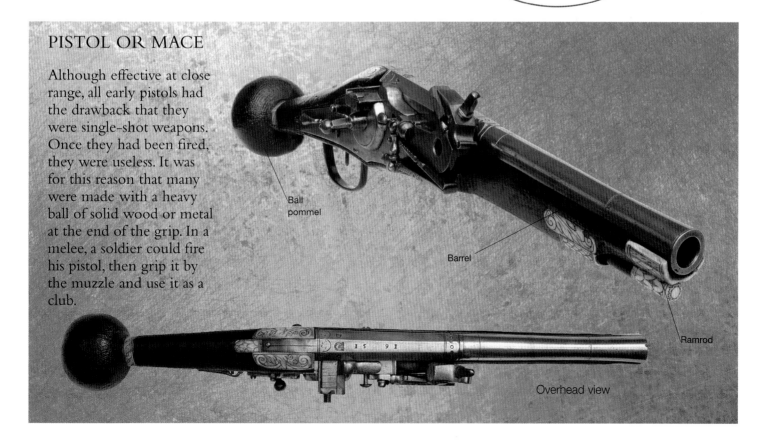

Ball pommel

Barrel

Ramrod

Overhead view

WHEEL LOCK WEAPONS

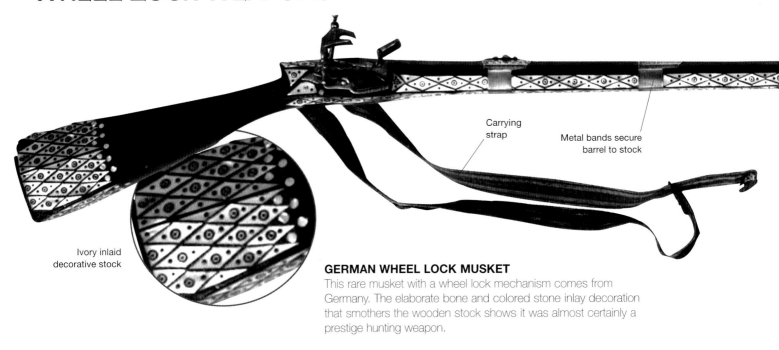

Carrying strap

Metal bands secure barrel to stock

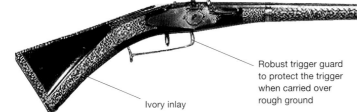

Ivory inlaid decorative stock

GERMAN WHEEL LOCK MUSKET

This rare musket with a wheel lock mechanism comes from Germany. The elaborate bone and colored stone inlay decoration that smothers the wooden stock shows it was almost certainly a prestige hunting weapon.

Robust trigger guard to protect the trigger when carried over rough ground

Ivory inlay

ITALIAN WHEEL LOCK HUNTING RIFLE

This elegant rifle was made in Italy. At this date rifles were not used by the military as the fouling caused by the gunpowder meant they had to be cleaned every six or so shots, something not practical on the battlefield.

Dog head holding pyrites to create spark

Iron barrel

Trigger guard

EARLY AUTOMATIC RIFLE

This ingenious hunting gun dates to about 1600. The rifled barrel was designed to take up to 16 cartridges that were set off one after another by the wheel lock mechanism. The trigger was pulled once, the resulting sparks fired the first cartridge which then set off a trail of powder that fired the second cartridge a second later, the third and subsequent cartridges following in turn. The ivory plaques show pictures of men hunting and natural motifs.

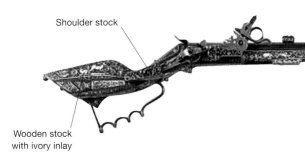

Shoulder stock

Wooden stock with ivory inlay

HUNTING RIFLE

This highly decorated wheel lock hunting rifle is from Austria. Note that the shoulder stock bends noticeably downward from the rear of the barrel. This allowed the user to peer along the length of the barrel to aim the gun without needing to bend his neck unduly downward.

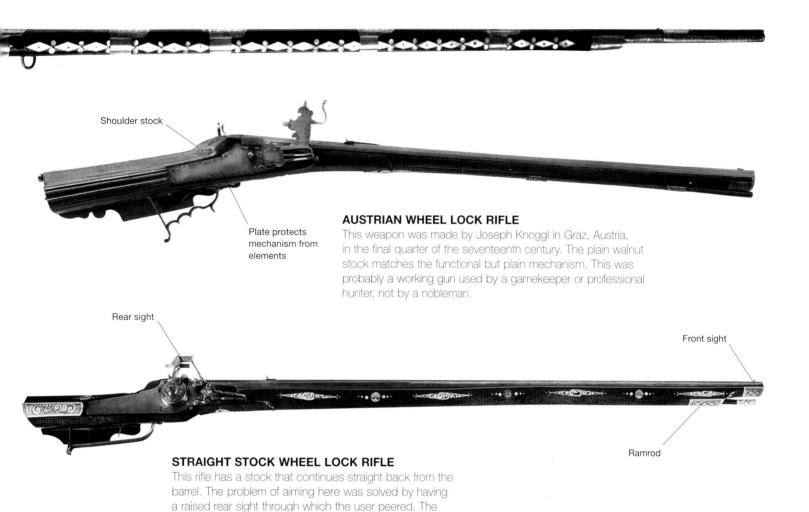

Shoulder stock

Plate protects mechanism from elements

AUSTRIAN WHEEL LOCK RIFLE

This weapon was made by Joseph Knoggl in Graz, Austria, in the final quarter of the seventeenth century. The plain walnut stock matches the functional but plain mechanism. This was probably a working gun used by a gamekeeper or professional hunter, not by a nobleman.

Rear sight

Front sight

Ramrod

STRAIGHT STOCK WHEEL LOCK RIFLE

This rifle has a stock that continues straight back from the barrel. The problem of aiming here was solved by having a raised rear sight through which the user peered. The inlay is of bone.

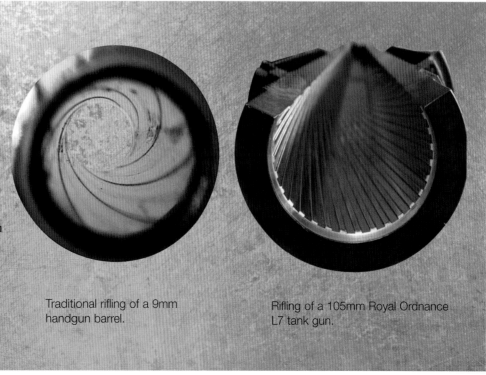

RIFLING

It had been known for centuries that if a projectile could be made to spin in flight it would be more accurate and have a greater range. Arrows were fitted with feathered "flights" at the rear that were set at an angle to give them this spin. The earliest guns were smoothbore, which meant the bullets did not spin. The first effort to spin a bullet was made in Augsburg in the 1490s, but it was not until the 1530s that German gunsmith August Kotter was able to produce barrels with accurate grooves inside that would spin a bullet properly.

Traditional rifling of a 9mm handgun barrel.

Rifling of a 105mm Royal Ordnance L7 tank gun.

EARLY COMBINATION WEAPONS

All firearms before the mid-nineteenth century could fire only one shot before they needed to be reloaded. Since this involved pouring powder down the barrel, followed by a bullet, and then wadding, all of which had to be rammed down securely to compress the powder, this was a time consuming business that could take up to thirty seconds. That time was not always available in a fight, so many firearms were made to include another weapon as well that could be used with murderous efficiency. Early wheel lock pistols usually had a club attached to the grip, but that was not the end of the early gunsmiths' imagination, as the examples here clearly show.

KEY PISTOL

Made in Scotland around 1730 this weapon combines a matchlock pistol with a key. The shank of the key forms the gun barrel. It is thought that this may have been used by the doorkeeper of a rich household so that he had a pistol immediately to hand when unlocking the front door in case criminals lurked outside.

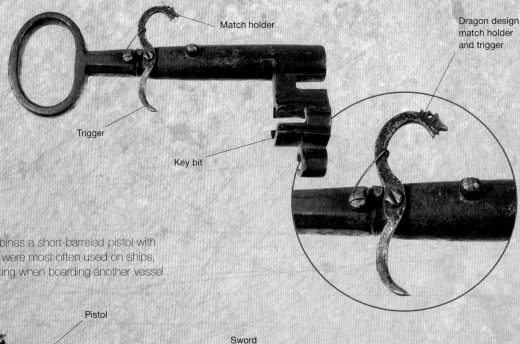

Match holder

Dragon design match holder and trigger

Trigger

Key bit

PISTOL SWORD

Made around 1750 this weapon combines a short-barreled pistol with a short sword blade. These weapons were most often used on ships, where the cramped conditions of fighting when boarding another vessel favored a shorter blade.

Pistol

Sword

Trigger

Ax head

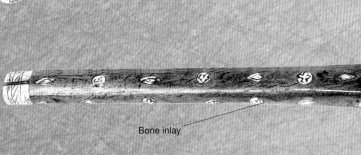

Bone inlay

GERMAN AX-PISTOL

This weapon was made in Silesia, then a part of Germany, in about 1650. The pistol fires out through the ax head. The trigger emerges only when the weapon is cocked, but otherwise lies snugly inside the wooden stock. The back of the ax features a spike able to punch through the plate armor of the period.

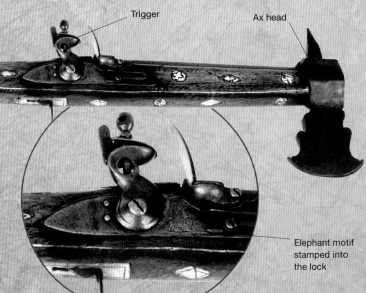

Elephant motif stamped into the lock

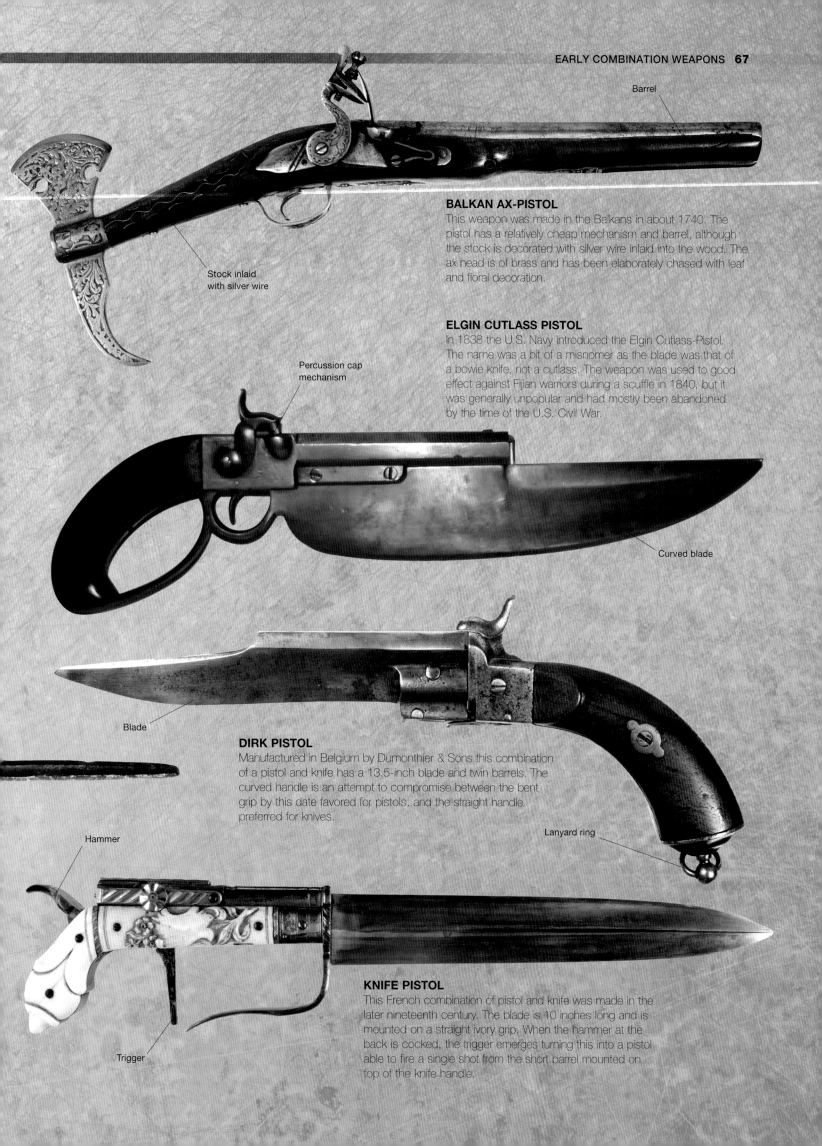

Barrel

Stock inlaid
with silver wire

BALKAN AX-PISTOL

This weapon was made in the Balkans in about 1740. The pistol has a relatively cheap mechanism and barrel, although the stock is decorated with silver wire inlaid into the wood. The ax head is of brass and has been elaborately chased with leaf and floral decoration.

ELGIN CUTLASS PISTOL

In 1838 the U.S. Navy introduced the Elgin Cutlass-Pistol. The name was a bit of a misnomer as the blade was that of a bowie knife, not a cutlass. The weapon was used to good effect against Fijian warriors during a scuffle in 1840, but it was generally unpopular and had mostly been abandoned by the time of the U.S. Civil War.

Percussion cap
mechanism

Curved blade

Blade

DIRK PISTOL

Manufactured in Belgium by Dumonthier & Sons this combination of a pistol and knife has a 13.5-inch blade and twin barrels. The curved handle is an attempt to compromise between the bent grip by this date favored for pistols, and the straight handle preferred for knives.

Lanyard ring

Hammer

KNIFE PISTOL

This French combination of pistol and knife was made in the later nineteenth century. The blade is 10 inches long and is mounted on a straight ivory grip. When the hammer at the back is cocked, the trigger emerges turning this into a pistol able to fire a single shot from the short barrel mounted on top of the knife handle.

Trigger

FLINTLOCK FIREARMS

While the wheel lock produced an effective and reliable method of firing a gun, it was expensive to produce and, containing delicate moving parts, was susceptible to damage if dropped or mishandled. In 1610 the French gunsmith Marin le Bourgeoys produced a new mechanism for firing a gun and presented it to King Louis XIII.

This was the flintlock, a relatively simple and robust mechanism that quickly proved to be popular. By the 1670s, the flintlock had replaced all other forms of firing a gun and was being used in pistols, muskets, and even cannon. It would remain the principle mechanism for firing a gun right through to the 1840s.

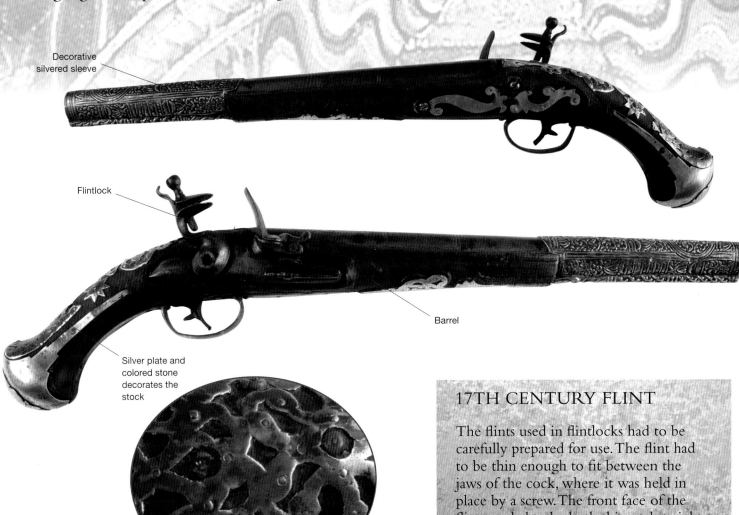

Decorative silvered sleeve

Flintlock

Silver plate and colored stone decorates the stock

Barrel

WOODEN FLINTLOCK PISTOL

This highly decorated flintlock pistol was made in central Europe in the later seventeenth century. The barrel is encased in an elaborately chased and silvered sleeve that would have sparkled and caught the sunlight when in action. The wooden stock is similarly decorated with pierced silver plates embellished with colored stones.

17TH CENTURY FLINT

The flints used in flintlocks had to be carefully prepared for use. The flint had to be thin enough to fit between the jaws of the cock, where it was held in place by a screw. The front face of the flint needed to be both thin and straight, allowing it to create the maximum number of sparks when the trigger was pulled and the flint was propelled against the steel face of the frizzen.

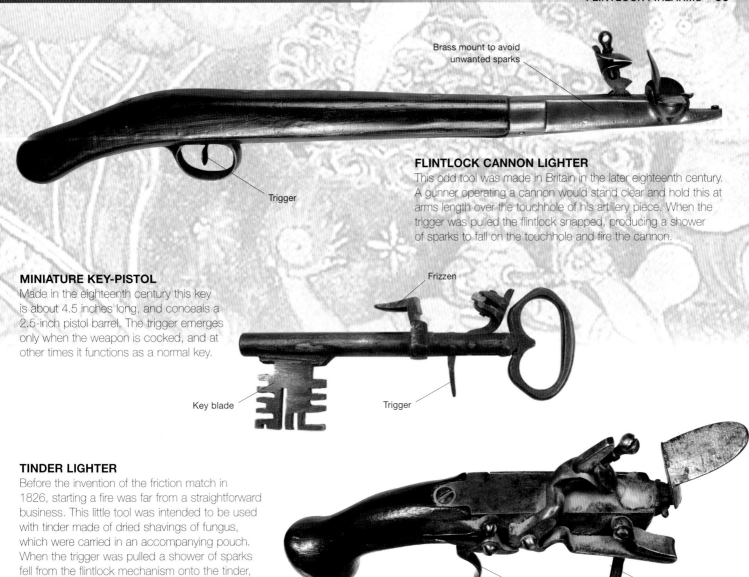

Brass mount to avoid
unwanted sparks

Trigger

FLINTLOCK CANNON LIGHTER

This odd tool was made in Britain in the later eighteenth century.
A gunner operating a cannon would stand clear and hold this at
arms length over the touchhole of his artillery piece. When the
trigger was pulled the flintlock snapped, producing a shower
of sparks to fall on the touchhole and fire the cannon.

MINIATURE KEY-PISTOL

Made in the eighteenth century this key
is about 4.5 inches long, and conceals a
2.5-inch pistol barrel. The trigger emerges
only when the weapon is cocked, and at
other times it functions as a normal key.

Frizzen

Key blade

Trigger

TINDER LIGHTER

Before the invention of the friction match in
1826, starting a fire was far from a straightforward
business. This little tool was intended to be used
with tinder made of dried shavings of fungus,
which were carried in an accompanying pouch.
When the trigger was pulled a shower of sparks
fell from the flintlock mechanism onto the tinder,
which then caught fire and could be used to set
light to straw or wood.

Trigger

Spring

FLINTLOCK MECHANISM

The flintlock worked by using
a spring to power a hammer, or
cock. Once the gun was loaded,
the frizzen was lifted and a pinch
of powder placed in the pan.
The frizzen was then lowered
and held in place by a spring to
keep the powder dry and secure.
When the trigger was pulled, the
hammer was jerked forward by
a more powerful spring. As the
hammer came down, the flint it
held struck the frizzen. This both
lifted the frizzen to expose the
loose powder and also created a
shower of sparks that ignited the
powder. The flame then flashed
through the touchhole to ignite
the main charge and fire the gun.

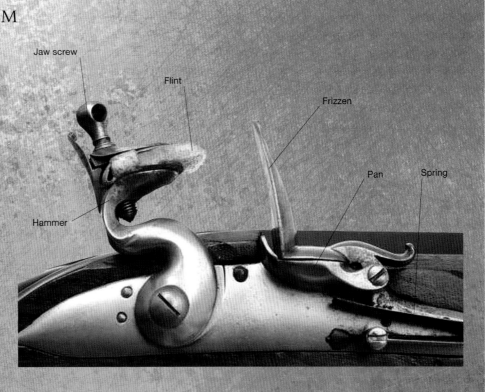

Jaw screw

Flint

Frizzen

Pan

Spring

Hammer

FLINTLOCK FIREARMS

WEST EUROPEAN FLINT GUN
Made in the seventeenth century this flintlock pistol retains a layout that was more common in earlier years. The grip is only slightly downturned from the line of the barrel, and the trigger is set quite far back. The solid wooden ball at the butt end acted both as a counterweight to the long barrel, and as a club once the gun had been fired.

MR. AND MRS. ANDREWS
This portrait of a wealthy English couple was painted by Thomas Gainsborough in 1748. They are shown in the middle of their estate; Mr. Andrews holds his flintlock hunting musket and is accompanied by his hunting dog. Hunting was a popular pastime among the gentry at this date, and the flintlock gun made it a productive way to bring home small game for the kitchens.

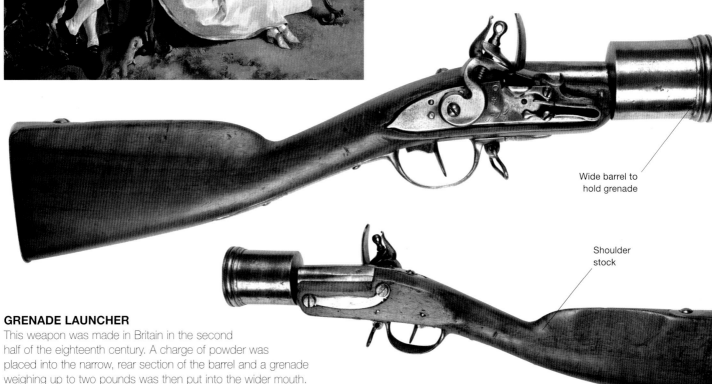

Wide barrel to hold grenade

Shoulder stock

GRENADE LAUNCHER
This weapon was made in Britain in the second half of the eighteenth century. A charge of powder was placed into the narrow, rear section of the barrel and a grenade weighing up to two pounds was then put into the wider mouth. An assistant lit the fuse on the grenade before the firer pulled the trigger and launched the grenade at the enemy.

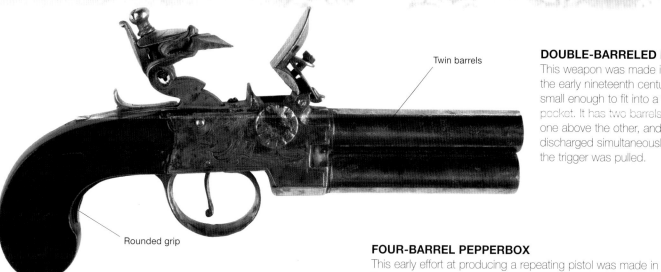

Twin barrels

Rounded grip

DOUBLE-BARRELED PISTOL
This weapon was made in Europe in the early nineteenth century and was small enough to fit into a waistcoat pocket. It has two barrels, mounted one above the other, and both discharged simultaneously when the trigger was pulled.

FOUR-BARREL PEPPERBOX
This early effort at producing a repeating pistol was made in Europe in the early nineteenth century. There are two triggers, each operating a separate hammer to fire one of the two top barrels. When both barrels had been fired, the barrels could be rotated to bring the bottom pair up to the top, ready to be fired.

Hammers

Triggers

Rifled barrels

DUCKFOOT PISTOL
Named for its physical similarity to a duck's foot, this pistol was designed to fire all four barrels simultaneously. The splayed design ensured that the bullets spread out to hit multiple targets. The weapons were intended for prison wardens and others who might face a hostile mob. This example was made by Goodwin & Co. in London in the first quarter of the nineteenth century.

Screw to hold flint in place

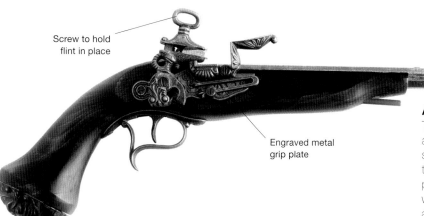

Engraved metal grip plate

ANTIQUE PISTOL
This small flintlock pistol has a stout wooden stock and elegantly engraved metal fixtures. The small size and smoothly rounded profile may indicate that this weapon was intended to be carried in a coat pocket. Note the spur on the trigger guard around which the middle finger could be curled to give added stability when firing.

FLINTLOCK PISTOLS

The development of the cheap, simple, and reliable flintlock mechanism meant that the more complex wheel lock quickly became redundant. Even pistols, where the wheel lock had been most popular, were soon being made with the flintlock that had become universal by about 1680. At the same time that the flintlock came into use for pistols, the shape of the weapon was also undergoing a change. The older style handles that ran straight back from the barrel, or had only a slight bend were replaced by a more definitely downward bending handle. There were several reasons for this change, not the least of which was that the user found it easier to cope with the recoil. Aesthetics and fashion also played their part.

Brass stock

Steel barrel

BRASS FLINTLOCK PISTOLS
This pair of pistols was made in France in the early eighteenth century. They retain the old-fashioned shape of grip, although they have the more modern forward positioning of the trigger. The stocks are made of cast brass instead of wood, which was more common.

Brass ramrod holder

FRENCH PISTOLS
This fine pair of pistols was made in France at the Royal Armory of Mauberge and were therefore intended for military use, a fact confirmed by the three fleur-de-lis embossed on the brass butt plate. Given the small size, they were probably intended for an infantry officer.

CANNON BARREL PISTOL

This little pistol, made by Patrick of Liverpool in 1805, is unusual for this date in two ways. First, it has a cannon-style barrel, which had gone out of fashion by this date. Second, the flintlock mechanism is mounted directly on top of the barrel rather than to one side, an uncommon feature at any date.

Cannon-shaped barrel

Military drum and flag engraved on side plate

Belt clip

SNAPCHANCE FLINTLOCK PISTOL

This small pistol was made in Spain in about 1710. The long steel clip on its left side is to attach the weapon to a belt. Note the fine brasswork on the butt and side plates. The small size and wide caliber indicates this was a short-range personal protection weapon.

Engraved brass fittings

Brass mount to fix barrel to stock and hold ramrod

PISTOLET

This small pistol, or pistolet, was made in 1790 at the Ateliers Nationaux, or national workshops, of France. It is thought that this was part of a batch made to be shipped to America to help arm the newly formed U.S. Army after thirteen of the British colonies in North America gained their independence as the United States of America.

SNAPHANCE MECHANISM

The snaphance mechanism appeared in the Netherlands around the year 1580, although its inventor is unknown. A flint was placed in a springloaded cock that was driven forward against a ridged steel plate to create a shower of sparks that ignited a pan of loose powder to fire the gun. It differed from the later flintlock in that the frizzen and pan cover were separate and needed to be adjusted to work properly. Also, the hammer could not be put to half cock to adjust the flint.

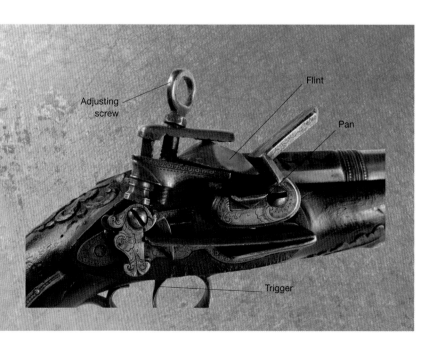

Adjusting screw

Flint

Pan

Trigger

FLINTLOCK PISTOLS

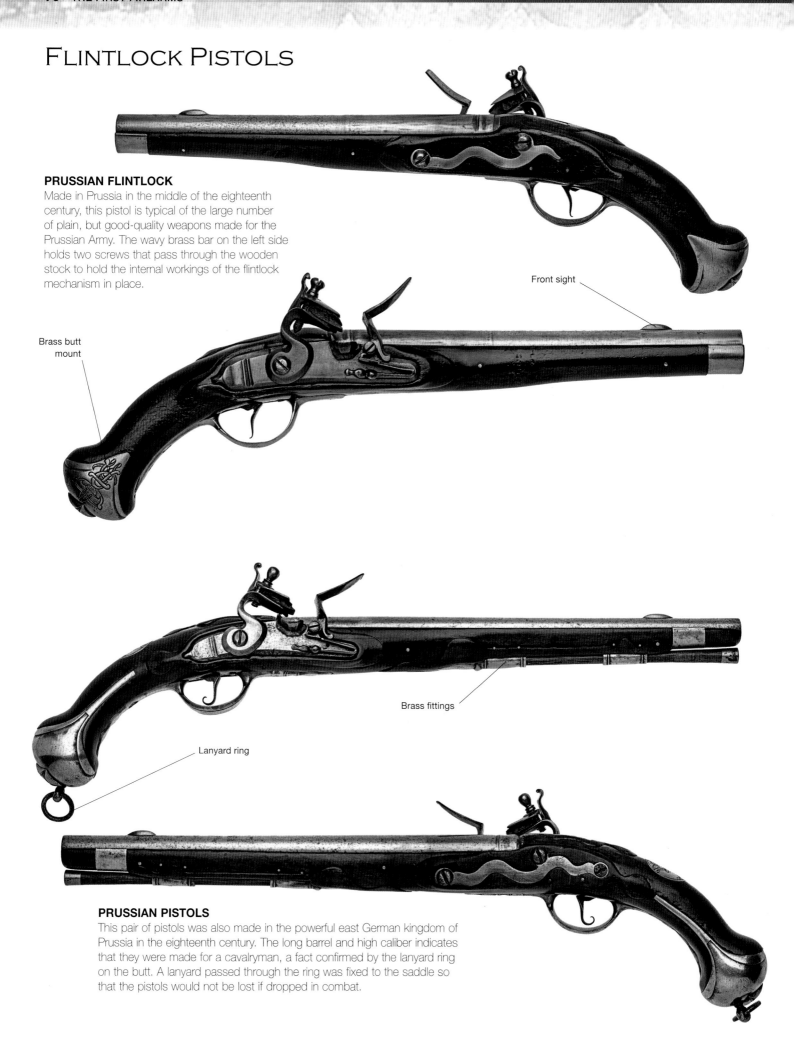

PRUSSIAN FLINTLOCK
Made in Prussia in the middle of the eighteenth
century, this pistol is typical of the large number
of plain, but good-quality weapons made for the
Prussian Army. The wavy brass bar on the left side
holds two screws that pass through the wooden
stock to hold the internal workings of the flintlock
mechanism in place.

Front sight

Brass butt
mount

Brass fittings

Lanyard ring

PRUSSIAN PISTOLS
This pair of pistols was also made in the powerful east German kingdom of
Prussia in the eighteenth century. The long barrel and high caliber indicates
that they were made for a cavalryman, a fact confirmed by the lanyard ring
on the butt. A lanyard passed through the ring was fixed to the saddle so
that the pistols would not be lost if dropped in combat.

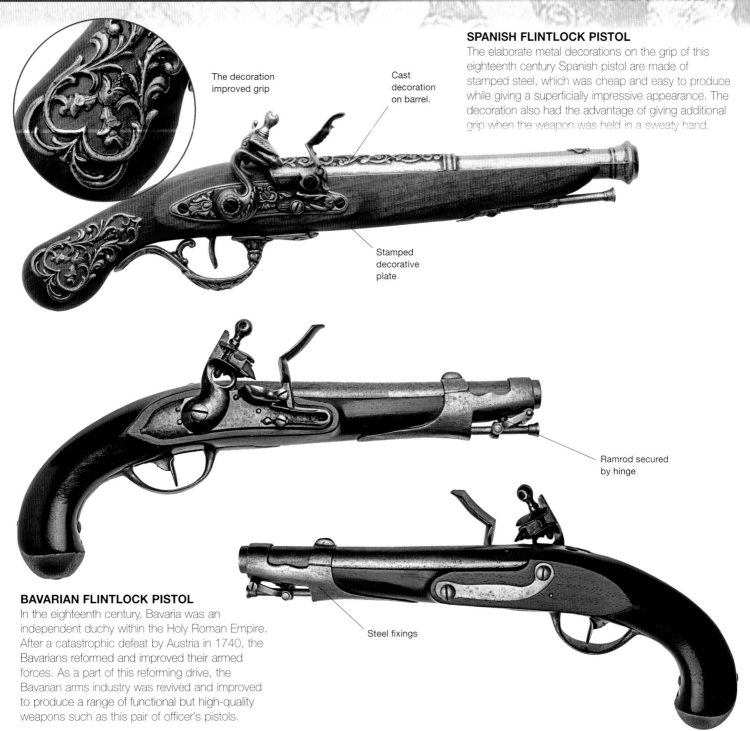

SPANISH FLINTLOCK PISTOL

The elaborate metal decorations on the grip of this eighteenth century Spanish pistol are made of stamped steel, which was cheap and easy to produce while giving a superficially impressive appearance. The decoration also had the advantage of giving additional grip when the weapon was held in a sweaty hand.

The decoration improved grip

Cast decoration on barrel.

Stamped decorative plate

Ramrod secured by hinge

BAVARIAN FLINTLOCK PISTOL

In the eighteenth century, Bavaria was an independent duchy within the Holy Roman Empire. After a catastrophic defeat by Austria in 1740, the Bavarians reformed and improved their armed forces. As a part of this reforming drive, the Bavarian arms industry was revived and improved to produce a range of functional but high-quality weapons such as this pair of officer's pistols.

Steel fixings

MIQUELET MECHANISM

The miquelet was a form of flintlock popular in the western Mediterranean area. It takes its name from the Spanish militia, the Miquelet, who fought alongside the British against the French in the Peninsular War of 1808–1814. The main differences between the miquelet and the flintlock are that the miquelet has the mainspring powering the hammer on the outside of the gun, and that the hammer is held in place when cocked by a pair of horizontal, not vertical, sears that engage into depressions on the hammer arm.

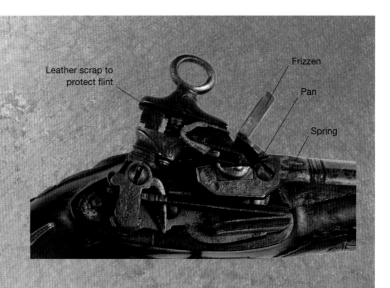

Leather scrap to protect flint

Frizzen

Pan

Spring

Flintlock Pistols

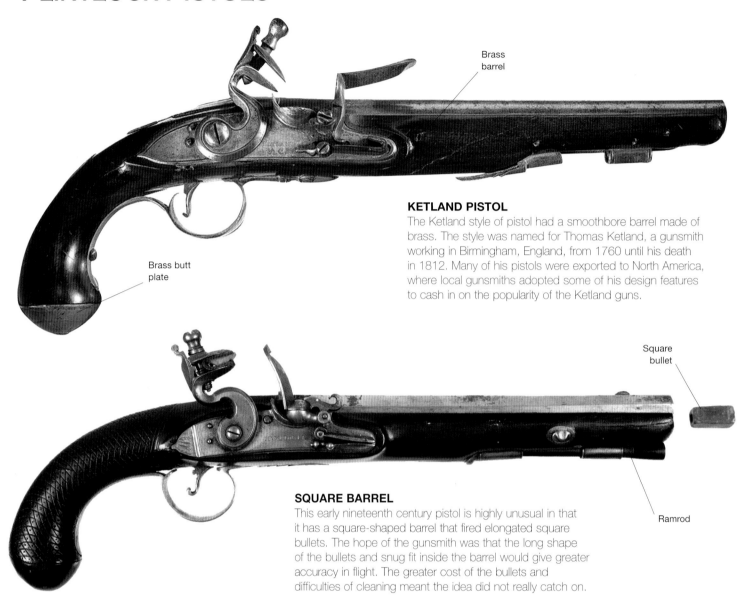

Brass barrel

Brass butt plate

KETLAND PISTOL
The Ketland style of pistol had a smoothbore barrel made of brass. The style was named for Thomas Ketland, a gunsmith working in Birmingham, England, from 1760 until his death in 1812. Many of his pistols were exported to North America, where local gunsmiths adopted some of his design features to cash in on the popularity of the Ketland guns.

Square bullet

Ramrod

SQUARE BARREL
This early nineteenth century pistol is highly unusual in that it has a square-shaped barrel that fired elongated square bullets. The hope of the gunsmith was that the long shape of the bullets and snug fit inside the barrel would give greater accuracy in flight. The greater cost of the bullets and difficulties of cleaning meant the idea did not really catch on.

Flared brass barrel

All wood stock

EUROPEAN PISTOL
This small pistol from the mid-eighteenth century is unusual in that it has a flared blunderbuss barrel. This may indicate that it fired a number of small shot rather than a single bullet. If so, it would have been hopelessly inaccurate at ranges over ten feet, and must have been intended for personal defense only.

AMERICAN FLINTLOCK

Made in the early nineteenth century this American pistol is fairly typical of the sort of pistol that would have been carried by a man when venturing into the less-settled parts of the continent. The stout construction would stand up to a fair degree of wear and tear, while the high caliber fired a heavy bullet able to stop a wild animal.

Steel bands secure barrel to stock

Ramrod

Snake-shaped hammer

SNAKEHEAD FLINTLOCK

This elaborately decorated pistol has its hammer in the shape of a striking snake, while snakes squirm around the trigger guard and lock plate. The wooden stock is unusually broad and is held to the barrel by pins, not bands.

Trigger guard

Snake motif decorative elements

Front sight

BRONZE FLINTLOCK

This small flintlock has a bronze barrel that has been fitted with a crude front sight in the form of a raised peg. At this date the accuracy of smoothbore muzzle loading pistols of this type was not very great. The utility of the sight must, therefore, be in doubt.

Brass fittings

Flintlock Pocket Pistols

Law and order was maintained well into the nineteenth century by local authorities who often had other matters they thought to be of higher priority. Therefore, protecting oneself from criminals was very much a personal matter, even in countries considered to be civilized. It was not until the 1780s that highwaymen ceased to be a common problem on British roads. In North America and Australia, outlaws and bushrangers continued to operate into the late nineteenth century. Travelers habitually carried firearms or swords when making journeys through open countryside as a result. Pocket pistols were generally small, rounded weapons that would fit easily into a pocket, and would not snag on fabric when pulled out in a hurry.

Brass fittings

Ramrod

Frizzen

Metal ramrod

Ramrod

Side plate

ITALIAN PISTOLS
This fine pair of pistols from Italy was made in the mid-eighteenth century. The barrels are short and the stocks are small and smooth. The barrels are of a caliber associated with full-sized weapons, so the ball fired would have had the stopping power of a full-sized pistol, although the weapon was less accurate.

CLERMONT PISTOL
This pistol is engraved with the name "Clermont," probably indicating that it was made in the French industrial town. This is a fairly unsophisticated weapon with working parts that have been well made, but with plain designs.

EUROPEAN FLINTLOCK
This stubby little pistol was made in Europe in the mid-eighteenth century. The only concession to decoration is the brass side plate with rudimentary engraving. The ramrod is fitted into a hole drilled through the stock under the barrel.

DOG HEAD PISTOL

The majority of pistol butts ended in a rounded head, usually encased in brass or steel to prevent the wood splitting if roughly handled. This French pistol, however, has a walnut butt carved into the shape of a dog's head. The pistol is otherwise a rather standard example of mid-eighteenth century French workmanship.

Carved butt

Flint

THREE-BARREL POCKET PISTOL

This little gun has three very short barrels that are all fired simultaneously by a single flintlock mechanism mounted on top of the gun. Ordinarily such barrels would be highly inaccurate, but these have been rifled in an attempt to improve accuracy.

Rifling

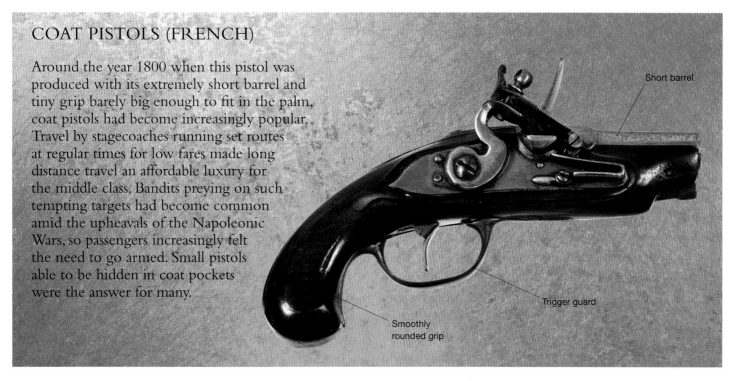

COAT PISTOLS (FRENCH)

Around the year 1800 when this pistol was produced with its extremely short barrel and tiny grip barely big enough to fit in the palm, coat pistols had become increasingly popular. Travel by stagecoaches running set routes at regular times for low fares made long distance travel an affordable luxury for the middle class. Bandits preying on such tempting targets had become common amid the upheavals of the Napoleonic Wars, so passengers increasingly felt the need to go armed. Small pistols able to be hidden in coat pockets were the answer for many.

Short barrel

Trigger guard

Smoothly rounded grip

TRAP GUNS

The idea of a trap gun was, in principle, quite simple, but in practice it could often turn out to be a fairly complex thing to operate successfully. The premise was that a gun was loaded and cocked and then left hidden out of sight. The trigger was connected to a trip wire, weight plate, or other device that would move when a game animal or person passed by. The trip wire would pull the trigger and fire the gun. Usually the gun was aimed at the tripping device, although sometimes it was loaded with powder only to scare intruders, be they animal or human. In practice, however, trap guns could not simply be left lying about. They needed to be placed in secure places where rainwater or dew could not dampen the powder in the pan, something that was not always possible in the woodlands where hunting traps tended to be set.

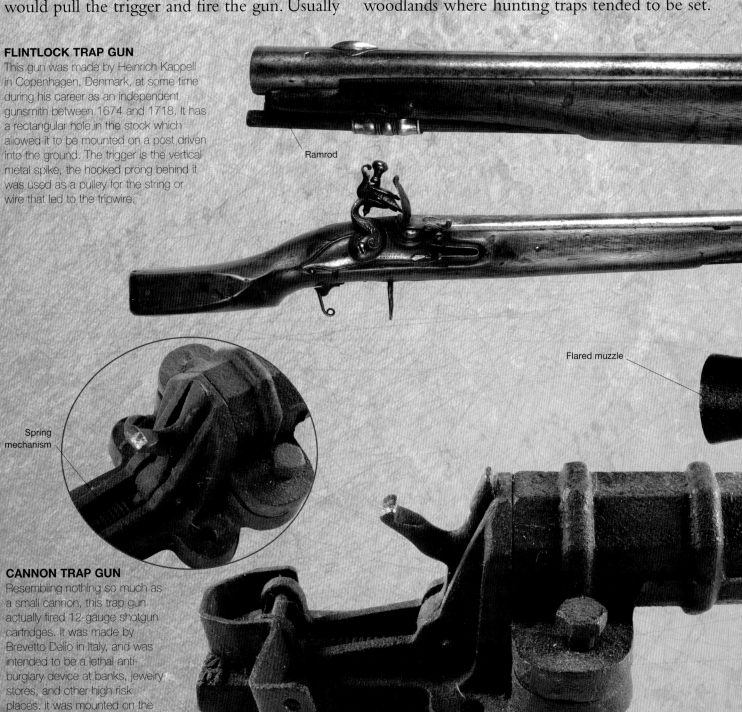

FLINTLOCK TRAP GUN
This gun was made by Heinrich Kappell in Copenhagen, Denmark, at some time during his career as an independent gunsmith between 1674 and 1718. It has a rectangular hole in the stock which allowed it to be mounted on a post driven into the ground. The trigger is the vertical metal spike, the hooked prong behind it was used as a pulley for the string or wire that led to the tripwire.

Ramrod

Flared muzzle

Spring mechanism

CANNON TRAP GUN
Resembling nothing so much as a small cannon, this trap gun actually fired 12-gauge shotgun cartridges. It was made by Brevetto Delio in Italy, and was intended to be a lethal anti-burglary device at banks, jewelry stores, and other high risk places. It was mounted on the floor pointing at the entrance, and was triggered by a wire leading to the door.

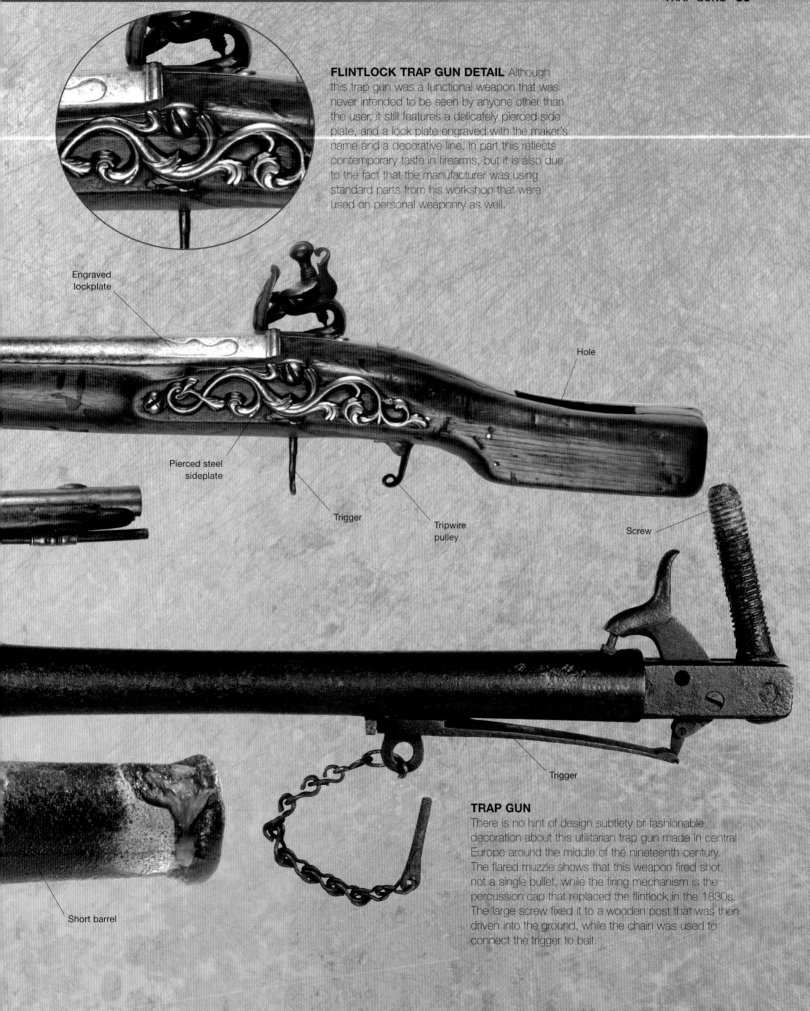

FLINTLOCK TRAP GUN DETAIL Although this trap gun was a functional weapon that was never intended to be seen by anyone other than the user, it still features a delicately pierced side plate, and a lock plate engraved with the maker's name and a decorative line. In part this reflects contemporary taste in firearms, but it is also due to the fact that the manufacturer was using standard parts from his workshop that were used on personal weaponry as well.

Engraved lockplate

Hole

Pierced steel sideplate

Trigger

Tripwire pulley

Screw

Trigger

Short barrel

TRAP GUN

There is no hint of design subtlety or fashionable decoration about this utilitarian trap gun made in central Europe around the middle of the nineteenth century. The flared muzzle shows that this weapon fired shot, not a single bullet, while the firing mechanism is the percussion cap that replaced the flintlock in the 1830s. The large screw fixed it to a wooden post that was then driven into the ground, while the chain was used to connect the trigger to bait.

Flintlock Rifles

The practice of putting spiral grooves inside a barrel to spin the bullet and make it more stable in flight had been around since the 1500s, but it was not until the early eighteenth century that the idea became popular for hunting weapons. The military avoided the new weapon for a number of reasons. First, the soot and other residues left by black gunpowder tended to clog the insides of barrels. With a smoothbore barrel this did not greatly affect the performance of the weapon, but a rifle could become unusable after as few as half a dozen shots. Another factor was the dense cloud of smoke thrown out by firing the gun. Once the first volley had been fired, a battalion of infantry was so swathed in smoke that the improved accuracy of the rifle would be negated by the lack of visibility.

AFRICAN TRADE RIFLE
This weapon was made by Lazarino in Italy in the seventeenth century. It has a hefty .72-inch caliber, but has a fairly lightweight construction. It was made to be taken to Africa as trade goods to be exchanged for ivory, gold, and other goods.

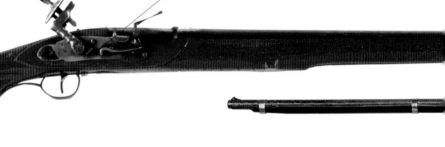

Flintlock mechanism

AFRICAN TRADE GUN
This eighteenth century musket was made in Italy for export to Africa. Weapons such as this were highly prized by the rulers of West African tribes as they gave their armies an advantage over rival tribes in the endemic warfare of the area. Increasingly, the goods exchanged for these guns were slaves, captured in the tribal wars.

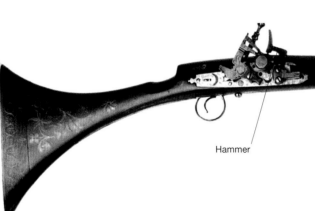

Hammer

ARAB MIQUELET
The mechanism of this weapon is what is known as a miquelet, a form of flintlock that has an external spring and horizontal sears holding the hammer in place. The wooden stock is decorated with inlaid silver wire, while the shoulder stock ends in a thick ivory plate.

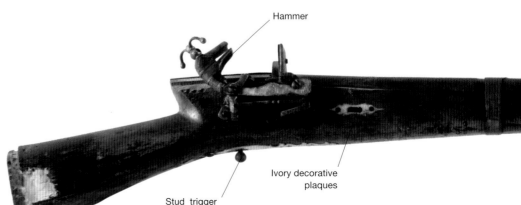

Hammer

Ivory decorative plaques

Stud trigger

AFRICAN SLAVE TRADE

Slavery has been common throughout Africa since prehistoric times. However, the trade taking slaves out of Africa did not become important until the fifteenth century when improved shipbuilding techniques made long-distance trading journeys possible. Europeans took slaves from West Africa to the Americas, while Arabs took slaves from East Africa to the Islamic world. At the height of the slave trade, as many as 70,000 Africans left the continent each year.

Ramrod

Shoulder stock

Front sight

Barrel

Barrel

SINGHALESE MUSKET
Made in Sri Lanka in about 1730, this musket has a side-mounted lock, and an elaborately decorated shoulder stock that splits into a typically Singhalese bifurcated curve. The exceptionally long barrel was intended to increase accuracy.

Brass banding

Ramrod

LATE EIGHTEENTH-CENTURY FRENCH MUSKET REPLICA
This modern replica of a late eighteenth-century French short-barreled musket has brass banding to secure the barrel to the stock. Replicas such as this allow experimental historians to discover the accuracy and firing characteristics of old weapons that are now too fragile or valuable to be fired.

ARABIAN RIFLE
This bulky, robust weapon was made in the later eighteenth century, and was used by mounted Arab warriors. The heavy wooden stock is decorated with ivory plates. Note the unusual stud trigger that emerged from the stock only when the weapon was cocked.

FLINTLOCK RIFLES

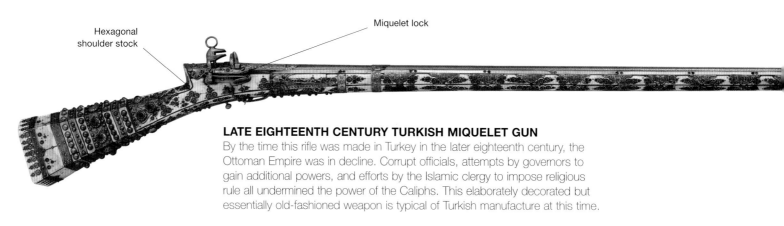

Hexagonal shoulder stock

Miquelet lock

LATE EIGHTEENTH CENTURY TURKISH MIQUELET GUN

By the time this rifle was made in Turkey in the later eighteenth century, the Ottoman Empire was in decline. Corrupt officials, attempts by governors to gain additional powers, and efforts by the Islamic clergy to impose religious rule all undermined the power of the Caliphs. This elaborately decorated but essentially old-fashioned weapon is typical of Turkish manufacture at this time.

PENNSYLVANIA LONGRIFLE

This unusually fine and elaborately decorated long rifle was made in Pennsylvania in the late eighteenth century. It is thought that the long rifle was first made in small craft workshops in Pennsylvania in about 1720. With their long barrels and rifling these guns were very accurate, but slow to reload and prone to fouling.

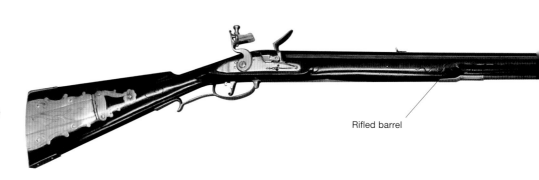

Rifled barrel

Brass barrel

Elaborate painted design

FLINTLOCK RIFLE FROM KUBACHI

This rifle was made by the Kubachi people of Dagestan in the early nineteenth century. At this date the area was part of the Khanate of Avaristan, which was coming under attack from Persia to the south and Russia to the north. Rifles such as this, in the hands of mountain tribesmen, held off foreign invasion until Dagestan fell to Russia in the 1860s.

Percussion mechanism

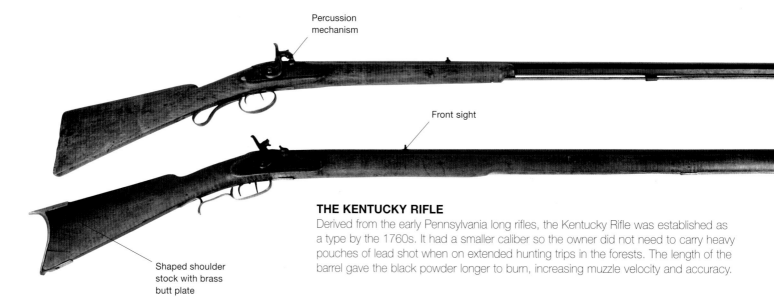

Front sight

THE KENTUCKY RIFLE

Derived from the early Pennsylvania long rifles, the Kentucky Rifle was established as a type by the 1760s. It had a smaller caliber so the owner did not need to carry heavy pouches of lead shot when on extended hunting trips in the forests. The length of the barrel gave the black powder longer to burn, increasing muzzle velocity and accuracy.

Shaped shoulder stock with brass butt plate

HUNTING RIFLE FLINTLOCK

With their increased accuracy and greater range, rifles were well suited to hunting. The fact that it took a long time to reload these weapons and that the barrels fouled after only a few shots were considered to be minor drawbacks. The length of the barrel would also increase accuracy, although many hunters preferred to have a shorter barrel as this was easier to handle in dense scrub or forest undergrowth.

A flintlock mechanism on an eighteenth-century rifle

Ramrod

Wooden stock

ARABIAN FLINT GUN

This long-barreled rifle was made in Arabia in the mid-nineteenth century. It has a traditional shape with an elegantly curved stock used by the lighter rifles favored by those who were rich enough to ride horses. Note that the stock runs the full length of the barrel to protect it from rough handling on horseback.

Shoulder stock

HUNTING RIFLE

European hunters in colonial areas soon found that the local wildlife included very dangerous animals such as tigers, lions, rhinoceros, and buffalo. Many men took to carrying short barreled, high-caliber weapons such as this to serve as a last line of defense against a sudden rush by a wounded killer.

Shoulder stock attached to pistol grip

Ramrod

THE REVOLUTIONARY WARS

By the mid-eighteenth century radical new ideas were circulating around Europe. These ideas, collectively termed "the Enlightenment," put logical reason and individual rights at the heart of a new way of looking at life. Tradition, religion, and monarchy were all subjected to critical study, and generally were condemned as outmoded, inefficient, and wrong. By and large the ideas were restricted to the middle class. In the British colonies in North America the new way of thinking led to an explosive situation where the generally middle-class colonists embraced the Enlightenment, while their monarch in Britain did not. In the 1770s the tension exploded into the American Revolution, which ended with a new republic being founded in North America. Back in Europe, the Enlightenment provided an intellectual basis for the grievances and unrest that caused the French Revolution of 1789, and the subsequent spread of liberty, warfare, and bloodshed across the continent.

24-inch barrel

AMERICAN CARBINE
This carbine was made in North America in the 1760s as a flintlock weapon, and was converted to percussion cap in the 1840s. The barrel is only 24 inches long, almost certainly so that it would be easier to use on horseback. The short bayonet would have been useless on horseback, so the weapon may have been intended for dragoons who were trained to fight as both cavalry and infantry.

Strap swivel

DRUMMER BOY RIFLE
This gun was captured from a French drummer boy at the Battle of Waterloo in 1815. As a rule, drummers were considered to be non-combatants and carried only short swords or pistols as personal protection weapons, so for a drummer to carry a weapon such as this was unusual. It is probably a cavalry carbine in origin due to its short barrel.

GUARD'S SWORD

This saber was made in the early nineteenth century for a guardsman in the Royal French Army. The arrangement of three fleur-de-lis was the symbol of the French monarchy from the thirteenth to the nineteenth century. The basket hilt combines lightness with a wide degree of protection to the hand of the user. The steel blade would have been single-edged with a slight curve.

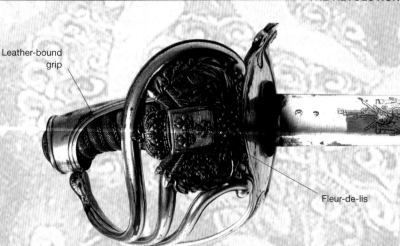

Leather-bound grip

Fleur-de-lis

Muzzle

Ramrod

VINTAGE KENTUCKY RIFLE

This Kentucky Rifle shows the key features of this type of weapon. The barrel is long; lengths of over 40 inches were not unusual and at least some were made with 48-inch barrels. The wooden stock runs almost the entire length of the barrel to give it added strength. The mechanism here is a flintlock, but after 1840 the guns were usually made as percussion cap guns.

Bayonet

Barrel

Trail

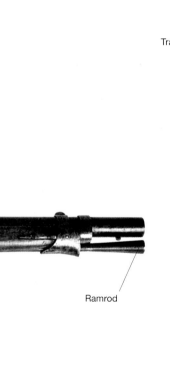

Ramrod

Gunstock

Steel rimmed spoked wheel

BRONZE ARTILLERY CANNON

By the year 1800 advances in metallurgy meant that gun barrels could be made lighter and slimmer than only a few decades earlier. This light cannon was made for the French Army. It has a bronze barrel that fires an 8-pound ball. The barrel is mounted on a carriage with large diameter wheels to allow it to pass smoothly over uneven terrain. The trail would be hitched to a wagon or caisson, which was pulled by horses.

THE REVOLUTIONARY WARS

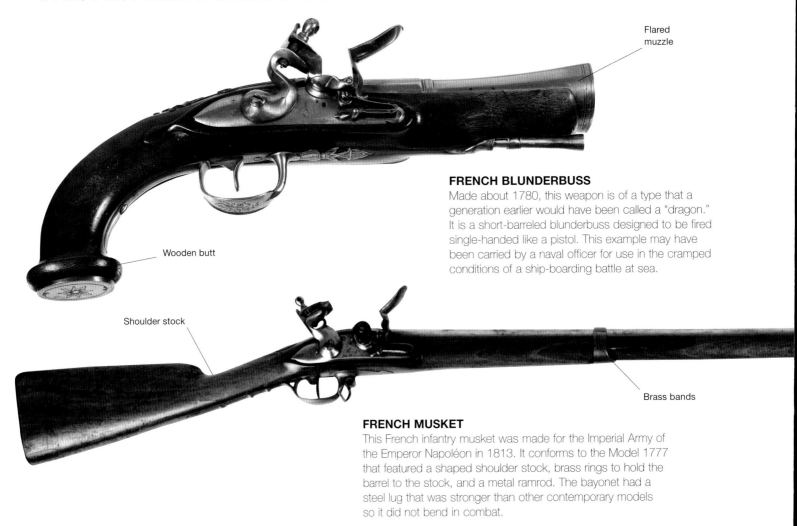

Flared muzzle

Wooden butt

FRENCH BLUNDERBUSS
Made about 1780, this weapon is of a type that a generation earlier would have been called a "dragon." It is a short-barreled blunderbuss designed to be fired single-handed like a pistol. This example may have been carried by a naval officer for use in the cramped conditions of a ship-boarding battle at sea.

Shoulder stock

Brass bands

FRENCH MUSKET
This French infantry musket was made for the Imperial Army of the Emperor Napoléon in 1813. It conforms to the Model 1777 that featured a shaped shoulder stock, brass rings to hold the barrel to the stock, and a metal ramrod. The bayonet had a steel lug that was stronger than other contemporary models so it did not bend in combat.

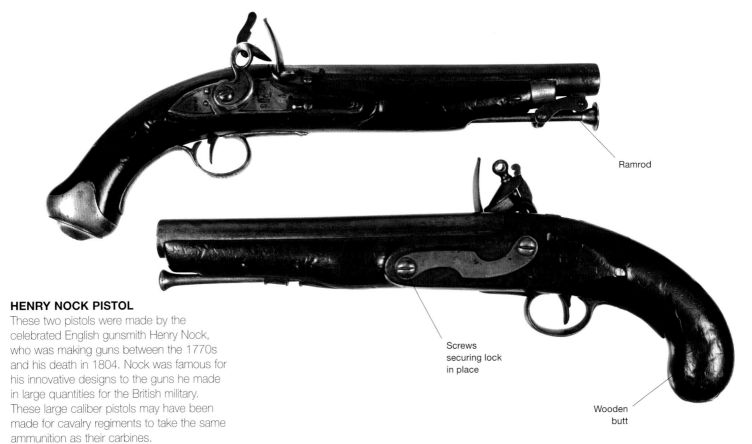

Ramrod

HENRY NOCK PISTOL
These two pistols were made by the celebrated English gunsmith Henry Nock, who was making guns between the 1770s and his death in 1804. Nock was famous for his innovative designs to the guns he made in large quantities for the British military. These large caliber pistols may have been made for cavalry regiments to take the same ammunition as their carbines.

Screws securing lock in place

Wooden butt

REVOLUTIONARY WAR FLINTLOCK

This pistol was used during the American Revolutionary War, although it may have been made some decades earlier. The brass fitting around the muzzle firmly fixes the barrel to the stock. The ring on the butt was attached to a lanyard that ran to the user's belt so the weapon was not lost if dropped in combat.

Lanyard ring

Brass muzzle band

Bayonet

BOSTON MASSACRE

On March 5, 1775, Private Hugh White got into an argument with a local apprentice boy while he was guarding the Customs House in Boston. A crowd of fifty Bostonians gathered, took the side of the apprentice, and threw stones at White. White sent for support, bringing a captain and seven men to his side. The crowd continued to throw objects and shout insults. In circumstances that remain controversial, the British soldiers opened fire. Five men were killed and six injured. The crowd fell back, but hundreds more poured into the streets along with hundreds of soldiers. After a tense standoff, the crowd dispersed. In a subsequent trial, two of the soldiers were convicted of manslaughter. American patriots used the incident to emphasise the brutal nature of British rule.

NAVAL SIDEARMS

By the eighteenth century, warships were armed with large caliber, muzzleloading cannon that could fire balls weighing up to 32 pounds more than a mile. The balls could inflict heavy damage on the fabric of enemy ships and great casualties among the rival crew. However, most of the damage was done above the waterline, so ships rarely sank in combat. A captain might surrender to prevent further casualties, but very often it was necessary to board an enemy vessel to secure control of it. In the cramped conditions of a ship, weapons designed for use on land were often cumbersome and unwieldy. A specialist range of shipboard sidearms developed that proved to be deadly and effective in confined spaces.

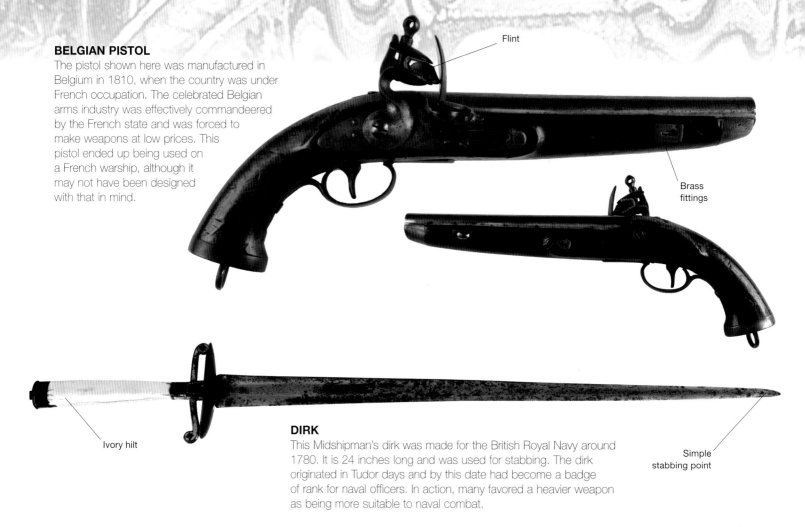

BELGIAN PISTOL

The pistol shown here was manufactured in Belgium in 1810, when the country was under French occupation. The celebrated Belgian arms industry was effectively commandeered by the French state and was forced to make weapons at low prices. This pistol ended up being used on a French warship, although it may not have been designed with that in mind.

Flint

Brass fittings

DIRK

This Midshipman's dirk was made for the British Royal Navy around 1780. It is 24 inches long and was used for stabbing. The dirk originated in Tudor days and by this date had become a badge of rank for naval officers. In action, many favored a heavier weapon as being more suitable to naval combat.

Ivory hilt

Simple stabbing point

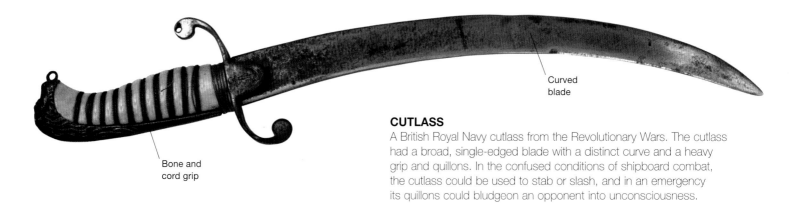

CUTLASS

A British Royal Navy cutlass from the Revolutionary Wars. The cutlass had a broad, single-edged blade with a distinct curve and a heavy grip and quillons. In the confused conditions of shipboard combat, the cutlass could be used to stab or slash, and in an emergency its quillons could bludgeon an opponent into unconsciousness.

Curved blade

Bone and cord grip

BOARDING AX AND GUN

This combination weapon was made for the British Royal Navy around 1770. The gun fired through the top of the ax. During combat, axes such as this were used to cut away broken rigging or hack off the lines holding grappling irons as well as to attack enemy sailors.

Spike for boarding

Ax blade

BOARDING PIKES

Many warships had short-hafted pikes stored in lockers on the deck. These weapons were therefore at hand to be grabbed by gunners and others if enemy sailors came onboard. The boarding pike, as it was known, was shorter than infantry pikes, rarely being more than 6 feet long, and had simple spike heads.

Head

Shaft

BOARDING THE CHESAPEAKE

On June 1, 1813, HMS *Shannon* was cruising off Boston when the USS *Chesapeake* sailed out to challenge her. Both ships were 38-gun frigates, but the American vessel had 379 men to the British 330. The two ships opened fire almost simultaneously as they sailed side by side, barely 100 feet apart. The British shot away the American ship's wheel, leaving her unable to steer. The *Shannon* poured devastating fire into the American ship, then both captains gave the order to board the other ship. The British got the upper hand and eleven minutes after the first shot was fired, the *Chesapeake* surrendered. The Americans lost their captain and 48 men, the British lost 23 sailors.

NAVAL SIDEARMS

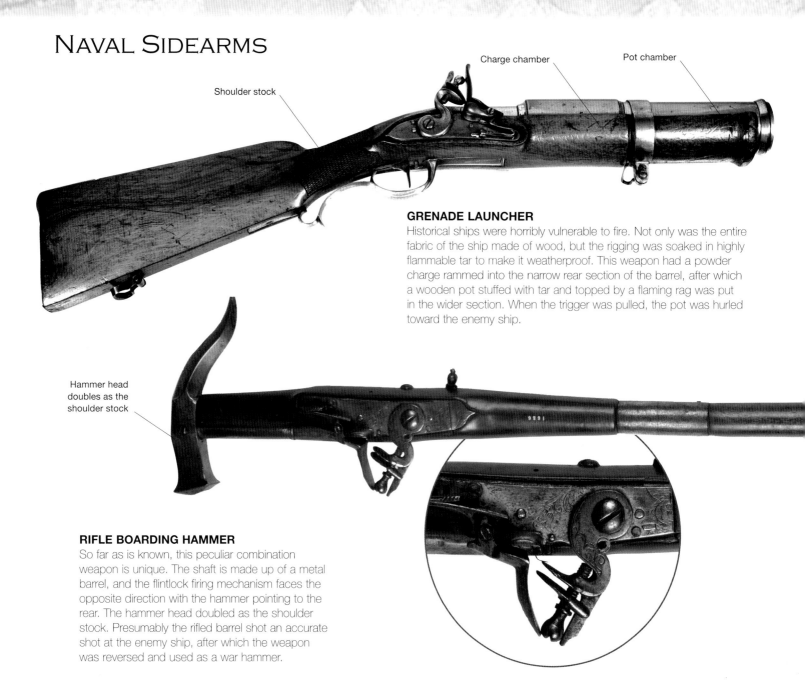

Shoulder stock

Charge chamber

Pot chamber

GRENADE LAUNCHER

Historical ships were horribly vulnerable to fire. Not only was the entire fabric of the ship made of wood, but the rigging was soaked in highly flammable tar to make it weatherproof. This weapon had a powder charge rammed into the narrow rear section of the barrel, after which a wooden pot stuffed with tar and topped by a flaming rag was put in the wider section. When the trigger was pulled, the pot was hurled toward the enemy ship.

Hammer head doubles as the shoulder stock

RIFLE BOARDING HAMMER

So far as is known, this peculiar combination weapon is unique. The shaft is made up of a metal barrel, and the flintlock firing mechanism faces the opposite direction with the hammer pointing to the rear. The hammer head doubled as the shoulder stock. Presumably the rifled barrel shot an accurate shot at the enemy ship, after which the weapon was reversed and used as a war hammer.

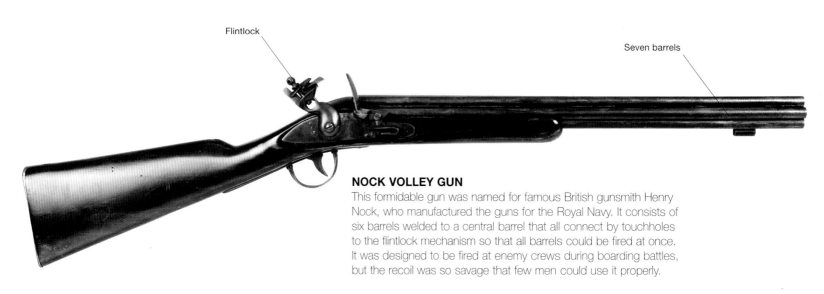

Flintlock

Seven barrels

NOCK VOLLEY GUN

This formidable gun was named for famous British gunsmith Henry Nock, who manufactured the guns for the Royal Navy. It consists of six barrels welded to a central barrel that all connect by touchholes to the flintlock mechanism so that all barrels could be fired at once. It was designed to be fired at enemy crews during boarding battles, but the recoil was so savage that few men could use it properly.

Flared muzzle

Ramrod

AMERICAN BLUNDERBUSS

This naval blunderbuss was made in 1814 at the U.S. Armory at Harpers Ferry, which had opened in 1802. At first the Armory consisted of twenty-five men and one room, but by 1814 it was growing rapidly and was soon producing 10,000 weapons a year.

Muzzle

THE DEATH OF NELSON

Admiral Horatio Nelson was the most successful and charismatic British naval commander since Sir Francis Drake two centuries earlier. After winning a string of naval victories, Nelson faced the mighty combined war fleets of Spain and France off Cape Trafalgar on October 21, 1805. The battle turned out to be his greatest triumph as the enemy ships were effectively annihilated, but at the moment of his victory Nelson was shot down by a musket ball fired from the French ship *Redoutable*. He died three hours later, soon after learning of the scale of his victory.

Cavalry Sidearms

Men fighting from horseback had special requirements of their weapons. They needed to be small enough and light enough to wield from horseback, and to leave the man free to control his horse at the same time. They also needed to be deadly and effective in what was often a fast-moving combat as the men passed at the speed of a galloping horse. These needs were often contradictory and resulted in a wide range of weaponry types as designers sought to make their weapons useful to men who served as members of a cavalry force.

Ramrod swivel

Brass butt plate

BRITISH PISTOLS

These two pistols were both used by British cavalry. The upper weapon is the standard 1796 Pattern pistol manufactured in large numbers to be used by horsemen. It has a ramrod secured in place by a swivel. The lower gun is a non-standard pistol bought privately. Both pistols have a large caliber to take the same balls used for the carbine, allowing the cavalryman to carry only one set of ammunition.

Wooden butt

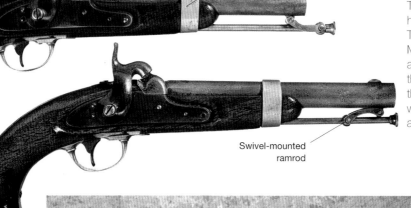

Brass fittings

TWO U.S. ASTON MODEL 1842 SADDLE PISTOLS

These pistols conform to the 1842 Pattern for holster pistols to be used by the U.S. Cavalry. They were made by Aston-Johnson in Middlefield, Connecticut, and are part of an order for 34,000 pistols completed by the company. They are smoothbore weapons that fired a .54-inch ball. The heavy caliber was demanded as the U.S. Cavalry wanted a pistol that could kill a horse.

Swivel-mounted ramrod

FRENCH HUSSAR

A French hussar of the 1790s canters into action. Note he wields a curved saber while his carbine dangles from a baldric, and his pistols are strapped to the saddle. Hussars were light cavalry who had the task of scouting ahead of the army to find the enemy forces, identify camping grounds, test the strength of bridges and carry out a host of other duties. Hussars tended to be smaller men mounted on fast horses and most of their equipment was designed to be lightweight. Their uniforms were deliberately showy and gaudy to attract the most dashing and courageous recruits.

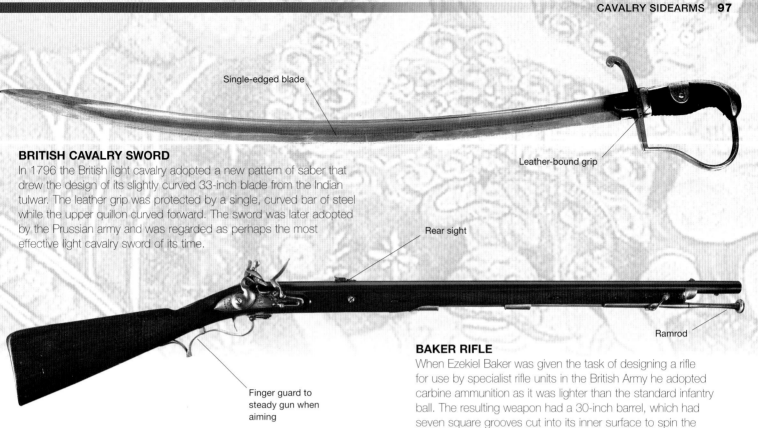

Single-edged blade

Leather-bound grip

BRITISH CAVALRY SWORD

In 1796 the British light cavalry adopted a new pattern of saber that drew the design of its slightly curved 33-inch blade from the Indian tulwar. The leather grip was protected by a single, curved bar of steel while the upper quillon curved forward. The sword was later adopted by the Prussian army and was regarded as perhaps the most effective light cavalry sword of its time.

Rear sight

Ramrod

Finger guard to steady gun when aiming

BAKER RIFLE

When Ezekiel Baker was given the task of designing a rifle for use by specialist rifle units in the British Army he adopted carbine ammunition as it was lighter than the standard infantry ball. The resulting weapon had a 30-inch barrel, which had seven square grooves cut into its inner surface to spin the bullet. Unlike contemporary muskets, it had a folding back sight as well as a front sight, and came with a cleaning kit to get rid of the fouling that caused problems in action.

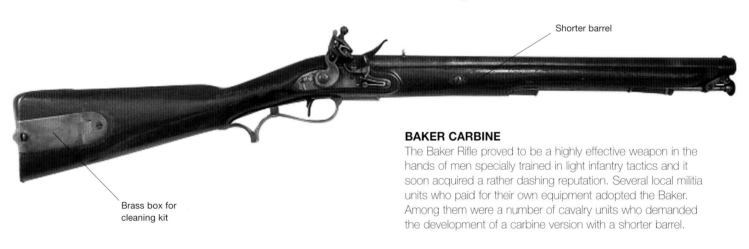

Shorter barrel

Brass box for cleaning kit

BAKER CARBINE

The Baker Rifle proved to be a highly effective weapon in the hands of men specially trained in light infantry tactics and it soon acquired a rather dashing reputation. Several local militia units who paid for their own equipment adopted the Baker. Among them were a number of cavalry units who demanded the development of a carbine version with a shorter barrel.

PRESENTATION WEAPONS

The practice of giving highly decorated weapons to an individual in recognition of an achievement or act of bravery dates back centuries, but weapons began to be made specifically for this purpose as recently as the eighteenth century. They remained real weapons of war despite their ceremonial purpose. This decorated Turkish blunderbuss was presented to French Marshal Aimable Pélissier in the 1850s.

DUELING PISTOLS

Dueling saw men meet with the intention of fighting, often to the death, to settle a dispute. The concept seems bizarre to us today, especially when the disputes were often over minor points of honor or honesty. However they developed, duels were considered to be better than the murderous brawls with drawn daggers that they replaced. Duels were fought with strict rules that sought to remove any advantage one man might have over another. Crucially, they were arranged to take place many hours or days after the initial incident in order to give tempers time to cool, which often resulted in no fight actually taking place at all.

Barrel extension

Spur

LONG-BARRELED PERCUSSION PISTOL
This pistol was made in the mid-nineteenth century in France. The 6-inch barrel extension could be screwed on for dueling, making the weapon more accurate, or removed for normal use to make the gun handier to carry about. The spur on the trigger guard helped steady the gun when the heavy extension was added.

Bayonet

PAIR OF DUELING PISTOLS
John Twigg was born in Lincolnshire UK in 1732, moved to Ireland to learn the craft of gunsmith, and then in 1755 settled in London to practice his trade. Twigg was renowned for making high-quality pistols to the specifications given him by customers who often had their own ideas of what they wanted. This pair of small dueling pistols with spring-loaded bayonets is typical of his work.

Folding trigger

Hatched wooden grip

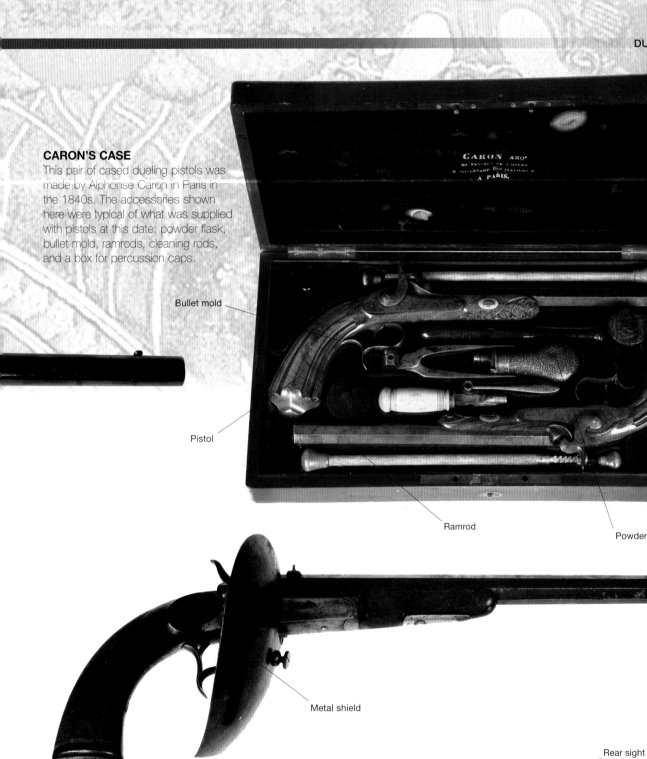

CARON'S CASE

This pair of cased dueling pistols was made by Alphonse Caron in Paris in the 1840s. The accessories shown here were typical of what was supplied with pistols at this date: powder flask, bullet mold, ramrods, cleaning rods, and a box for percussion caps.

Bullet mold

Pistol

Ramrod

Powder flask

Metal shield

Rear sight

Front sight

RARE PAIR

This pair of pistols was made in Belgium in the early nineteenth century with percussion cap mechanisms. They were designed to be used to teach men how to duel with pistols. The guns fired wax bullets which would mark the clothing and show if a hit had been scored. The metal shields fitted over the triggers and protected the hands from injury.

DUELING PISTOLS

WOGDON PISTOL

Robert Wogdon began making pistols in London in the 1760s and was famed for his high-quality dueling pistols. This example is fitted with a detachable shoulder stock to allow the pistol to double as a carbine. Made in the later eighteenth century, it was converted to a percussion cap mechanism sometime in the early nineteenth century.

Percussion hammer

Ramrod

Shoulder stock

THE FAMOUS BURR-HAMILTON DUEL

One pair of Wogdon dueling pistols had a tragic role in American history. In 1804, former Secretary of the Treasury Alexander Hamilton insulted Vice President Aaron Burr at a private dinner. A man who had been present referred to the insult, without repeating it, in a letter to the *Albany Register* newspaper. Burr demanded an apology, Hamilton refused on the grounds that he was not responsible for how another man interpreted his words. Burr challenged Hamilton to a duel. Hamilton chose a pair of Wogdon pistols and fired first. He missed, although whether intentionally or not is unclear. Burr then returned fire, hitting Hamilton fatally in the abdomen.

The duel between former Secretary of the Treasury Alexander Hamilton, and sitting Vice President Aaron Burr, on July 11, 1804.

The Wogdon pistols that were used to fatal purpose in both the Burr-Hamilton duel, and the duel that killed Hamilton's son, Philip, three years earlier.

Percussion
hammer

Wooden stock

BELGIAN PISTOLS

This pair of dueling pistols was produced in Belgium in the
1830s. They feature the then-new percussion cap firing
system, have engraved wooden grips, and a spur on the
trigger guard for a second finger to steady the aim. These
weapons have a hair (or set) trigger that would fire at the
slightest pressure.

FRENCH DUELING PISTOLS

This unusual pair of pistols was made in
France in about 1840. They show many
of the typical features of a dueling
weapon—set trigger, trigger guard spur,
and so forth—but they are very plain and
unadorned weapons, which is rare in
dueling weapons of this date. They may
have been made for personal protection
and only later used for dueling.

Front sight

Trigger guard spur

Twin barrels

Ivory grip

ANTIQUE DUELING PISTOL

This exquisitely decorated little
pistol has an engraved ivory hilt and
elaborate chasing over the body of
the weapon. The flintlock mechanism
is mounted on top of the gun and
fires both barrels at the same time.

THE BLUNDERBUSS

A blunderbuss was a weapon commonly made for civilian use during the flintlock era. The name comes from the Dutch "donderbus," meaning "thunder-stick." It is not entirely certain that the weapon originated in the Netherlands, although the gunsmiths of the area certainly produced many of the earliest examples. The weapon fired lead shot or pellets that spread out on being fired. The purpose of the flared muzzle is much debated. It does not seem to spread the shot much, but does serve to make the sound of the shot louder and certainly looks intimidating to anyone staring down the muzzle. Given the use of blunderbusses as personal protection weapons it may be that the intimidation of a foe was the main purpose.

INDIAN BLUNDERBUSS
The proper name for a blunderbuss made to be fired with one hand like a pistol is a "dragon." This example is from eighteenth century India. The barrel has a damascened pattern on the metal but it is otherwise a fairly plain weapon. The folding trigger emerged when the weapon was at half cock, as shown here.

Damascened barrel

Trigger

Inlaid shell decoration

Whip

FLINTLOCK BLUNDERBUSS
This elaborately decorated blunderbuss was made in India about 1780. The decoration is prolific but of relatively low quality on an otherwise workmanlike weapon. The whip attached to the stock indicates this was used by a wagon driver, presumably to deter attack by bandits or wild animals.

CAUCASIAN MOUNTAINEER'S BLUNDERBUSS

Made in Russia in the later eighteenth century, this weapon was destined for the Christian states of the Caucasus Mountains and is decorated in the style favored there. At this date the Christian kingdoms of Georgia and Ossetia were coming under attack from Islamic Persia, and Russia was keen to arm and assist their fellow Christians.

Etched wooden pattern

Engraved silver plates

Brass barrel

FLINTLOCK BLUNDERBUSS PISTOL

By the time this weapon was made by London gunsmith Thomas Richards, probably in the 1760s, the term "dragon" for a pistol-style blunderbuss was falling out of use. The brass muzzle is widely flared and firmly fixed to the wooden stock. The weapon is in near perfect condition and so has seen little use.

Ramrod

Flared brass barrel with cast decoration

ENGLISH FLINTLOCK BLUNDERBUSS PISTOL

A modern replica of a blunderbuss pistol made around 1750 in England. This level of cast decoration is unusual on an English weapon, which tended to be plainer in design, so it may have been manufactured for export to Hispanic countries where this style was more popular.

Embossed lock plate

Flared muzzle

Shoulder stock

BLUNDERBUSS

This weapon has a widely flared barrel made of brass. Despite its short length, it was fired from the shoulder with the second hand gripping the stock near the muzzle. Its age and origin are uncertain, although it may have been made in Germany around the 1750s.

THE BLUNDERBUSS

FLINTLOCK BLUNDERBUSS
This English blunderbuss of the mid-eighteenth century was made in Nottingham by the Daykin workshop. It has a wooden ramrod with a brass tip. The bayonet along the top of the barrel is spring loaded so that it flicks forward and locks into position at the press of a button.

Bayonet

Ramrod

Etched decoration on barrel

Ramrod

EUROPEAN SHORT BLUNDERBUSS
Made in London around 1800 this blunderbuss is very short and has a greatly flared muzzle. It was almost certainly made for coach or wagon drivers who traveled the long highways and, even at this late date, were wary of armed robbers.

Bayonet

Flintlock

Bayonet

BLUNDERBUSS WITH BAYONET
Made around 1810, this weapon is of a higher quality than most blunderbusses, and may have been made for a coachman driving a nobleman or other wealthy person. The bayonet is spring-loaded while the brass barrel and lock mechanism are both of high quality manufacture.

Bayonet

Shoulder stock

BRITISH BLUNDERBUSS

This weapon was made by Patrick of Liverpool, gunmaker to Prince William, Duke of Gloucester. This weapon was not a weapon made to order, but a routine piece of workmanship, and although of good quality was probably made for a middle-class customer.

Flintlock mechanism

Brass barrel

Strap loop

BRASS BARRELED BLUNDERBUSS

This weapon was made by Bird & Ashmore of Birmingham, England, in about 1810. In addition to the usual features of a short-barreled blunderbuss, this weapon has metal loops to which can be fixed a shoulder strap. It may have been used by a person who traveled on horseback, rather than a coach or carriage driver.

EARLY BLUNDERBUSS

This weapon has an early eighteenth-century style grip. The style of decoration indicates that it may have been made in the Iberian Peninsula. Note the cast decoration on top of the brass barrel, and the decorated trigger guard.

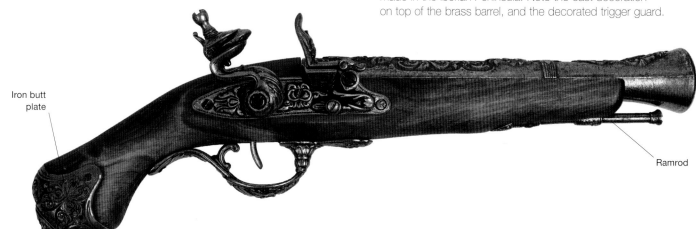

Iron butt plate

Ramrod

PERCUSSION WEAPONS

Although the flintlock mechanism was superior to anything invented earlier it still had its problems. The most obvious of these was its lack of reliability in damp weather, and its total inability to fire in heavy rain. Scottish clergyman Reverend Alexander Forsyth noticed that birds resting on the ground would take flight as soon as they saw the spurt of smoke from the priming pan, which came a fraction of a second before the weapon fired. This was enough to allow many birds to escape, which annoyed Reverend Forsyth. He then invented fulminate of mercury, which detonates when hit. Using this instead of powder in the pan eliminated the puff of smoke that had previously alerted the birds.

Cap hammer

Pan

SPANISH DUAL IGNITION

This Spanish pistol combines the Forsyth mechanism—a small pan holding fulminate of mercury—with the later percussion cap system. It is likely that at the date this was made, percussion caps were expensive and in short supply, so the less-reliable pan was included for when caps could not be obtained.

Percussion nipple

Bayonet

SPANISH BLUNDERBUSS

This unostentatious blunderbuss pistol was made in Spain in the late eighteenth century. It was later converted to a percussion cap firing system, but was otherwise left unaltered. It has a wooden ramrod with a brass tip, and a steel bayonet mounted on a spring.

Matchlock lever

Barrel

Trigger

Hammer

CONVERTED MATCHLOCK

This rather unusual weapon was made in China in the early eighteenth century as a matchlock weapon, then converted around 1840 to use percussion caps. The lock has been modified, not replaced. The old lever remains and has to be pulled back by hand to cock the trigger. When the trigger is pulled, the lever falls forward to hit the nipple.

Brass fittings

RUSSIAN PISTOL

Made around the year 1840, this pistol was manufactured in Russia and used by an infantry officer. It features a typical early-style percussion cap mechanism with a spur at the rear of the hammer to allow it to be more easily cocked. The weapon is otherwise of a design familiar from the later eighteenth century.

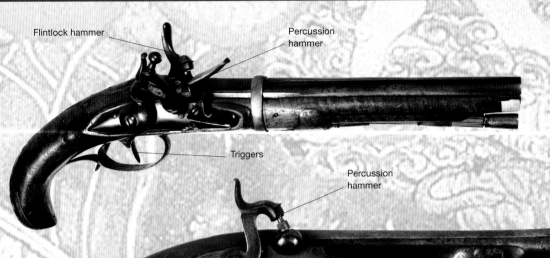

Flintlock hammer

Percussion hammer

Triggers

DUAL FIRE PISTOL

This weapon was made in Switzerland about the year 1840. It has both a flintlock and a percussion cap. The flintlock is in the usual position to the right of the breech of the barrel, while the percussion hammer strikes down on top of the barrel from the left side. The triggers for the two mechanisms are distinct.

Percussion hammer

Ramrod secured by swivel

BOUTET

Nicolas-Noël Boutet joined the French Royal Army in the 1780s as a private soldier, but in the wake of the Revolution he was moved to work at—and after 1798 to supervise—the Armory at Versailles. This pistol is typical of the designs he produced at Versailles and was used by an infantry officer.

Percussion hammer

CAP AND BALL PISTOL

"Cap and ball" was a term used to describe guns that used the percussion cap firing mechanism, but which were otherwise similar to the older flintlock design with smoothbore, muzzleloaded barrels firing round lead balls. This example was made around 1840 and has a relatively small caliber.

Wooden grip

PERCUSSION CAP MECHANISM

The percussion cap was the first method of firing a gun that worked in rain, and worked on muzzleloading guns. The cap contained a mixture of fulminates that exploded when struck sharply. The cap was put mouth down over a hollow nipple which had a hole that led into the barrel. The snug fit of cap over nipple excluded water from getting at the powder in the barrel. When the hammer struck the cap a flash of hot gas traveled down the nipple tube to ignite the main charge inside the barrel and fire the gun.

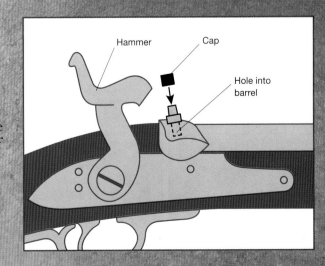

Hammer

Cap

Hole into barrel

PERCUSSION WEAPONS

Hammer

Nipple

Stud trigger

PERCUSSION PISTOL

This simple early percussion pistol has little in the way of sophistication. The hammer is powered by a spring and hits the nipple at the rear of the barrel. The weapon is small and has a small caliber and stud trigger. It was a cheap weapon produced to be carried in a pocket.

Hammer

Revolving pan

INDIAN COMBINATION RIFLE

Made in the late eighteenth century as a flintlock weapon, this rifle was later converted into a dual flintlock/percussion cap gun. The hammer had a flint held in its jaws, with the percussion hammer formed on the lower jaw. The powder pan can revolve to bring the nipple to the top.

Front sight

Rear sight

SILVER-PLATED SINGLE-SHOT PISTOL

Joshua Stevens founded his gun-making business in Massachusetts in 1864 making cheap pistols and rifles. In 1880 the company's fortunes improved when it began making top quality, single-shot target pistols such as this silver-plated example.

Stud trigger

Hammer

Trigger

AMERICAN LONG-BARRELED PISTOL

This long-barreled pistol was made by Joshua Stevens to fire the 410 gauge shotgun cartridge, introduced in 1892. This cartridge fires only eight pellets and has a small charge of powder, resulting in a weak shot and small spread. Weapons such as this were often given to boys for shooting vermin.

Barrel

PERCUSSION PISTOL

The case of this British weapon is cast in a single piece of brass. Its small size indicates that it was intended to be carried in a coat pocket. The short barrel means that this single-shot weapon would have been inaccurate at ranges over 20 feet.

Lanyard ring

RUSSIAN FLINT PISTOL

This 1858 Russian pistol is something of a curiosity. Its short barrel would have been inaccurate, yet it is fitted with a front sight. Its small size indicates it was used by an infantry officer, yet it has a lanyard ring more usually associated with cavalry weapons. Although made as a flintlock, it has been adapted to be a percussion cap weapon.

Lead ball

Brass ramrod

SMALL BLACK POWDER PISTOL WITH SHOT

This small pistol was made around 1840 to be fired by percussion cap, although its design could date to the eighteenth century. The round lead balls are typical of ammunition that was fired by pistols from about 1500 to the introduction of cartridges in the 1850s.

PERCUSSION BREECHLOCK FIREARMS

Throughout history, firearms had been loaded from the muzzle. First the powder was poured in, then ball and wadding were pushed down and rammed firmly into place. This system had obvious problems. It took a long time and gave great scope for human error when it came to spilling powder, dropping balls, or forgetting to remove the ramrod. The introduction of the percussion cap allowed gunsmiths to start experimenting with loading a gun through the breech. Breech loading allowed for more secure positioning of the powder and ball, but in time would also allow for enclosed cartridges to be inserted, with consequent elimination of human error, and an increase in speed of the reloading process.

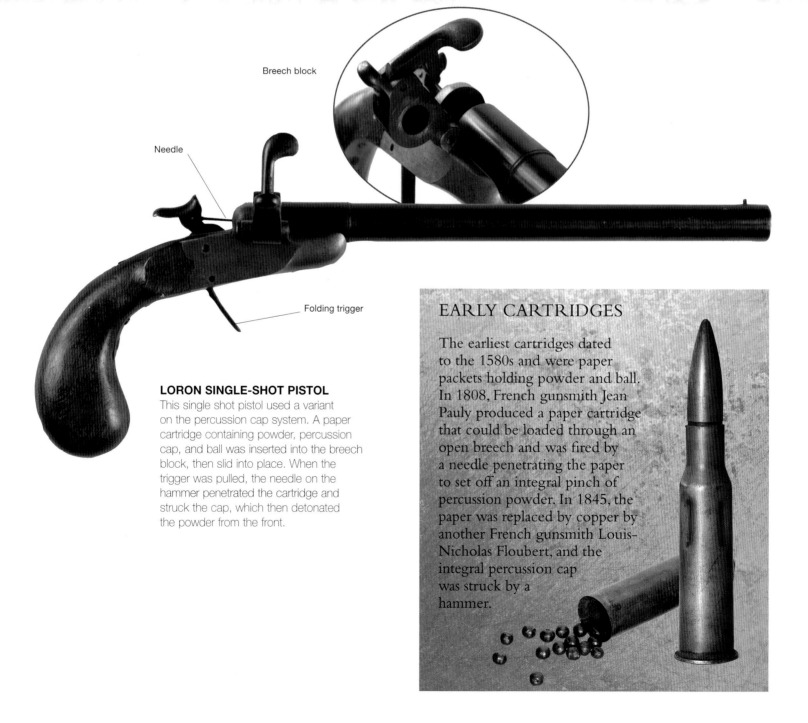

Breech block

Needle

Folding trigger

LORON SINGLE-SHOT PISTOL

This single shot pistol used a variant on the percussion cap system. A paper cartridge containing powder, percussion cap, and ball was inserted into the breech block, then slid into place. When the trigger was pulled, the needle on the hammer penetrated the cartridge and struck the cap, which then detonated the powder from the front.

EARLY CARTRIDGES

The earliest cartridges dated to the 1580s and were paper packets holding powder and ball. In 1808, French gunsmith Jean Pauly produced a paper cartridge that could be loaded through an open breech and was fired by a needle penetrating the paper to set off an integral pinch of percussion powder. In 1845, the paper was replaced by copper by another French gunsmith Louis–Nicholas Floubert, and the integral percussion cap was struck by a hammer.

Clip

Lanyard
ring

Hinge

Trigger

LANCASTER PISTOL
Dating around 1845 this Lancaster
Pistol was made in England for use
in the colonies of the British Empire.
The four barrels hinge down for
loading, and are held in place by a
clip when fired. The cartridges used
had an integral percussion cap,
together with powder and lead ball.

EARLY BREECH-LOADING MECHANISM

This very early breech-loading
mechanism was made in England
around 1715 for a flintlock rifle. The
powder, ball, and priming powder
were loaded into the separate cartridge
chamber, then the cartridge was inserted
into the rear of the breech before firing.
The wooden stock was hinged in front
of the trigger guard. This mechanism
brought several advantages, including
that the hunter could keep the chamber
dry in a leather pouch if it was raining.
He could also carry several pre-loaded
chambers, which greatly speeded up the
business of reloading. Although useful,
the concept was expensive and was
soon abandoned by gunsmiths.

Rifle opened to
receive new chamber

Spare
chamber

PERCUSSION BREECHLOCK FIREARMS

Hinged wooden stock

Separate cartridge chamber

BREECH-LOADING FIREARM OF PHILIP V OF SPAIN
This unusual breech-loading hunting rifle was made by Tienza of Madrid for King Philip V of Spain in 1715. This weapon is typical of the luxury goods that Philip would have acquired as King of Spain.

BELGIAN DOUBLE-BARREL PISTOL
Made in Belgium in the later nineteenth century, this double-barreled pistol is loaded by pushing the trigger guard forward to unlock the barrels so that they swing up and expose the breech. The cartridges are inserted into the barrel, which is then locked into position for firing.

Etched wooden grip

Rear sight

MAYNARD BREECH-LOADING RIFLE
This weapon was dubbed the "Model 1865" when manufactured by Edward Maynard in Massachusetts, although it entered production in 1863. Pulling down the trigger guard lever raised the rear of the barrel allowing for a cartridge to be pushed into place, or the old one to be removed. This example has interchangeable barrels. The upper has a shrouded front sight for longer-range accuracy.

Trigger guard lever

Firing pins

Hammers

Barrels tipped forward

DOUBLE-BARREL PISTOL WITH FIRING PINS

This neat pistol was made in Belgium about 1850. The barrels fold down to allow metal-jacketed center-fire cartridges to be inserted. The trigger has a double action to operate the two hammers, which swing forward to hit firing pins that then drive forward to hit the cartridges. It may have been adapted from an original design that used percussion caps.

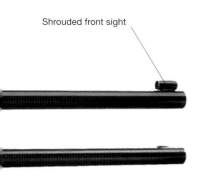

Shrouded front sight

RIFLE BREECH MECHANISM

Loading a gun through the breech with a prepared cartridge could speed up reloading and improve accuracy. The Ferguson Rifle of 1770 was an early effort to produce such a weapon. It saw action at Saratoga in 1777, but problems with manufacturing the precision parts led to the weapon being abandoned.

The breech screw was lowered by rotating the trigger guard

PERCUSSION CAP RIFLES

The percussion cap greatly improved the reliability of firearms and was first taken up by hunters who valued its ability to fire in damp weather. By the early nineteenth century when percussion caps entered production most hunters were using rifled weapons that gave greater accuracy at the cost of speed of reloading. For this reason, many of the first Percussion cap weapons were hunting rifles. The military, who favored speed of fire over accuracy, were slower to adopt the Percussion cap rifle and retained the smoothbore musket for many years after it had gone out of use in the civilian market.

Folding rear sight

BRUNSWICK RIFLE
The first Percussion cap rifle to enter service with the British Army was the Brunswick Rifle of 1840. Although it was a heavy weapon firing a low-velocity round, the Brunswick proved to be reliable and accurate, so it remained in service to 1860, and with second rank units to 1885.

Metal frame

GERMAN RIFLE
This intriguing hunting gun was made in Germany about 1850. It has two barrels, each fired by a separate hammer operated by its own trigger. One of the barrels fires rifled bullets, the other is a smoothbore barrel for firing shotgun cartridges. The shoulder stock is wood, although the frame of the gun is metal.

Triggers

Percussion cap mechanism

Smoothbore barrel

Ramrod

1839 TOWER CONVERSION MUSKET
This is a modern replica of the original 1839 Pattern Musket. The gun was based on the 1802 New Land Pattern musket that had been issued to the Guards regiments. This model featured a modern percussion cap mechanism attached to the barrel and stock of the old gun. It was manufactured up to 1851 and saw extensive service in the American Civil War, as well as with the British army.

Deeply scalloped
shoulder stock

Ramrod

HALF STOCK PERCUSSION CAP TARGET RIFLE

This target rifle was made by Leo O. Leonard of Keene, New
Hampshire, in the 1860s. The heavy octagonal barrel has a
post sight which is dovetailed to the front of the barrel, and a
rear "V" notched sight with a peep sight below. It is mounted
to a threaded post on the barrel's rear tang mount.

TARGET RIFLE

Emil Pachmayr began making sporting guns in Traunstein,
Bavaria, in 1831, and the company he founded is still operating
in Salzburger Strasse. This quality target rifle was made in the
early twentieth century and features a number of quality details
not found on cheaper weapons.

Ramrod

Round eye cup

Cheek rest

Double triggers

Ornamental clasps

HAWKEN RIFLE

Jacob and Samuel Hawken began making their quality
muzzleloading rifles in St. Louis, Missouri, in 1815 and
continued to 1858 when the business switched to
retailing guns made by others. The guns became
synonymous with the Western Frontier, and were prized
for their light weight and long-range accuracy.

Rawhide
carrying sling

PERCUSSION CAP RIFLES

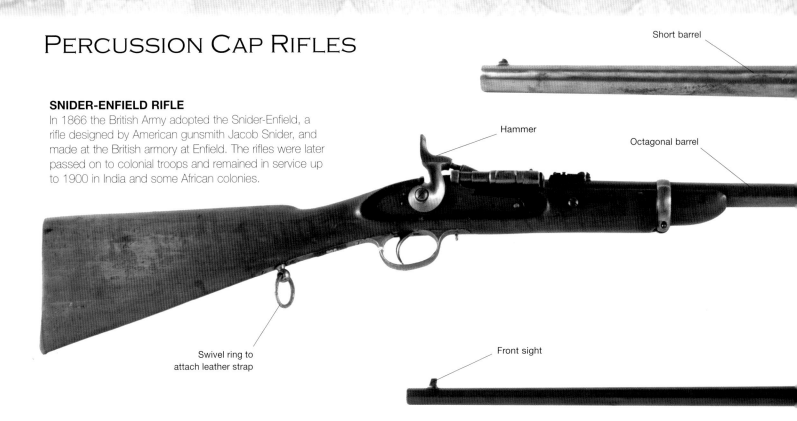

Short barrel

Hammer

Octagonal barrel

SNIDER-ENFIELD RIFLE

In 1866 the British Army adopted the Snider-Enfield, a rifle designed by American gunsmith Jacob Snider, and made at the British armory at Enfield. The rifles were later passed on to colonial troops and remained in service up to 1900 in India and some African colonies.

Swivel ring to attach leather strap

Front sight

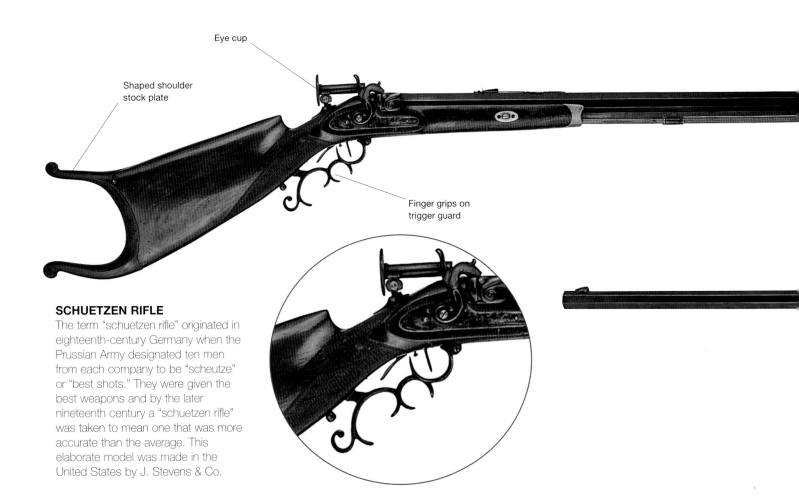

Eye cup

Shaped shoulder stock plate

Finger grips on trigger guard

SCHUETZEN RIFLE

The term "schuetzen rifle" originated in eighteenth-century Germany when the Prussian Army designated ten men from each company to be "scheutze" or "best shots." They were given the best weapons and by the later nineteenth century a "schuetzen rifle" was taken to mean one that was more accurate than the average. This elaborate model was made in the United States by J. Stevens & Co.

Percussion hammer

Front sight

MUTZIG FRENCH CARBINE

In 1791 Cardinal de Rohan, Bishop of Strasbourg, fled the French Revolution and moved to live in a German part of his diocese. His old palace at Mutzig was seized by the French state and converted to an arms factory, which it remained for over a century. This percussion cap cavalry carbine was made in the Mutzig factory in the mid-nineteenth century.

Detachable barrel

REMINGTON RIFLE

This repeating rifle was made in 1941 to take .22 sporting cartridges and was intended for hunters. It features a takedown design in which the barrel can be removed and the stock comes apart. It was designed to be carried disassembled in a suitcase for easy transport on trains to a hunting region.

Percussion hammer

Short wooden stock

HERZBERG PERCUSSION RIFLE

Throughout the nineteenth century Herzberg was one of the most important industrial cities in Saxony. At this date Saxony was an independent kingdom, but squeezed between the larger states of Prussia and Austria, it invested heavily in its armed forces. This muzzleloading rifle was made in Herzberg in the early nineteenth century and was issued to light infantry units.

REPEATING WEAPONS
1840-1914

Until the mid-nineteenth century all efforts to speed up the business of firing one shot after another had concentrated on making the loading of single-shot weapons faster and easier. It was the invention of the integrated cartridge that made it possible to consider weapons that could hold more than one cartridge at a time, making swift reloading a mechanical action of the repeating gun.

BATTLE OF GETTYSBURG
Fought in 1863 as part of the American Civil War, the Battle of Gettysburg saw the limited use of some early repeating weapons.

PEPPERBOXES

One of the earliest attempts to produce a handgun that would fire multiple times before being reloaded was the pepperbox (also known as a pepperpot)—named for its resemblance to a domestic pepper grinder. The system had three or more barrels fixed to a central rod around which they could be rotated. When the gun was fired, the barrels rotated so that a fresh barrel was brought to the top, and would come in line with the firing mechanism. In this way, each barrel could be fired in turn before the weapon needed to be reloaded. The earliest pepperboxes were made around 1490, but problems with the matchlock and the likelihood of other barrels being set off by the first meant that pepperbox pistols did not become common until these problems were solved in the later eighteenth century.

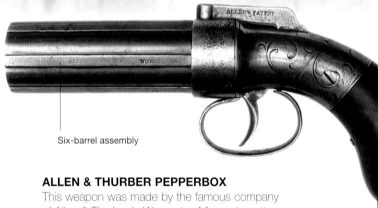

Six-barrel assembly

ALLEN & THURBER PEPPERBOX

This weapon was made by the famous company of Allen & Thurber in Worcester, Massachusetts, around 1850. The pepperbox mechanism used here was patented by Ethan Allen in 1837 and remained in use until the 1870s.

Wooden butt

Firing hammer

Trigger

SIX-BARRELED PEPPERBOX

This Allen & Thurber pistol was made around 1856. The pistol has six barrels—all machined out of a single piece of steel and each firing a .36 ball. By the time this gun was being made, Ethan Allen was taking a back seat as he was handing over the company to his two sons-in-law, Sullivan Forehand and H. Wadsworth.

FOUR-BARRELED DERRINGER-STYLE PISTOL

By the time this gun was made in the mid-nineteenth century the word "derringer" had come to mean almost any pistol that was small enough to fit into a pocket. This highly unusual weapon has four barrels that are fired independently by four hammers striking four different nipples for percussion caps. The four hammers are pulled back together; then each time the trigger is pulled, a different hammer is released.

JOHAN ENGHOLM GUN

This pepperbox was made by Swedish gunsmith Johan Engholm in the middle of the nineteenth century. Engholm began making guns in the 1840s and continued to do so into the twentieth century. He was particularly well known for his high-quality pepperbox guns.

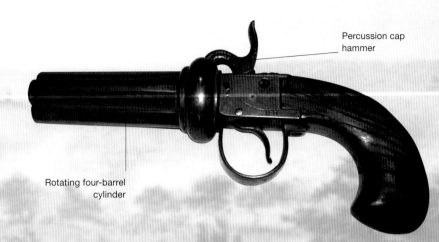

Percussion cap hammer

Rotating four-barrel cylinder

Short barrel assembly

POCKET PEPPERBOX

A fine example of an Allen & Thurber pocket pepperbox, or derringer. This example has a shorter barrel than most other Allen & Thurber guns, making it easier to conceal in a pocket or bag. The smooth outline of the weapon meant that it was unlikely to snag on cloth when it was needed in a hurry.

Curved wooden butt

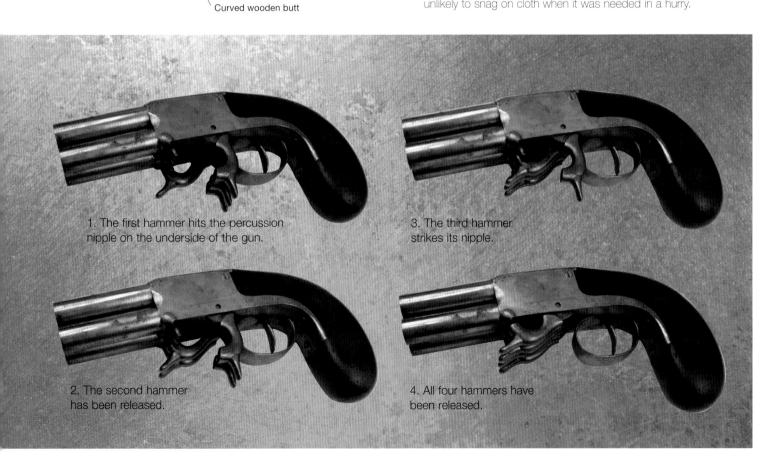

1. The first hammer hits the percussion nipple on the underside of the gun.

3. The third hammer strikes its nipple.

2. The second hammer has been released.

4. All four hammers have been released.

PEPPERBOXES

MARIETTE

In 1832 Gilles Mariette, a Belgian gunsmith working in Liege, Belgium, perfected a pepperbox system that was characterized by the way the barrels unclipped from the body of the gun for cleaning and reloading. This example is at the luxury end of the Mariette range, with damascened barrels and an engraved body.

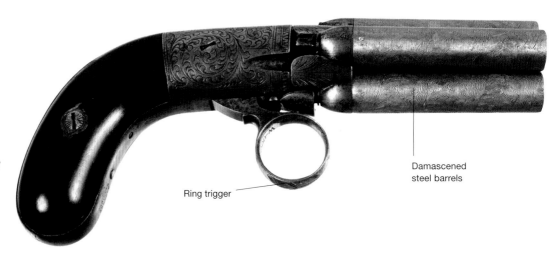

Ring trigger

Damascened steel barrels

MARIETTE BREVETÉ D26

This Mariette pepperbox is shown with the barrels on, and with the barrels removed (inset). Mariette patented his pepperbox mechanism in 1839, but was later sued for breach of copyright by American gunsmith Samuel Colt. Mariette won the action and continued to make his guns until 1865.

Central pivot

Wooden butt

Barrel assembly

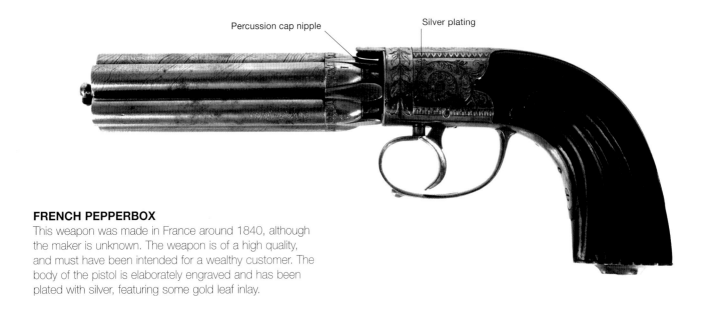

Percussion cap nipple

Silver plating

FRENCH PEPPERBOX

This weapon was made in France around 1840, although the maker is unknown. The weapon is of a high quality, and must have been intended for a wealthy customer. The body of the pistol is elaborately engraved and has been plated with silver, featuring some gold leaf inlay.

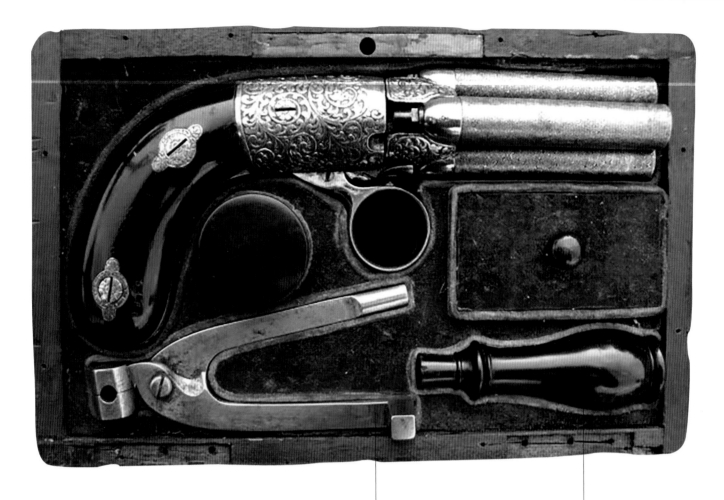

MARIETTE PEPPERBOX IN CASE
This elegant little pepperbox by Gilles Mariette was made in about 1850. It is shown here in its original traveling box, which contains a powder flask, bullet mold, and boxes for other accessories.

Bullet mold

Powder flask

Percussion nipples

Ring trigger

MARIETTE 18-SHOT PEPPERBOX
This extraordinary little pistol by Gilles Mariette contains no fewer than eighteen barrels set around the central spindle. The barrels are set in two rows, but the percussion nipples are in one line to allow the single hammer action. As with all Mariette pistols, there is a ring trigger and a simple cylindrical body. The barrels are of damascened steel.

PEPPERBOXES

COOPER PEPPERBOX PISTOL
The English gunsmith J. R. Cooper manufactured pepperboxes that fired the bottom barrel on the cylinder, not the top barrel. These guns used an underhammer, striking forward from beside the ring trigger.

Recess for fixing percussion cap to nipple

Underhammer

Damascened barrels

Engraved body

ENGRAVED J. R. COOPER DOUBLE ACTION PEPPERPOT
This pistol features a double-action trigger, which means that pulling the trigger performs the double action of cocking the hammer and then releasing it to fire the gun. This contrasts with the single-action trigger that releases only the hammer, which needs to be cocked by another mechanism.

Ring trigger

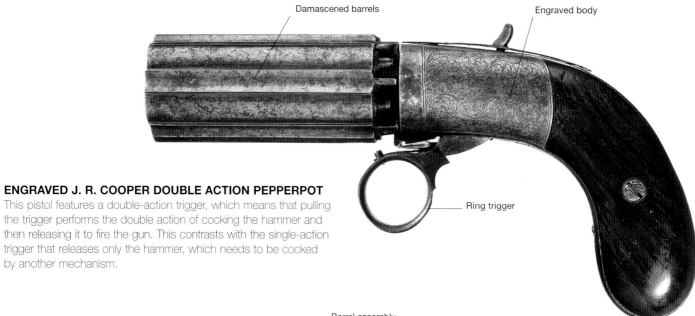

Barrel assembly

Recess to engage percussion caps

ENGRAVED J. R. COOPER PEPPERPOT
This tiny English pepperbox was made around 1850 by J. R. Cooper of Birmingham, England. This weapon has a nickel-silver frame that has been engraved with foliate designs. The ring trigger operates an underhammer. The barrel assembly needs to be twisted around by hand to bring the next barrel into line with the firing mechanism.

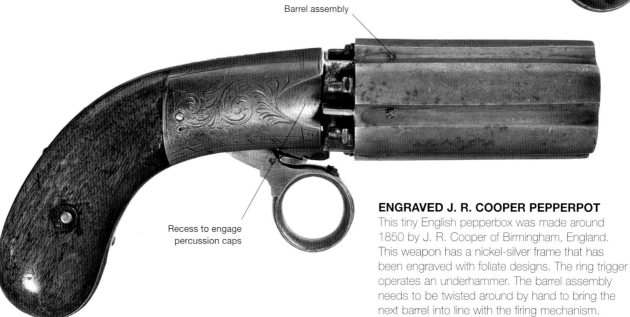

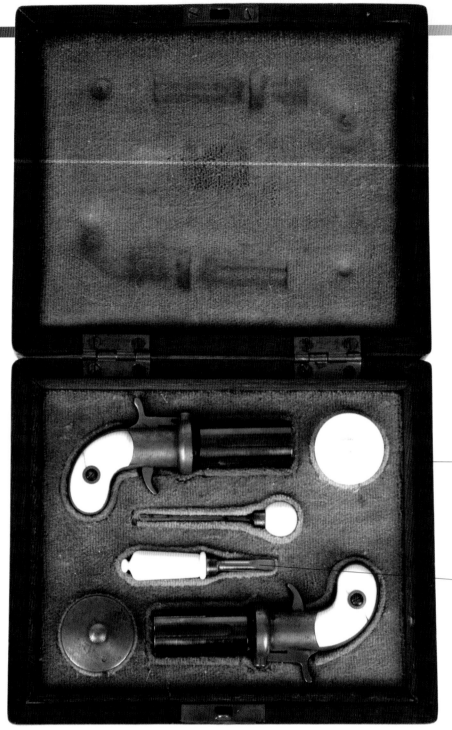

ENGLISH MINIATURES

This tiny pair of pistols was manufactured by English gunsmith John Maycock. Each pistol has a six-barrel pepperbox assembly and an ivory grip. The barrels are only 1 inch long, and have been blued to resist rusting. The neat little box includes a cartridge box, cleaning rod, screwdriver, and other accessories.

Mahogany case

Screwdriver

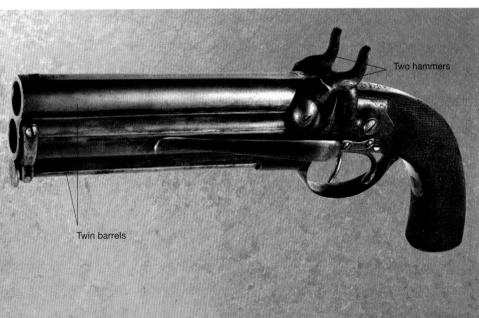

THE HOWDAH PISTOL

A howdah is the platform, often with a fabric roof, that rests on top of a tame elephant and carries passengers while the mahout, or driver, sits on the elephant's neck. The howdah pistol shows a different approach to firing more than one shot in quick succession. It was a heavy-caliber weapon designed to protect those traveling the wilder areas of southern Asia on a howdah from attack by wild animals or bandits.

Two hammers

Twin barrels

TURRET PISTOLS AND TURNOVERS

While pepperboxes had multiple barrels, the turret pistol design featured a single barrel. The multiple firing capability came from the revolving turret mounted between the barrel and the hammer. This turret consisted of a disc that contained a number of small cylinders; each could be loaded with powder and ball. As each shot was fired, the cylinder rotated around to bring another of the cylinders into line with the barrel, and the ball it contained could be fired. The hammer struck the nipple from the side. A turnover pistol used a similar action to the pepperbox, but instead of the rotating barrel assembly moving in steps, it was simply flipped over once.

ENGRAVED TURRET PISTOL
This neat little turret pistol has several interesting features. The barrel has a front sight, while the rear sight is mounted on top of the turret itself. The folding trigger is shaped so that when not in use, it lay flat against the bottom side of the turret. The turret and case of the gun have been elaborately engraved.

Folding trigger

Wooden grip

Turret

Barrel

ALLEN TURRET PISTOL
This turret pistol was made by C.B. Allen of Springfield, Massachusetts. The turret contained seven chambers, each holding powder and a .40-caliber ball. The sideways-mounted hammer can be seen in this view. The folding trigger is shown in the uncocked position.

FOUR-BARRELED TURNOVER

This turnover pistol has four barrels, two triggers, and two hammers. All four barrels were loaded with powder and ball. Each of the two triggers fired one of the upper barrels by striking a percussion cap. The barrel was then turned over to bring the unused barrels to the top. New percussion caps were then fitted to the nipples, the hammers were pulled back, and the gun was ready to fire again.

Percussion caps could be detonated by even a relatively gentle tap, so metal shields like this to protect the caps were necessary to prevent accidental firings.

Two hammers

Nipple guard

Double trigger

Hammer spur
for cocking

TURNOVER PISTOL

This small turnover pistol was made by London gunsmith Thomas Lloyd. The extremely short barrels and small grip show that it was intended as a pocket pistol.

Folding trigger in
closed position

Folding triggers were common on pocket pistols. They lay flush with the receiver so that they did not snag on fabric, but emerged when the hammer was cocked ready for the weapon to be fired.

POCKET-SIZED PISTOLS

Until London's police force was established in 1829 there was no modern-style law enforcement to be found anywhere. Some towns or cities had a watch service to patrol the streets, and some magistrates employed men to serve warrants and arrest wanted persons, but the imposition of law and order was generally in the hands of the local population. This uneven measure of justice meant that people who carried around jewelry, money, or other items worth stealing were well advised to also carry the means of defending themselves. For many citizens that meant a gun that was small enough to be tucked into a pocket, bag, or even a muff.

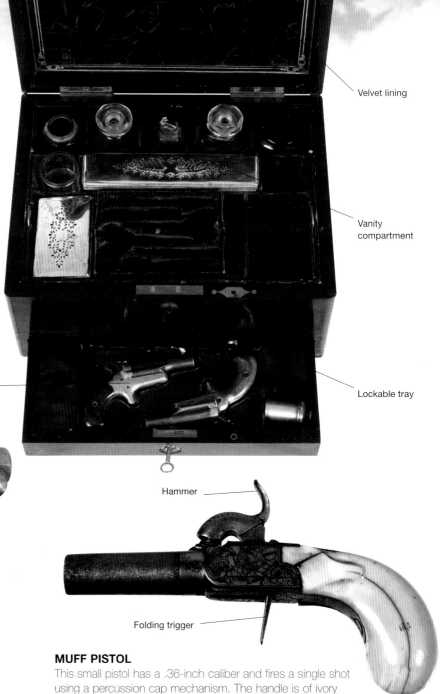

Velvet lining

Vanity compartment

Colt pistols

Lockable tray

LADIES' CASE WITH PISTOLS

In the nineteenth century, ladies who traveled much would have had a wooden case containing perfumes, makeup, needles and thread, and other essentials. This example was made by Halstaffe of Regent Street, London, and is unusual in having a concealed tray at the bottom that contains a pair of Colt Model No.3 derringer pistols.

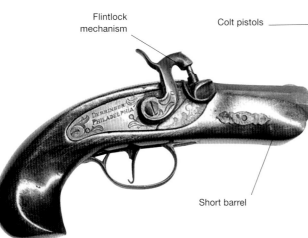

Flintlock mechanism

Short barrel

PHILADELPHIA DERINGER

In 1806 American gunsmith Henry Deringer opened his business on Tamarind Street, Philadelphia. At first he made pistols and muskets for the military, but in 1825 he invented the gun that made him famous. The Philadephia Deringer was a single-shot, muzzle-loading flintlock pistol that combined a very short barrel with a wide caliber. The result was a pistol small enough to be carried in the pocket but powerful enough to knock a man down.

Hammer

Folding trigger

MUFF PISTOL

This small pistol has a .36-inch caliber and fires a single shot using a percussion cap mechanism. The handle is of ivory and the plain barrel is steel. The folding trigger on the underside of the frame is in the closed position. These small, elegant guns were designed to be carried in a lady's muff.

Hammer spur

Hammer

Ivory handles

Folding trigger

PAIR OF MUFF PISTOLS

This pair of quality muff pistols show signs of exceptional workmanship. The hilts are of ivory, the barrels are damascened steel, and the cases have been engraved with foliate designs. The damascened steel used in gun barrels was made by welding together different pieces of metal, then twisting them to form the convoluted patterns of the finished product.

PERCUSSION CAP PISTOL

A simple but relatively well made single-shot pistol from the 1840s. This pistol is muzzle-loaded and works with a straightforward single-action trigger, working a hammer that strikes the percussion cap in line with the barrel.

Front sight

Hammer

Loading lever

Barrel

Magazine tube

REMINGTON PISTOL

This small pistol was made in the 1870s and has an unusual tube magazine action. The tube below the barrel holds five rounds in a spring-loaded case. By pushing down on the loading lever the breech block falls, ejecting the spent cartridge and chambering the next one pushed into place by the spring.

THE ASSASSINATION OF LINCOLN

On April 14, 1865, U.S. President Abraham Lincoln went to Ford's Theater in Washington, D.C., with his wife to watch the play "Our American Cousin." Watching President Lincoln was the Confederate spy John Wilkes Booth, who earned a living as an actor. At the intermission, the president's bodyguard slipped out to get a drink. Booth climbed the stairs and stealthily entered Lincoln's private box. He pulled out a Philadelphia Derringer that he habitually carried in his pocket, and at 1:13p.m. shot Lincoln in the back of the head. Major Henry Rathbone, who was also in the box, grabbed Booth, but the assassin stabbed him, leapt to the stage, and fled. Lincoln died the following morning without regaining consciousness. Booth was cornered ten days later and shot dead by troops sent to arrest him.

COLT'S REVOLVERS

The struggle to find a reliable method of producing a gun able to fire more than once without reloading was a long one for gunsmiths. The problem was finally solved by American gunsmith Samuel Colt when he combined the newly developed revolver mechanism and the newly invented metal-jacketed cartridge. It was the combination of these two developments in gun design that made the Colt revolver such a reliable, effective, and efficient weapon. Colt was not just a weapons designer, he was a manufacturer who revolutionized the business of making guns by replacing what had been a craft with industrial mass production. It was his new methods of making guns as much as his designs that were to be his legacy to the world of the weapons industry.

Bayonet

Revolving chamber

Hammer

PROTOTYPE COLT REVOLVER

While Colt was a good designer, he lacked the metal working skills to turn his designs into a reality. This 1831 prototype was actually made by John Pearson of Baltimore to a Colt design. This is one of several pre-patent examples to survive that show the way Colt was improving his design in stages before applying for a patent.

Loading lever

Hammer in resting position

COLT PATERSON

This gun is another example of the Texas Paterson. This slightly later model has a hinged loading lever and a capping window, which solved problems with the earlier model. The loading lever meant that it was no longer necessary to remove the revolving cylinder to load it, while the capping window allowed the gun to be carried safely when loaded as the hammer rested in the window and could not accidentally fire a chamber.

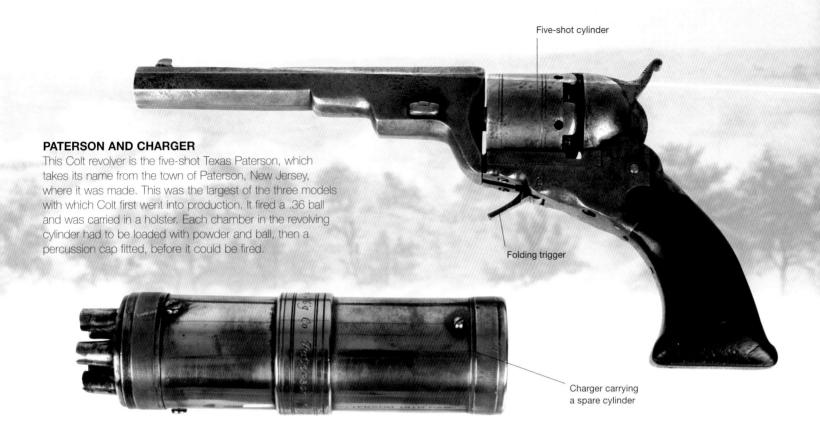

Five-shot cylinder

Folding trigger

Charger carrying
a spare cylinder

PATERSON AND CHARGER
This Colt revolver is the five-shot Texas Paterson, which takes its name from the town of Paterson, New Jersey, where it was made. This was the largest of the three models with which Colt first went into production. It fired a .36 ball and was carried in a holster. Each chamber in the revolving cylinder had to be loaded with powder and ball, then a percussion cap fitted, before it could be fired.

SAMUEL COLT

Samuel Colt was born in Hartford, Connecticut, in 1814 and at a young age became interested in weapons manufacturing. In 1830 he voyaged on the brig *Corvo* and was fascinated to see that whichever position the helm was in, the spoked wheel was able to engage with a clip that held it firm. It was this that gave him the idea of a pistol with a revolving cylinder holding chambers that engaged with a clip to hold it in a position so that each chamber lined up with the barrel in turn. Colt's idea proved to be the basis for the revolver pistol that made his name and his fortune. When Samuel Colt died in 1862 he was one of the richest men in the United States.

COLT'S NEW MODEL ARMY METALLIC CARTRIDGE REVOLVING PISTOL.

The Drawing is one-half the size of the Pistol.
cal. .45 inch.   Price $20,00.

COLT'S METALLIC CARTRIDGE ARMY PISTOL, WITH ATTACHABLE STOCK.

Colt's Revolvers

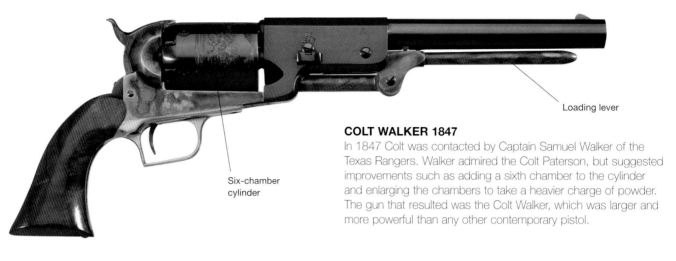

Loading lever

COLT WALKER 1847

In 1847 Colt was contacted by Captain Samuel Walker of the Texas Rangers. Walker admired the Colt Paterson, but suggested improvements such as adding a sixth chamber to the cylinder and enlarging the chambers to take a heavier charge of powder. The gun that resulted was the Colt Walker, which was larger and more powerful than any other contemporary pistol.

Six-chamber cylinder

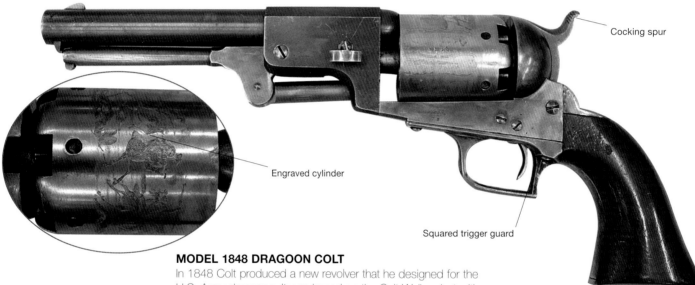

Cocking spur

Engraved cylinder

Squared trigger guard

MODEL 1848 DRAGOON COLT

In 1848 Colt produced a new revolver that he designed for the U.S. Army dragoons. It was based on the Colt Walker, but with improvements. The two most important were a 7.5-inch barrel instead of a 9-inch barrel, and a more secure locking mechanism for the loading lever. Taken together these made the pistol handier to use and less prone to jamming in action.

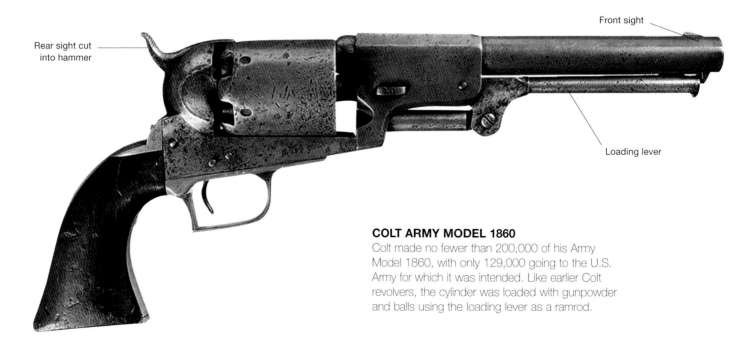

Front sight

Rear sight cut into hammer

Loading lever

COLT ARMY MODEL 1860

Colt made no fewer than 200,000 of his Army Model 1860, with only 129,000 going to the U.S. Army for which it was intended. Like earlier Colt revolvers, the cylinder was loaded with gunpowder and balls using the loading lever as a ramrod.

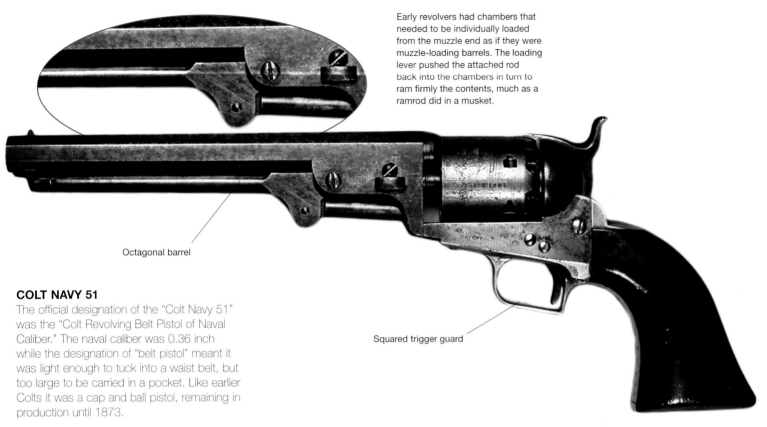

Early revolvers had chambers that needed to be individually loaded from the muzzle end as if they were muzzle-loading barrels. The loading lever pushed the attached rod back into the chambers in turn to ram firmly the contents, much as a ramrod did in a musket.

Octagonal barrel

COLT NAVY 51

The official designation of the "Colt Navy 51" was the "Colt Revolving Belt Pistol of Naval Caliber." The naval caliber was 0.36 inch while the designation of "belt pistol" meant it was light enough to tuck into a waist belt, but too large to be carried in a pocket. Like earlier Colts it was a cap and ball pistol, remaining in production until 1873.

Squared trigger guard

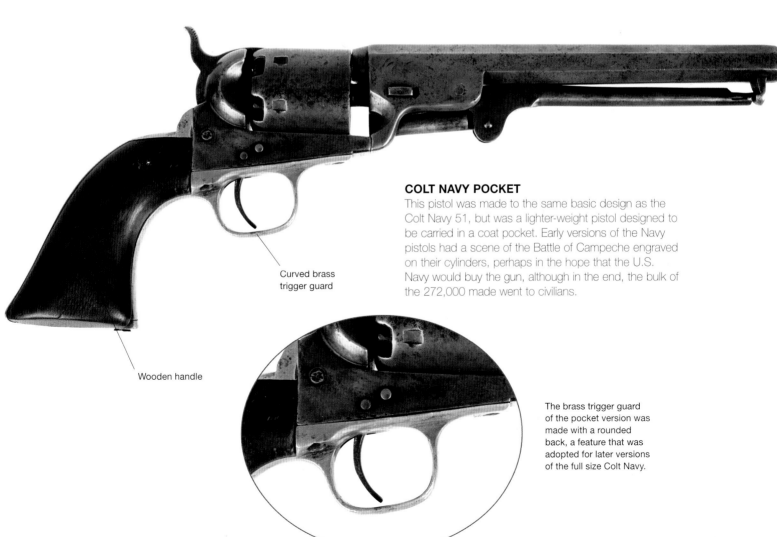

Curved brass trigger guard

COLT NAVY POCKET

This pistol was made to the same basic design as the Colt Navy 51, but was a lighter-weight pistol designed to be carried in a coat pocket. Early versions of the Navy pistols had a scene of the Battle of Campeche engraved on their cylinders, perhaps in the hope that the U.S. Navy would buy the gun, although in the end, the bulk of the 272,000 made went to civilians.

Wooden handle

The brass trigger guard of the pocket version was made with a rounded back, a feature that was adopted for later versions of the full size Colt Navy.

COLT'S REVOLVERS

Front sight

Cleaning rod

Lanyard ring

COLT NEW NAVY

The Colt New Navy, or M1892, was in production from 1892 to 1908. Unlike earlier Colts it was designed to fire metal-jacketed cartridges. This removed the need for a loading lever, which was replaced by a rod to extract any used cartridges that jammed inside the chamber. Unlike the original Navy Colt, this later model was adopted by the U.S. military.

Hammer spur

Octagonal barrel

Loading lever

COLT POCKET

This Pocket Model of 1849 has a five-chamber cylinder, and took cap and ball shots. It has an inscription recording that it was presented to an officer in the U.S. Army in May 1861 by the Ladies of Bristol, Pennsylvania. Its owner was killed eighteen months later at the Second Battle of Bull Run.

The front sights of the Colt Pocket were fixed and could not be altered. They were ranged for shots at 75 yards, which meant that at 25 yards the bullet struck the target about a foot above the aim spot.

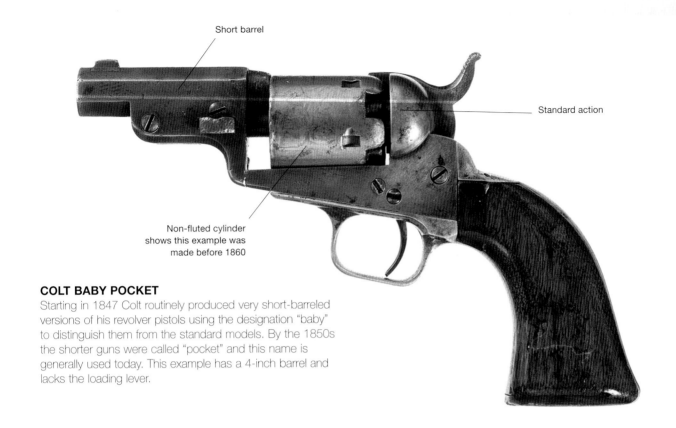

Short barrel

Standard action

Non-fluted cylinder shows this example was made before 1860

COLT BABY POCKET

Starting in 1847 Colt routinely produced very short-barreled versions of his revolver pistols using the designation "baby" to distinguish them from the standard models. By the 1850s the shorter guns were called "pocket" and this name is generally used today. This example has a 4-inch barrel and lacks the loading lever.

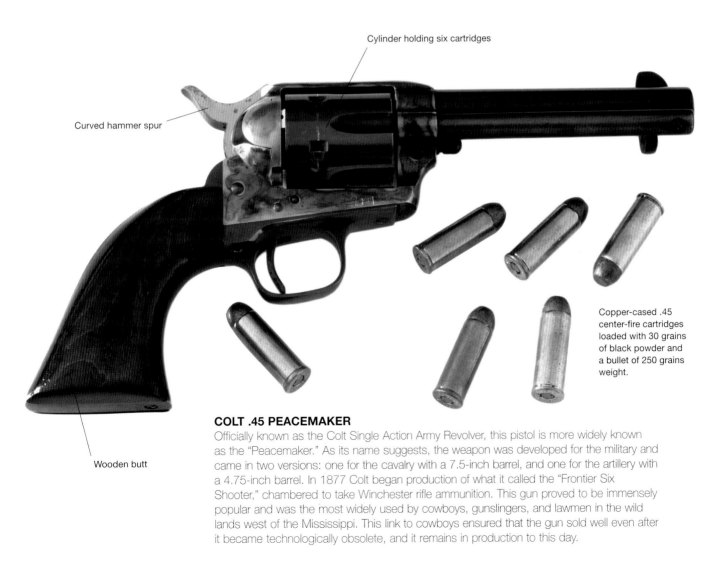

Cylinder holding six cartridges

Curved hammer spur

Copper-cased .45 center-fire cartridges loaded with 30 grains of black powder and a bullet of 250 grains weight.

Wooden butt

COLT .45 PEACEMAKER

Officially known as the Colt Single Action Army Revolver, this pistol is more widely known as the "Peacemaker." As its name suggests, the weapon was developed for the military and came in two versions: one for the cavalry with a 7.5-inch barrel, and one for the artillery with a 4.75-inch barrel. In 1877 Colt began production of what it called the "Frontier Six Shooter," chambered to take Winchester rifle ammunition. This gun proved to be immensely popular and was the most widely used by cowboys, gunslingers, and lawmen in the wild lands west of the Mississippi. This link to cowboys ensured that the gun sold well even after it became technologically obsolete, and it remains in production to this day.

Colt's Revolvers

Front sight

Short-barrel model

NEW DOUBLE-ACTION REVOLVER

The Colt Lightning Revolver was the version of the M1877 chambered to take the .38 Long Colt cartridge. This was the first Colt revolver to have a double action, in which pulling the trigger turned the cylinder around, cocked the hammer, and then released the hammer to fire the gun. The mechanism proved to be delicate and broke easily.

Front sight

"Colt DA41" etched on barrel

COLT DA 41 REVOLVER

The Colt Double-Action Revolver entered production in 1899 and ten years later was adopted by the U.S. Army in slightly modified form as the M1909. The gun was available in various calibers—this one takes .41 cartridges, but it could also take .38 and .45 cartridges.

Rubber grip

Colt logo

MODEL 1855 CARBINE

The Colt Model 1855 combined the cylinder action of the pistol with the longer barrel and shoulder stock of the rifle. Over the ten years the model was in production about 4,435 were made. This is one of the rare Dragoon Carbines, with its cut-down barrel.

Cylinder

Folding rear sight

Cap nipple

Cylinder axis rod

BILLY THE KID

Through the course of his short but violent life, the outlaw known as Billy the Kid used a variety of guns, but he seems to have preferred Winchester rifles and Colt revolvers. He was born William McCarty, but is better known as William Bonney, a name he adopted when on the run. Many legends surround Billy, including that he shot twenty-one men (more likely he killed nine), and that he escaped his final, fatal encounter with Sheriff Pat Garrett in 1881 to live until the 1950s. His sobriquet of "the Kid" came from his youth. He went on the run at age fourteen and was killed when he was twenty-one.

WORLD REVOLVERS

It was Samuel Colt who developed and perfected the revolver mechanism for handguns. This gave the user a great advantage in combat as he could reliably fire his gun five or six times when an opponent could only fire once before reloading. This made Colt's guns very popular and it was not long before other manufacturers were imitating the revolver. Colt had a policy of aggressively protecting his patents, taking to court anyone who produced anything similar to a Colt design. Once Colt's patents ran out, however, there was a rush of companies making revolvers, some of them direct copies of Colt originals.

Front sight

Gems

COLT IMITATION
This gun was made by Eibar in Spain in the 1920s. It is an almost direct copy of a Colt original, though the owner has modified it slightly by having semi-precious stone set into the handle.

Hammer

BELGIAN PISTOL
Made in the 1840s in Belgium, this pistol has a side-mounted hammer that hits the percussion cap of the topmost chamber in the revolving cylinder. The chambers were loaded with powder, ball, and wad, which was then compacted by pulling down the side-mounted loading lever to drive the ram into the chamber.

Loading lever

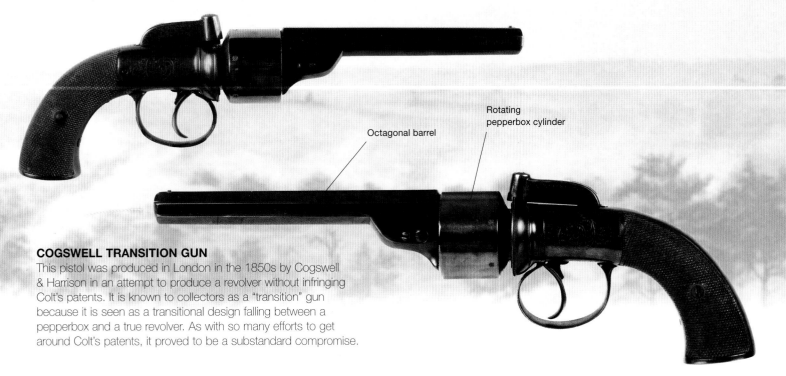

Octagonal barrel

Rotating
pepperbox cylinder

COGSWELL TRANSITION GUN

This pistol was produced in London in the 1850s by Cogswell & Harrison in an attempt to produce a revolver without infringing Colt's patents. It is known to collectors as a "transition" gun because it is seen as a transitional design falling between a pepperbox and a true revolver. As with so many efforts to get around Colt's patents, it proved to be a substandard compromise.

Hammer

Percussion cap nipple

MASSACHUSETTS ARMS COMPANY .28

This small .28 pistol was made by the Massachusetts Arms Company of Chicopee Falls. In an effort to evade Colt's lawyers, the pistol has a single percussion cap nipple on the frame, which directs the hot gasses down a channel to a chamber in the rotating cylinder. Colt won the subsequent legal action.

Nipple

Loading lever

FIVE-SHOT COOPER REVOLVER

This gun, made in Birmingham, England, by J. R. Cooper, copies many features from Colt's design. The swing-hinged loading lever, the ratcheted cylinder drive mechanism, and rear-mounted nipples are all taken from Colt's designs.

WORLD REVOLVERS

Hammer

SLOCUM
In 1863 the Brooklyn Arms Company produced this small revolver that they named the "Slocum" in honor of the general who was leading troops from Brooklyn in the American Civil War. The cylinder contained sliding tubes that moved forward over a fixed ejection system.

Sliding tubes

Hammer

MOORE
In the 1860s Daniel Moore of the New York company Moore's Patent Firearms developed a metal-jacketed cartridge that had a rounded base from which projected a small knob, or teat, containing the priming charge. This meant that the cylinders on his revolvers were loaded from the front, not the rear, as in other models.

Stud trigger

WILLIAMS & POWELL REVOLVER
The British gunsmith William Tranter of Birmingham, England, produced a number of innovative designs, and after his death in 1890 other companies rushed to copy his work. This double-action pistol was made by Williams & Powell of Liverpool in the 1890s, and in many respects is a near copy of a Tranter design.

Five-shot cylinder

Ejector mechanism

Two-stage trigger

Front sight

Hammer

Six-shot cylinder

Lanyard ring

BELGIAN REVOLVER

This revolver was manufactured in Belgium for the military market in the third quarter of the nineteenth century. The lanyard ring on the butt allowed the weapon to be connected by a cord to the belt or webbing of the army officer who used it. Therefore, the gun would not be lost if it was dropped in action.

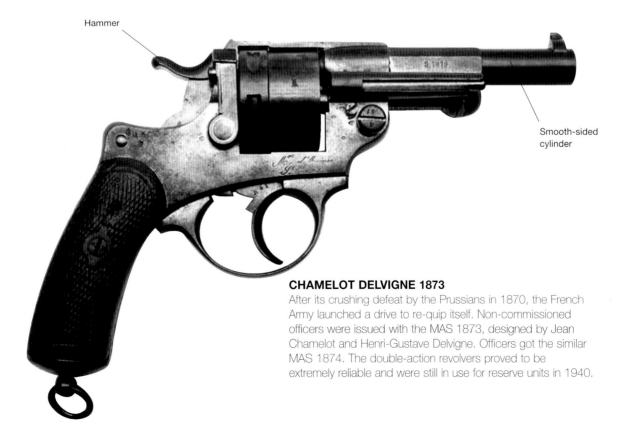

Hammer

Smooth-sided cylinder

CHAMELOT DELVIGNE 1873

After its crushing defeat by the Prussians in 1870, the French Army launched a drive to re-quip itself. Non-commissioned officers were issued with the MAS 1873, designed by Jean Chamelot and Henri-Gustave Delvigne. Officers got the similar MAS 1874. The double-action revolvers proved to be extremely reliable and were still in use for reserve units in 1940.

WORLD REVOLVERS

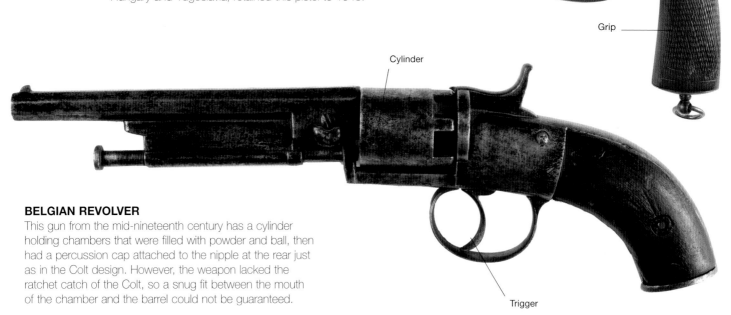

RAST & GASSER

This M1898 revolver was the standard issue sidearm for officers and non-commissioned officers in the Austro-Hungarian Army from 1898 to 1912. Large numbers of this robust and reliable weapon were made and it remained in use throughout World War I. Successor states, such as Hungary and Yugoslavia, retained this pistol to 1945.

Eight-shot cylinder

Grip

Cylinder

BELGIAN REVOLVER

This gun from the mid-nineteenth century has a cylinder holding chambers that were filled with powder and ball, then had a percussion cap attached to the nipple at the rear just as in the Colt design. However, the weapon lacked the ratchet catch of the Colt, so a snug fit between the mouth of the chamber and the barrel could not be guaranteed.

Trigger

Octagonal barrel

Acanthus leaf decoration

BELGIAN COPY

This weapon was made in Belgium in the late nineteenth century, but is an almost direct copy of the French Chamelot-Delvigne Model 1872. Note the elegant acanthus leaf carved onto the wooden butt, as well as the hatched markings to improve grip.

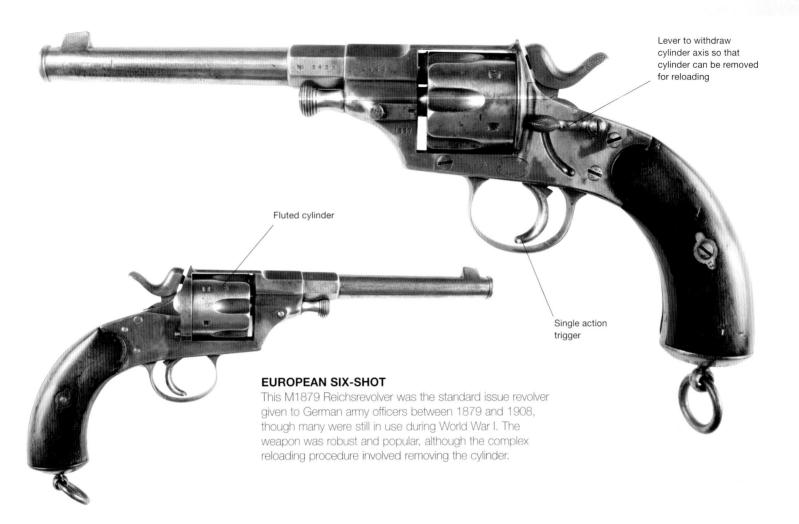

Lever to withdraw cylinder axis so that cylinder can be removed for reloading

Fluted cylinder

Single action trigger

EUROPEAN SIX-SHOT
This M1879 Reichsrevolver was the standard issue revolver given to German army officers between 1879 and 1908, though many were still in use during World War I. The weapon was robust and popular, although the complex reloading procedure involved removing the cylinder.

GARFIELD ASSASSINATION

On July 2, 1881, President James Garfield (in black top hat below) was walking to a train at the Washington terminal of the Baltimore and Potomac Railroad when he was shot twice from behind by Charles Guiteau. Guiteau was arrested on the spot, making a series of bizarre statements that led some to conclude he was deranged. His gun, a Webley .450 "British Bull Dog" revolver (see right) was wrestled from him. The second bullet could not be found and extracted, and the wound became infected. After weeks of bedridden pain, Garfield died on September 19th. A jury rejected Guiteau's defense of insanity and found him guilty of murder. He was executed on June 30, 1882.

WORLD REVOLVERS

TIP-UP REVOLVER

In 1860 the gunsmith, Albert Spirlet of Liege, Belgium, filed a patent for a style of revolver that had a trigger guard that swung aside to allow the barrel and cylinder to tip up so the cartridges could be removed and reloaded. Spirlet registered follow up patents until 1876, but when these ran out the design was copied by many other European manufacturers.

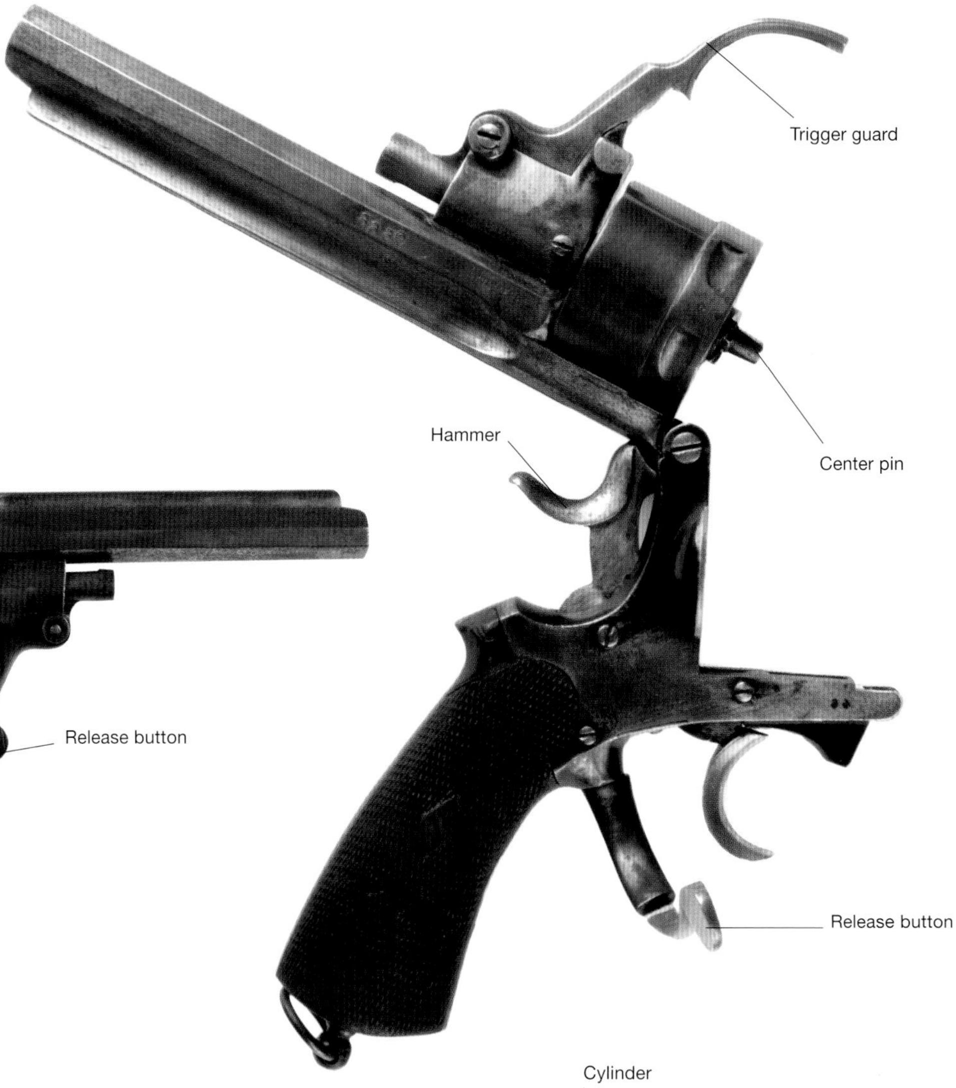

Trigger guard

Hammer

Center pin

Hammer

Release button

Release button

Cylinder

BLACK METAL REVOLVER

This large caliber revolver was made by Tipping & Lawden at their works on Constitution Hill, Birmingham, England, in the 1870s. The company later merged with others to form the Birmingham Small Arms Trading Company. This example is stamped "John Clarke, Newton Abbot," presumably this being the name and hometown of the owner.

Lanyard ring

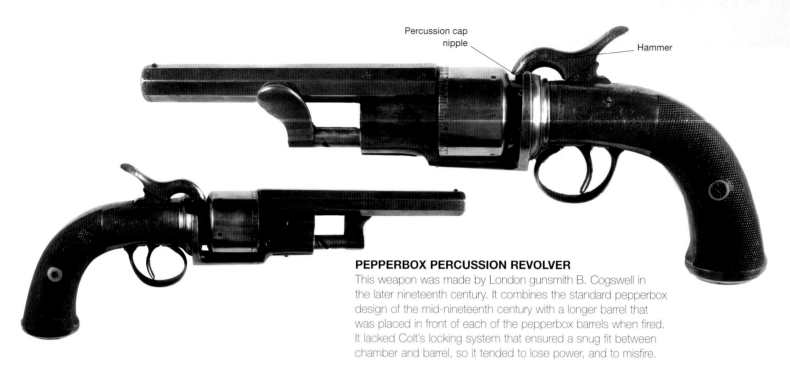

Percussion cap nipple

Hammer

PEPPERBOX PERCUSSION REVOLVER

This weapon was made by London gunsmith B. Cogswell in the later nineteenth century. It combines the standard pepperbox design of the mid-nineteenth century with a longer barrel that was placed in front of each of the pepperbox barrels when fired. It lacked Colt's locking system that ensured a snug fit between chamber and barrel, so it tended to lose power, and to misfire.

Ejection rod

HUSQVARNA 1433 REVOLVER

The Husqvarna Works were founded in 1689 by King Charles XI of Sweden to manufacture muskets for the Swedish Army. The factory began making civilian arms in 1864 and by 1900 was making bicycles, stoves, and sewing machines. This pistol is the 1887 Nagent Model, of which about 14,000 were made for the Swedish Army until 1905.

The cylinder on the Husqvarna was advanced by an arm attached to the trigger. As the trigger was pulled, the arm pushed up against the notch at the rear of the cylinder, advancing the cylinder to bring a fresh cartridge in line with the hammer.

Lanyard ring

Octagonal, then round barrel

DANISH DOUBLE-ACTION PISTOL

Jean-Baptiste Ronge was a gunsmith based in Liege, Belgium, who in 1891 won the contract to supply pistols to the Danish Navy—a contract the Belgian company kept right up until the fall of Denmark to the German invasion of 1940. The pistol was a variant of the Levaux pistol made by several companies in Belgium. Those destined for the Danes were stamped "DENMARK," with a crown over the word.

Clip to break pistol to load or unload

THE AMERICAN CIVIL WAR

The American Civil War divided the nation, split families apart, and caused huge casualties among the combatant states. The conflict was fought between states wishing to secede from the Union (the Confederacy) and those states that did not want them to go (the Union). Among the reasons for the high casualty rates was the fact that weapons technology was advancing rapidly, but the ways men were deployed on the field of battle was not. Dense phalanxes of men designed for the era of inaccurate smoothbore muskets were exposed to concentrated fire from increasingly accurate small arms that were able to inflict hideous damage in short stretches of time. The men who marched up the ridge at Gettysburg were entering a new era of weapons and warfare for which neither they, nor their commanders, were fully prepared.

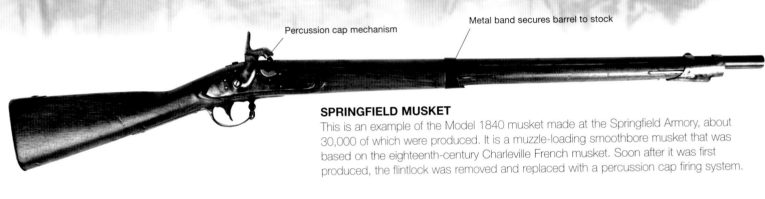

Percussion cap mechanism

Metal band secures barrel to stock

SPRINGFIELD MUSKET

This is an example of the Model 1840 musket made at the Springfield Armory, about 30,000 of which were produced. It is a muzzle-loading smoothbore musket that was based on the eighteenth-century Charleville French musket. Soon after it was first produced, the flintlock was removed and replaced with a percussion cap firing system.

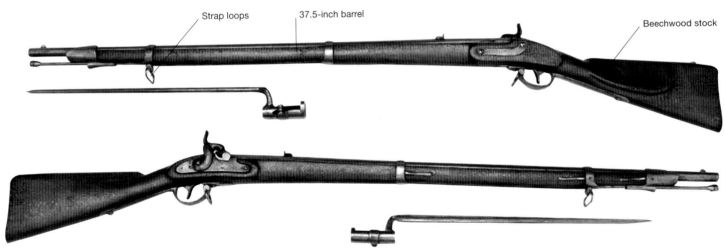

Strap loops

37.5-inch barrel

Beechwood stock

LORENZ RIFLE MUSKET

Entering service with the Austro-Hungarian Army in 1855, the Lorenz Rifle was a precision weapon and highly advanced for its time. Unfortunately the gunsmiths of Austria-Hungary were not up to the demands of precision engineering and many rifles proved to be substandard. However, the American states had a great demand for new guns, so they bought Lorenz rifles in huge numbers—the Union bought 240,000 and the Confederacy about 100,000. The muzzle-loading percussion cap design fired a .54-inch lead ball.

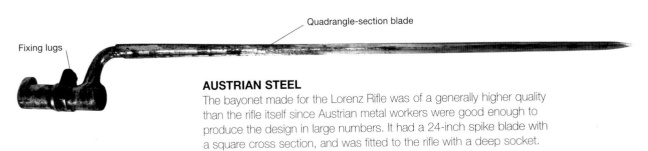

Quadrangle-section blade

Fixing lugs

AUSTRIAN STEEL

The bayonet made for the Lorenz Rifle was of a generally higher quality than the rifle itself since Austrian metal workers were good enough to produce the design in large numbers. It had a 24-inch spike blade with a square cross section, and was fitted to the rifle with a deep socket.

MAYNARD CARBINE
This type of carbine was used extensively by the Confederate cavalry although it was made by the Massachusetts Arms Company, as the weapons had been bought before the war. It was a breechloader that used a tough brass cartridge that could be loaded and reloaded with powder and ball up to 100 times before it wore out. This example was made for Emperor Napoleon III of France, and has his crest on the butt.

Lever is pulled down to open breech

Silver plate with Imperial crest

Folding rear sight in raised position

Front sight

SPENCER CARBINE
The Spencer repeating mechanism had seven .56 copper-jacketed cartridges stored in a tube in the stock. When the trigger guard was pulled down, the falling block opened, ejecting the spent cartridge and loading the next. It came in two models: the carbine shown here with a 22-inch barrel, and an infantry rifle with a 30-inch barrel.

HOMEMADE BLADES
The farmers who made up a large portion of the Confederate forces were accustomed to a make-do-and-mend approach to tools. They brought along a wide variety of tools and weapons to use while in service. These knives were homemade; the one on the right being influenced in its shape by the famous Bowie Knife, while the one below is a simple stabbing weapon.

Wooden hilt

Wooden scabbard

BATTLE OF FORT SUMTER

When several southern states announced their secession from the Union, there followed a tense standoff. The states claimed government property inside their state belonged to them, the Union government declared it did not. After four months, the issue came to a head at Fort Sumter in South Carolina. On April 11, 1861, the South Carolina authorities demanded that Major Robert Anderson hand over Fort Sumter. He refused and next day the South Carolinians opened fire. The bombardment of the fort is shown here. Anderson surrendered the following day. The incident meant that the disputed secession had become a war.

THE AMERICAN CIVIL WAR

LEMAT PISTOL

The style of pistol developed in New Orleans by French gunsmith Alexander Francois LeMat proved to be very popular with Confederate officers. The upper barrel fires .40 bullets from a nine-shot revolving cylinder using a percussion cap system. The lower barrel takes a shotgun cartridge and can be fired only once without reloading.

Lever on hammer selects which barrel will be fired

Trigger spur

Nipple for percussion cap

8-inch barrel

REMINGTON NEW ARMY

After the Colt Factory burned down in 1864, the Union Army turned to Remington of New York to manufacture officer pistols. This New Model Army pistol had six chambers in the cylinder. Each one loaded from the front with powder and ball contained in a paper cartridge that burned away when the weapon was fired, leaving the chamber empty for the next loading.

SMITH & WESSON MODEL NO.2

Based in Springfield, Massachusetts, Smith & Wesson perfected a system of loading metal-jacketed cartridges into a revolving cylinder. This is a Model No.2, introduced in the 1850s and used in small numbers during the Civil War. The barrel swung up, allowing the cylinder to be removed for reloading.

Spoke for pushing out spent cartridges

Stud trigger

TRANTNER

This pistol was made in Birmingham, England, by gunsmith William Trantner. It has an interesting double action with the lower trigger cocking the hammer, and the upper trigger releasing it to fire the gun. Many thousands of these pistols were bought by the Confederacy to arm its officers.

Five-shot cylinder

Octagonal barrel

Lanyard ring

SAVAGE-NORTH REVOLVER

This pistol was made by the Savage Revolving Arms Company of Middletown, Connecticut, for the U.S. Navy, although in fact the Army bought many more than did the Navy. It held a six-shot, percussion cap cylinder. The lower ring trigger advanced the cylinder and cocked the hammer, which was then fired by the upper trigger.

Large trigger guard

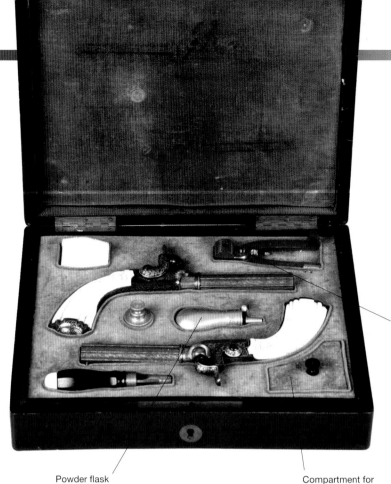

Powder flask

Compartment for
percussion caps

Bullet mold

JEFFERSON DAVIS' PISTOLS

This beautiful pair of pistols was made in Belgium for Jefferson Davis,
President of the Confederacy. They were intended as a diplomatic gift and
so were made to luxury specifications with carved ivory handles, gold leaf
decoration, and damascened steel barrels. They never reached Davis as
the ship carrying them over the Atlantic was captured by a U.S. Navy ship.

GATLING GUN

Two Gatling guns entered service near
Petersburg toward the end of the U.S.
Civil War. The weapon consisted of six
or ten barrels around a central shaft
that rotated as the handle was turned.
Cartridges fell into each barrel in turn
from a hopper, then were ejected after
firing. It could fire 200 rounds per
minute, but was so large and heavy
that it was not able to keep up with
infantry forces in the field.

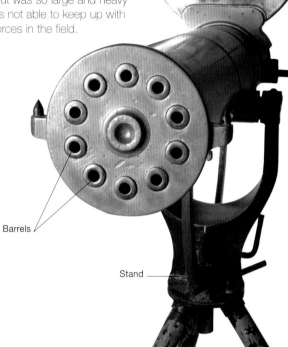

Hopper

Barrels

Stand

GETTYSBURG

The Battle of Gettysburg, seen
here from behind Union lines in
a painting by Thure de Thulstrup,
was fought between Union General
George Meade with 93,000 men,
and Confederate General Robert
E. Lee with 71,000 men. Lee was
invading the northern states to
threaten Philadelphia, Baltimore, and
Washington, D.C., and to capture
large food supplies. Learning of
Lee's move, Meade moved to screen
Washington and the two armies
met by accident at Gettysburg. The
resulting battle lasted three days and
climaxed in a massed assault by Lee's
infantry, which was driven off. Both
sides lost about 23,000 men killed
or wounded, but the battle was a
defeat for Lee, who had to call off his
invasion and was forced to thereafter
fight on the defensive.

HANDGUNS OF THE AMERICAN WEST

Movies and novels have accustomed modern readers to imagine Western handguns being used in vicious shoot outs by gunslingers, bandits, rustlers, and heroic lawmen. In fact, the vast majority of handguns used on the Western Frontier were used by farmers, cowboys, and travelers to give them protection against wild animals, or for use with livestock. Reliability and ruggedness were prized over more glamorous concepts such as being fast on the draw. That said, some handguns were used by lawmen and by bandits, or in battles fought between the settlers and the indigenous tribes of the area.

ADAMS REVOLVER

The British company of Robert Adams produced a range of pistols specifically for export to the Americas. They were percussion cap revolvers that had a double-action trigger and were famously hard wearing. Adams guns were favored by army officers for their reliability, though others found them to lack the stopping power needed to deal with larger animals.

Loading lever

Brass trigger and guard

Metal frame to butt

Cylinder

LITTLE-BIGHORN COLT

This Colt percussion cap revolver was found by an archaeologist on the field of the Battle of the Little Bighorn in Montana. On June 25, 1876, the 7th Cavalry commanded by General George Armstrong Custer attacked a force of Lakota, Cheyenne, and Arapaho that turned out to be larger than expected. Custer and his command were wiped out.

Cylinder

Hinge

SCHOFIELD MODEL 3

The Schofield Model 3 pistol shown here was a variant of the Smith & Wesson Model 3 that included changes designed by Major George Schofield of the U.S. Cavalry. The pistol had an improved catch where the weapon broke for reloading, and used a shorter .45 brass cartridge. The gun remained a standard issue for cavalrymen until the end of the 1898 Spanish-American War, after which all remaining guns of this type were sold off by the Army.

Catch

Octagonal barrel

Wooden travel box

Powder flask

Cylinder

BELLE STARR GUN

This 36 Navy Model Revolver is said to be the gun carried by the notorious female outlaw Belle Starr during the time she was married to Texas bandit and rustler Jim Reed. This pistol was made by the Manhattan Firearms Company and is a single-action, five-shot percussion cap weapon. In 1880 Belle married a Cherokee rustler named Sam Starr and moved to Indian Territory. She was shot dead by an unknown person in February 1889.

THE INDIAN WARS

The arrival of settlers from Europe on the east coast of North America led to a series of wars between the newcomers and the indigenous tribes, termed "Indians" by the settlers. The wars were fought for a variety of reasons, but the underlying issue was that of land. The settlers wanted the land occupied by the Indians. European-style farming and industry could support a greater population than Indian-style methods, so the settlers always had an advantage in terms of numbers, and often of weapons technology. After 1820 most wars were fought against the Plains Tribes or the Apache, and it is these wars that feature most heavily in movies or novels. The wars ended with the total defeat of the Indians, who now make up barely 1 percent of the population of the United States. This contemporary print shows a confrontation near Moravian Town in 1812.

THE WINCHESTER RIFLE

Although the Winchester Repeating Arms Company made a whole range of weapons, the term "Winchester Rifle" usually refers to the lever action rifles made by the company from 1866 to the present day. The basic design of the rifles has remained much the same, although the details have changed over the years. The most controversial change came in 1964 when expensively machined parts were replaced with cheaper stamped components in an effort to compete in price with other rifle manufacturers. The move outraged Winchester fans who had long regarded the brand as a prestige product, but now considered it to be on par with so many others. A long, slow decline set in and in 2006 the company folded, the factory closed, and production stopped. The remaining assets were bought by the Olin Corporation, which then began limited production of some Winchester products.

WINCHESTER 66 (THE YELLOW BOY)

The Winchester Model 1866 quickly acquired the nickname of "Yellow Boy" due to the yellowish color of the gunmetal receiver. The tubular magazine held fifteen rounds, loaded into the firing chamber by way of a falling block design operated by the trigger guard. This example is a presentation model made for Czar Alexander II of Russia.

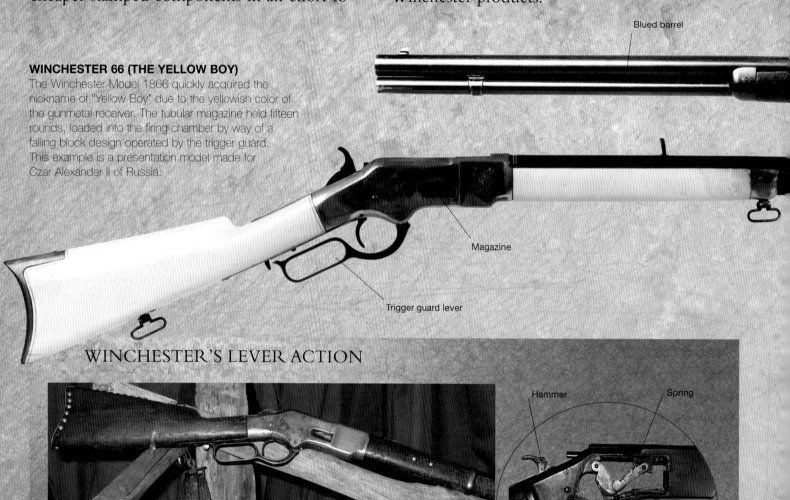

Blued barrel

Magazine

Trigger guard lever

WINCHESTER'S LEVER ACTION

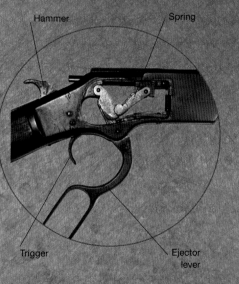

Hammer

Spring

Trigger

Ejector lever

What made the Winchester Rifle so important was that it was the first repeating rifle that was effective and remained usable in field conditions. This rugged reliability was down in part to the gun's lever action. When a shot had been fired, the ejector lever behind the trigger was pulled down to eject the spent cartridge and allow the spring in the tubular magazine to push the next cartridge into position. The lever was then pushed back up, raising the block and new cartridge back into position and at the same time cocking the hammer ready to be fired by pulling the trigger. This same basic lever mechanism would be used in all future Winchester models.

WINCHESTER 73 PRESENTATION RIFLE

Known affectionately as the "Winchester 73," this was the most famous of all the Winchester models. Although later models were introduced, the 73 remained popular in the American West and was in production until 1919. In 2013 production was restarted under license by the Miroku Corporation of Japan. This particular weapon was a presentation gun made for Albert Edward, Prince of Wales, who later became King Edward VII of Britain. The silver plate set into the stock is engraved with three ostrich feathers, the royal emblem of the Prince of Wales. The gun was selected as a premier example and given a special blued finish.

WINCHESTER 73

The enduring fame of the Model 1873 as a key weapon of the Wild West led Universal to make a big-budget western movie about the gun starring James Stewart and Shelley Winters, both top Hollywood stars of the time. The film followed the career of a single Winchester 73 rifle as it passed through the hands of a cowboy, bandit, lawman, Indian, soldier, and saloon girl. The film proved to be enormously popular, but today is best known for early roles by future stars Tony Curtis, James Best, and Rock Hudson.

Hammer

The silver plaque carries the royal badge of the Prince of Wales, three ostrich feathers.

Silver plaque

OLIVER WINCHESTER

The great gunsmith Oliver Winchester was born in Boston in 1810, and moved to New York at a young age to start a business making clothes. The business prospered and he moved to larger premises in New Haven, Connecticut, with his wife and three young children. Winchester then heard that the Volcanic Repeating Arms Company was in financial trouble due to persistent failures with their designs. Winchester put together a consortium that bought the company, and then he hired the talented young designer Benjamin Henry to sort out the technical issues while he solved the financial mess. Henry produced a new brass cartridge and redesigned the Volcanic rifle. This solved some of the problems and produced the Henry Rifle. By the early 1860s, Winchester had the company on a firm financial footing. Around the same time another designer, Nelson King, perfected a sealed magazine that loaded via a side gate. The company was now renamed the Winchester Repeating Arms Company and the Model 1866 was produced. The gun proved to be immensely popular and earned Winchester a fortune. He followed it up with the even-better

1873 model and entered politics, becoming Lieutenant Governor of Connecticut. He died in 1880 and left the company to his son, William.

RIFLES OF THE AMERICAN WEST

While pistols used on the Western Frontier have acquired an image of use in gunfights, shootouts, and all manner of movie violence, the rifles tend to be neglected by movie makers and novelists. In truth, however, it was the rifles and carbines carried by settlers, mountainmen, cowboys, and others that did more to turn the wild lands of the West into the productive farmlands and wilderness areas that they are today. Pistols might be more convenient to carry around, but for range and stopping power when hunting deer, bear, bison, wolf, or puma nothing could touch the rifle.

WINCHESTER 1873

The most popular and best known of all the frontier rifles was the Winchester Model 1873. The earlier models used the .44-40 cartridge, though later variants were chambered for .38-40 and .32-20 handgun cartridges. This example is a carbine with a 20-inch barrel. The rifle had a 24-inch barrel.

WINCHESTER 86

For the Model 1886, Winchester incorporated improvements made by the gunsmith John Browning, soon to be famous in his own right. It was chambered to take the powerful .45-70 government cartridge that was used in U.S. Army rifles. A later variant of the 1886 could take the even more powerful .50-110, which Winchester produced as a rival to the British "elephant round" for big game hunters. It was used mostly to shoot buffalo on the western plains.

KENTUCKY RIFLE

By the later nineteenth century the traditional Kentucky Rifle was entering a decline. Although its accuracy and range were never in doubt, it was an expensive weapon to make by a skilled gunsmith, and it required an experienced marksman to get the best out of it. By contrast, the mass-produced rifles of Winchester, Remington, and Colt were cheaper and more reliable in the hands of less-skilled users. By 1900 only half a dozen men were left alive who could make a rifle such as this.

Hammer

Loading gate

Wooden stock

Loading gate

Percussion cap mechanism

Front sight

Cleaning rod

ELIPHALET REMINGTON

Born in 1793 in Suffield, Connecticut, Eliphalet Remington followed his father into the blacksmith trade, but in 1816 he made his first rifle and never looked back. By 1840 Remington's business was employing a number of men and soon adopted the manufacturing techniques of the industrial revolution to produce good quality sporting rifles at low cost. Eliphalet died in 1861, handing the business to his three sons: Philo, Eliphalet III, and Samuel. The company later expanded into making bicycles and typewriters, but to this day produces rifles and shotguns, as well as ammunition. The Remington Small Arms Company is now the oldest business in the United States to continue making the original product: rifles.

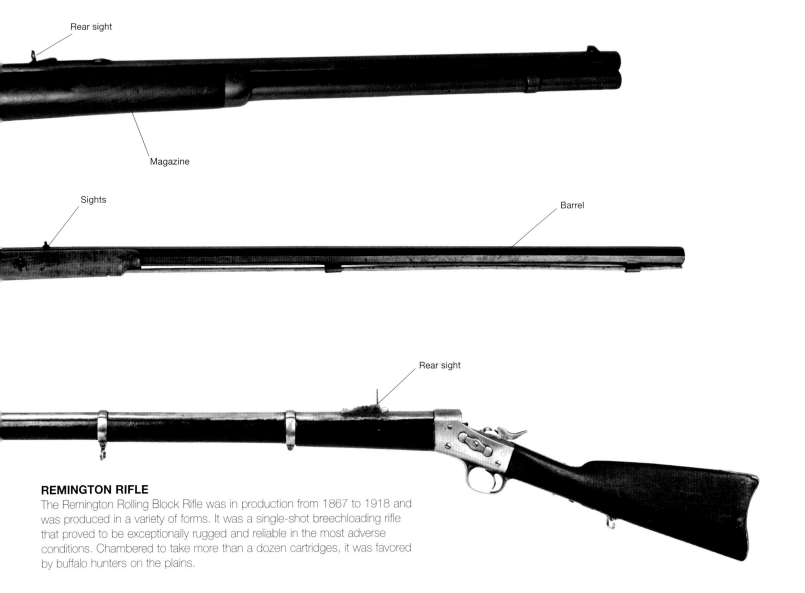

Rear sight

Magazine

Sights

Barrel

Rear sight

REMINGTON RIFLE

The Remington Rolling Block Rifle was in production from 1867 to 1918 and was produced in a variety of forms. It was a single-shot breechloading rifle that proved to be exceptionally rugged and reliable in the most adverse conditions. Chambered to take more than a dozen cartridges, it was favored by buffalo hunters on the plains.

RIFLES OF THE AMERICAN WEST

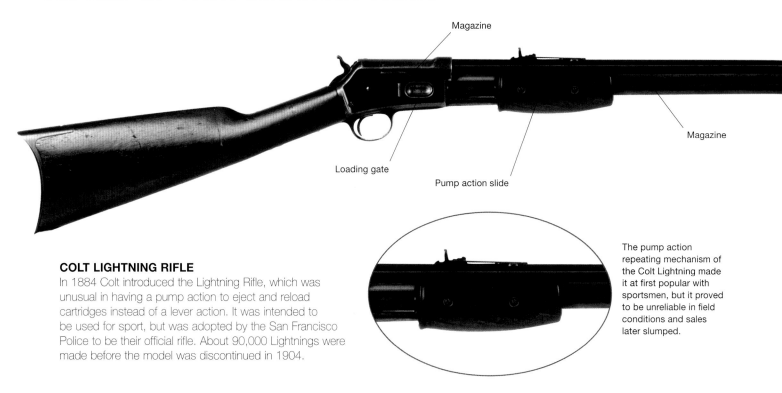

Magazine

Magazine

Loading gate

Pump action slide

COLT LIGHTNING RIFLE

In 1884 Colt introduced the Lightning Rifle, which was unusual in having a pump action to eject and reload cartridges instead of a lever action. It was intended to be used for sport, but was adopted by the San Francisco Police to be their official rifle. About 90,000 Lightnings were made before the model was discontinued in 1904.

The pump action repeating mechanism of the Colt Lightning made it at first popular with sportsmen, but it proved to be unreliable in field conditions and sales later slumped.

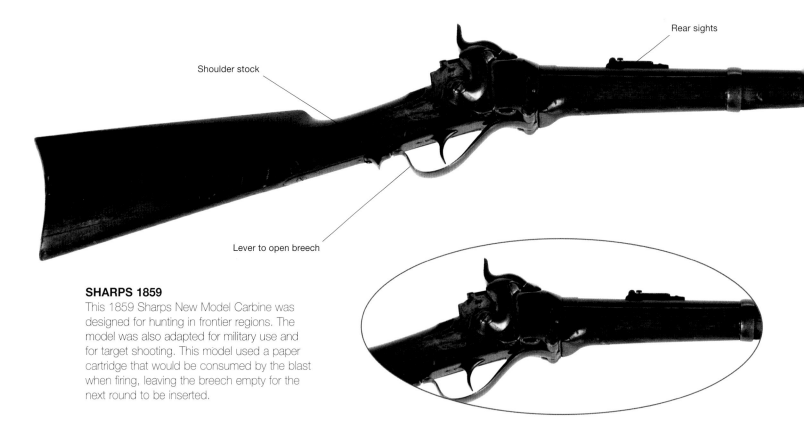

Rear sights

Shoulder stock

Lever to open breech

SHARPS 1859

This 1859 Sharps New Model Carbine was designed for hunting in frontier regions. The model was also adapted for military use and for target shooting. This model used a paper cartridge that would be consumed by the blast when firing, leaving the breech empty for the next round to be inserted.

The Sharps was loaded by pulling down the trigger guard, causing the breech block to fall and reveal the breech itself. The paper cartridge was then pushed into the breech and the lever pulled up, which automatically flipped a percussion cap into place.

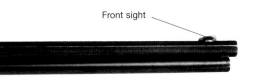

Front sight

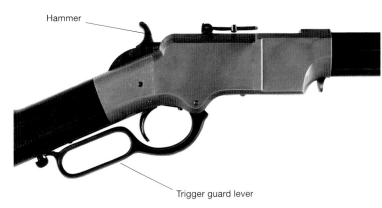

Hammer

Trigger guard lever

HENRY RIFLE

In 1860 gunsmith Benjamin Henry produced a .44 repeating rifle that used a lever action to eject and load metal-jacketed cartridges. Pulling the trigger guard down opened the falling block breech, while lifting it again closed the breech. A key problem with the action was that there was no safety catch. If the hammer was cocked it would go off if dropped, while if uncocked a blow to the hammer would fire the gun. Despite this, the 16-shot Henry proved very popular throughout the U.S. Civil War.

SHARPS .50-90 CARTRIDGES

As cartridges came to be mass produced with a metal case and integral percussion cap, manufacturers sought to popularize the use of specific cartridges with their weapons. The .50-90 was made to fit Sharps rifles, and was marketed as being powerful enough to kill a buffalo. On June 29, 1874, hunter Billy Dixon shot dead a Comanche warrior during the Battle of Adobe Walls at a range of just over a mile using a .50-90 to make what was called "the shot of the century."

BUFFALO BILL

William Cody was widely known as Buffalo Bill and was one of the most colorful figures of the American West. Cody was born in Iowa in 1846, moving to Kansas with his family in 1853. After his father's death in 1857, Cody became a messenger, carrying messages on horseback around Kansas. He spent the next few years in a variety of ways such as gold prospecting, buffalo hunting, and scouting for the Army, though some of the tales he told later were probably invented. In 1873, he put together a show of former soldiers, Indians, and cowboys who toured the Eastern States putting on displays of Western life. He later took the show to Europe, where it was a sensation. He died in 1917. Buffalo Bill is shown here in the clothes he wore for his Wild West show in 1903.

MAUSERS

The Mauser rifle revolutionized the arms trade in the late nineteenth century. The key development of the rifle was its bolt action. The breech of the rifle is formed of a rod that is locked into place by an interrupted thread. A handle projecting from the side of this bolt is lifted to unlock the thread, then pulled back to open the breech. The spent cartridge is ejected as the bolt is pulled back, clearing the way for a new cartridge to be inserted.

The bolt is then pushed forward again to close the breech and cock the gun, while the handle is pulled down to re-engage the thread. The action is rugged, reliable, and simple, meaning it can handle more powerful cartridges than comparable systems, and is able to be dismantled for cleaning and reassembled quickly and easily. It was for this reason that the Mauser bolt action proved to be so popular with the military.

CZECHOSLOVAKIAN VZ24 MAUSER
This variation on the Mauser was designed in Czechoslovakia in 1920, just after the country gained its independence from the Austro-Hungarian Empire. It was based on the German KAR98K, and used the same 8mm cartridge.

Receiver

Bolt handle

Bolt handle

Bolt

Tapering stock

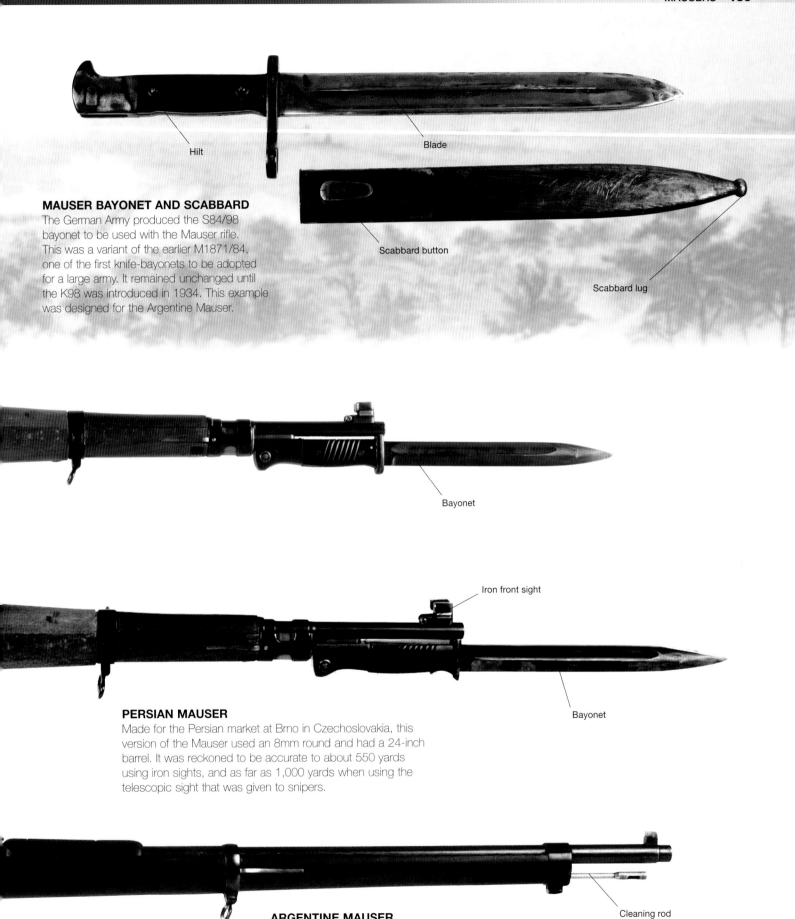

Hilt

Blade

MAUSER BAYONET AND SCABBARD

The German Army produced the S84/98 bayonet to be used with the Mauser rifle. This was a variant of the earlier M1871/84, one of the first knife-bayonets to be adopted for a large army. It remained unchanged until the K98 was introduced in 1934. This example was designed for the Argentine Mauser.

Scabbard button

Scabbard lug

Bayonet

Iron front sight

PERSIAN MAUSER

Made for the Persian market at Brno in Czechoslovakia, this version of the Mauser used an 8mm round and had a 24-inch barrel. It was reckoned to be accurate to about 550 yards using iron sights, and as far as 1,000 yards when using the telescopic sight that was given to snipers.

Bayonet

Cleaning rod

ARGENTINE MAUSER

In 1891 the Argentine Army placed a large order with Mauser, but insisted on some modifications. The most important regarded the cartridge. This was the new 7.65 x 53mm "Argentine," which was rimless and could be mounted into five-round stripper clips. This greatly speeded up the business of reloading the magazine, and so increased the rate of fire.

MAUSERS

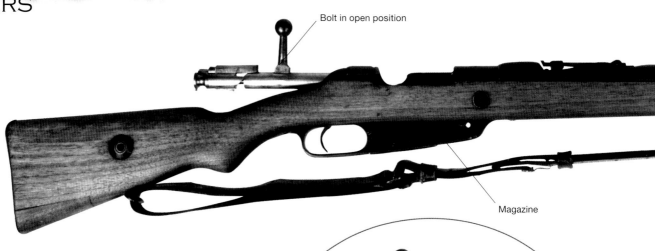

Bolt in open position

Magazine

SWEDISH MAUSER

When the Swedish government placed an order for 12,000 rifles with Mauser they demanded some variations that proved so popular that the rifle remained in service with Swedish armed forces until 1995. The Swedish Mauser fired the 6.5×55mm SAAMI cartridge with its round nose and reduced charge. The barrels had to be made using a steel alloy that included nickel, copper, and vanadium for added strength and reduced corrosion.

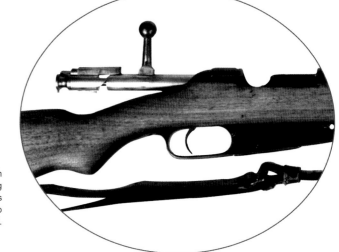

The bolt of the Swedish Mauser was made using Swedish iron ore which has the correct trace elements to make strong, durable steel.

Tapered stock

Cleaning rod

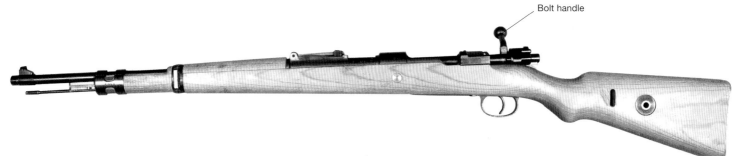

Bolt handle

MAUSER KARABINER 98K, 1940

The Karabiner 98 Kurz, usually referred to as the 98K, was the standard rifle used by the Germany Army from 1935 to 1945. It was a short (kurz) version of the Gewehr 98 Mauser, which had been the standard issue German army rifle from 1898 to 1935. The 98K had a 24-inch barrel—5 inches shorter than its predecessor—and an improved bolt handle, but was otherwise similar. This example is a Swedish Army 98K that has been rechambered to fire the Swedish 8×63mm cartridge.

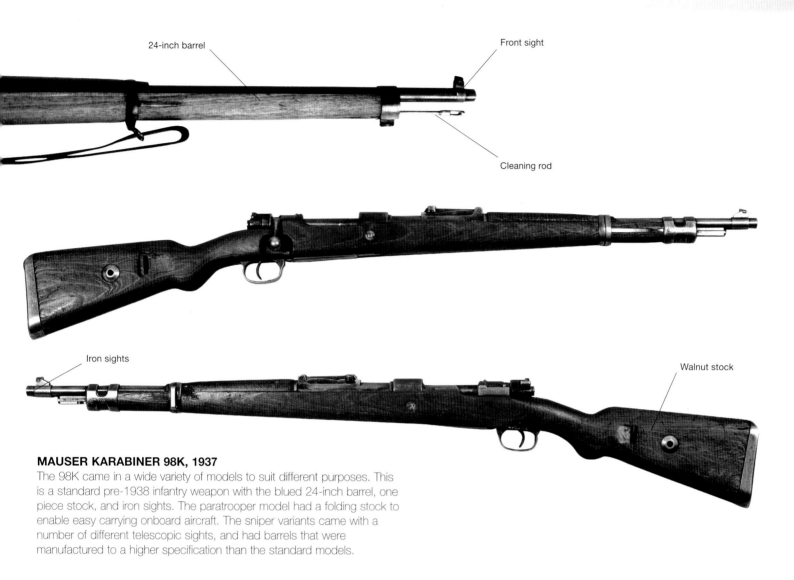

24-inch barrel

Front sight

Cleaning rod

Iron sights

Walnut stock

MAUSER KARABINER 98K, 1937

The 98K came in a wide variety of models to suit different purposes. This is a standard pre-1938 infantry weapon with the blued 24-inch barrel, one piece stock, and iron sights. The paratrooper model had a folding stock to enable easy carrying onboard aircraft. The sniper variants came with a number of different telescopic sights, and had barrels that were manufactured to a higher specification than the standard models.

PAUL MAUSER

Paul Mauser was born in Württemburg, Germany, in 1838. He followed his father into the gunsmith trade and was then conscripted into the Württemburg Army. It was while in the army that he developed the idea for a turning bolt breech design, based on the Dreyse needle gun. When he left the army, he tried to get his idea into production but it was not until he formed a partnership with his brother Wilhelm in 1870 that the business began to prosper. A massive order from the Prussian Army for the new bolt-action rifle established the brothers' fortune and before long they bought the Württemburg state arsenal where Paul had worked as a conscript. Paul continued to work as the chief designer, while Wilhelm handled the financial side of the business. Wilhelm died in 1882, after which Paul floated the company on the stock exchange. Paul Mauser died in 1918.

BAYONETS

When firearms were first introduced to the battlefield in the form of matchlocks and arquebuses they had a number of drawbacks. The most critical of these for the survival of the man using them was that they made the gunman vulnerable to attack by cavalry. Once a gun had been fired it took time to reload, during which time a horseman could gallop up to skewer the gunman with a lance or

sword. Moreover, horses that would shy away from a glittering sharp point would barge past a dull gun barrel. The bayonet was the answer to these problems. At its most basic, it took the form of a sharp point attached to the front of the barrel. The word bayonet comes from the French city of Bayonne, where early versions of the bayonet were made in the seventeenth century.

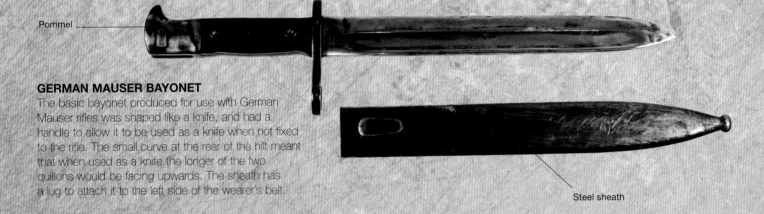

Pommel

GERMAN MAUSER BAYONET
The basic bayonet produced for use with German Mauser rifles was shaped like a knife, and had a handle to allow it to be used as a knife when not fixed to the rifle. The small curve at the rear of the hilt meant that when used as a knife the longer of the two quillons would be facing upwards. The sheath has a lug to attach it to the left side of the wearer's belt.

Steel sheath

THE BATTLE OF GROSSBEEREN

By August 1813, the allied enemies of French Emperor Napoléon I were gathering in central Europe, ready to march on France. Napoléon decided to pre-empt them by sending Marshal Oudinot with 60,000 men to capture the Prussian capital of Berlin. Due to flooding, Oudinot divided his army into three columns advancing on separate roads. At Grossbeeren the 27,000 men under General Reynier ran headlong into 38,000 Prussians commanded by General von Bulow. Reynier occupied the village, but could advance no further. Bulow ordered an assault on the French. The Prussian infantry advanced in columns with fixed bayonets. The climax of the battle came when the Prussians charged into the village and fought the French infantry in a savage bayonet battle with little or no firing, as shown right. The bayonets proved able to drive the

French out of defended households, and the churchyard where musket fire had failed. Oudinot ordered a retreat and Berlin was saved.

STEYR MANNLICHER BAYONET

The ten-inch blade of this Hungarian bayonet is unusual in that the sharp edge faces up when it is fixed to the Steyr Mannlicher M1895 rifle for which it was produced. This blade was developed for the Imperial Austro-Hungarian Army in 1895, but continued in use with both the Austrian and Hungarian armies after the Empire broke up in 1918.

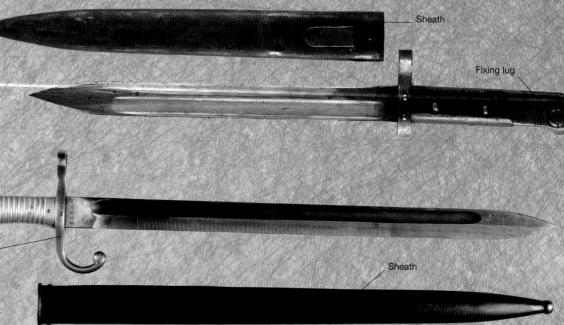

Sheath

Fixing lug

Quillon

Sheath

ARGENTINIAN MAUSER BAYONET

In the 1880s Argentina was engaged in diplomatic disputes with Chile that threatened to erupt into war at any time over a disputed boundary. The Argentinians therefore purchased large numbers of Mausers for their army. The president of Argentina, Julio Roca, was an army general who insisted on a long bayonet for the rifle. The result was this elegantly shaped bayonet with a 10-inch blade, which gave the Argentinian Mauser a greater bayonet reach than others.

MAUSER PIONEER BAYONET

In 1905 the German Army introduced a new style bayonet for use by pioneers, and soldiers trained in engineering and construction techniques. This consisted of a longer 10-inch blade that had a sawback and a broader tip. The weapon lacked a barrel ring, which was considered to be unwieldy when the weapon was used as a tool. Instead, the grooved lug on top of the handle had to take the entire pressure of use.

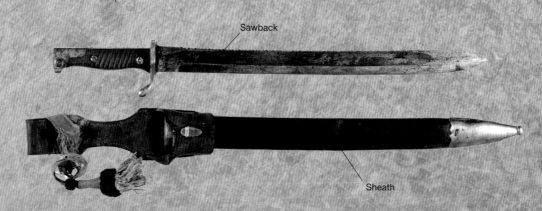

Sawback

Sheath

Sinuous curved shape

CHASSEPOT BAYONET

The Chassepot was a breech loading, single-shot rifle that was the standard French army rifle during the Franco-Prussian War of 1870–1871. The Chassepot came with an elegantly curved 20-inch bayonet, known as a "sword bayonet." At this date most armies believed that reach was all important in bayonet fighting, which is why this weapon was so long. The Chassepot was shorter than earlier rifles, so the long bayonet was deemed necessary to keep the weapon the same overall length. It was thought that in a bayonet to bayonet combat, the man with the longer weapon would have a clear advantage as he could strike his opponent when still out of reach of his weapon. The sword bayonet, unlike the spike bayonet, enabled the user to slash at the enemy as well as to thrust.

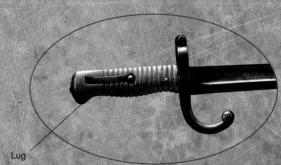

Lug

Magazine Rifles

By the end of the nineteenth century it was clear that the bolt action rifle had important advantages over the rival lever action and pump action models. The bolt action was cheap to make, easy to maintain, and with fewer working parts was less likely to go wrong in action. These advantages were of particular interest to the military as they tended to use guns in bad weather conditions and where maintenance facilities were poor. The addition of a magazine under the bolt with a spring to push cartridges up into the breech as each spent cartridge was ejected greatly speeded up the rate of fire of bolt action rifles and made them even more effective on the battlefield than they had been before.

Bolt

Iron sights

M1903 SPRINGFIELD
The adoption of the M1903 Springfield by the U.S. Army ended decades in which different units had used different weapons, with resulting problems for ammunition supply and maintenance. It proved to be popular and efficient, serving as the standard U.S. rifle throughout World War I and for much of World War II, with the sniper version remaining in use well into the Vietnam War.

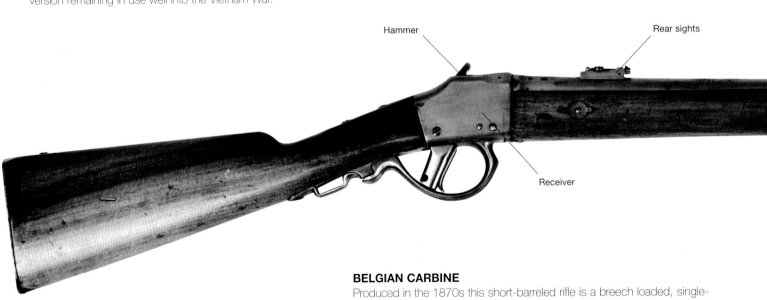

Hammer

Rear sights

Receiver

BELGIAN CARBINE
Produced in the 1870s this short-barreled rifle is a breech loaded, single-shot weapon. The short barrel is supported along its length by a wooden stock that is in three parts to ease manufacturing. The rear sights are shown here folded down flat, but when raised can be adjusted to ranges delineated in meters. The receiver is a single-shot, breech-loading mechanism taking .45 center-fire cartridges.

WINCHESTER MODEL 70

The iconic Model 70 was introduced by Winchester in 1936 and remained in production until 2006, and since 2008 has been made under license in Belgium. Among the features that make this a classic sporting rifle is the clawed feeder that pushes the new round into the chamber, and the blade ejector that flips the used cartridge out. Together these give a smooth, reliable reloading action that ensures the nose of the bullet is not snagged or damaged in any way. When shooting large or dangerous game, such as bears, this is considered essential.

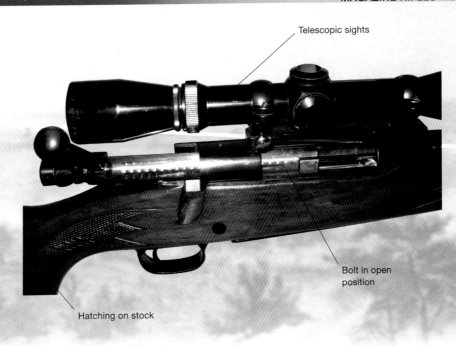

Telescopic sights

Bolt in open position

Hatching on stock

Magazine holding five rounds

Sight protection ears

ENFIELD PATTERN 1914

In 1914, the British Army was about to start re-equipping its infantry with the Enfield Pattern 1914, which was more durable and more accurate than the SMLE rifle that equipped the infantry at the time. However, the outbreak of war caused the move to be postponed, and then abandoned. As a result, most of these rifles went to the export market in the 1920s.

Swivel mounts for carrying strap

Strong bolt

31.5-inch barrel

Iron sights

ARISAKA TYPE 38

The Arisaka Type 38 was the standard Japanese army rifle from 1906 to 1945. It was rushed into production after the Type 30 was found to have serious problems with jamming during the Russo-Japanese War of 1904–05. The new rifle did not jam, but was heavy and at 50.4 inches was longer than the rifle of any other modern nation.

MAGAZINE RIFLES

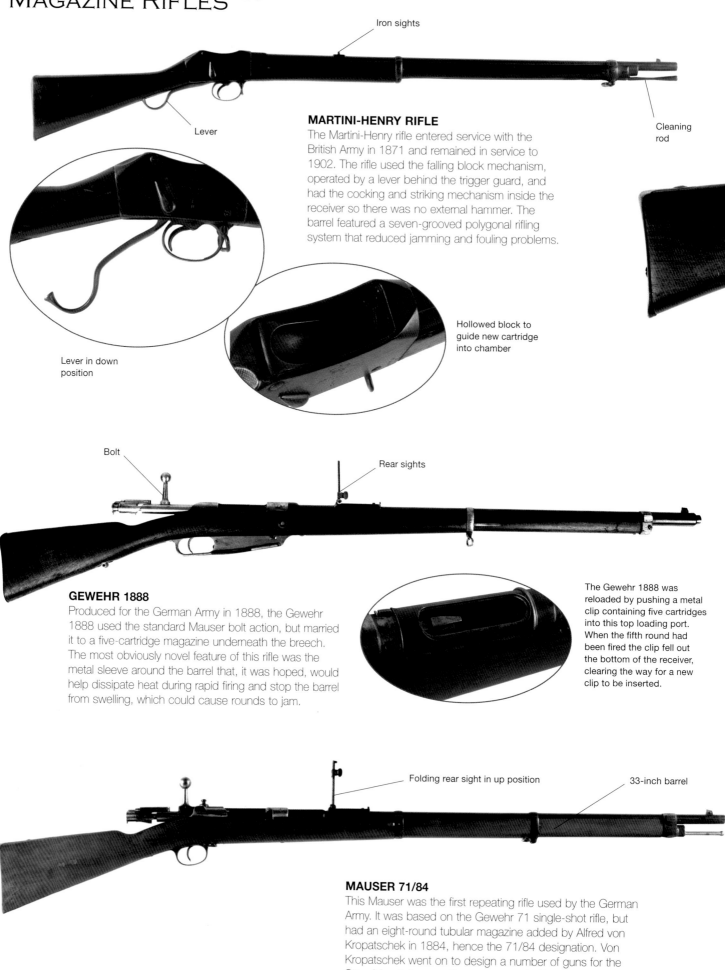

Iron sights

Lever

Cleaning rod

Lever in down position

Hollowed block to guide new cartridge into chamber

MARTINI-HENRY RIFLE

The Martini-Henry rifle entered service with the British Army in 1871 and remained in service to 1902. The rifle used the falling block mechanism, operated by a lever behind the trigger guard, and had the cocking and striking mechanism inside the receiver so there was no external hammer. The barrel featured a seven-grooved polygonal rifling system that reduced jamming and fouling problems.

Bolt

Rear sights

GEWEHR 1888

Produced for the German Army in 1888, the Gewehr 1888 used the standard Mauser bolt action, but married it to a five-cartridge magazine underneath the breech. The most obviously novel feature of this rifle was the metal sleeve around the barrel that, it was hoped, would help dissipate heat during rapid firing and stop the barrel from swelling, which could cause rounds to jam.

The Gewehr 1888 was reloaded by pushing a metal clip containing five cartridges into this top loading port. When the fifth round had been fired the clip fell out the bottom of the receiver, clearing the way for a new clip to be inserted.

Folding rear sight in up position

33-inch barrel

MAUSER 71/84

This Mauser was the first repeating rifle used by the German Army. It was based on the Gewehr 71 single-shot rifle, but had an eight-round tubular magazine added by Alfred von Kropatschek in 1884, hence the 71/84 designation. Von Kropatschek went on to design a number of guns for the Steyr Mannlicher munitions company in his native Austria.

BELGIAN POLICE CARBINE

This carbine was manufactured in 1858 for the mounted arm of the Belgian police. At the time, Belgium was undergoing rapid industrializaton as the coal deposits and iron ore mines began to be exploited. There was much civic unrest in this period and the police used mounted patrols to keep an eye on the more troublesome areas.

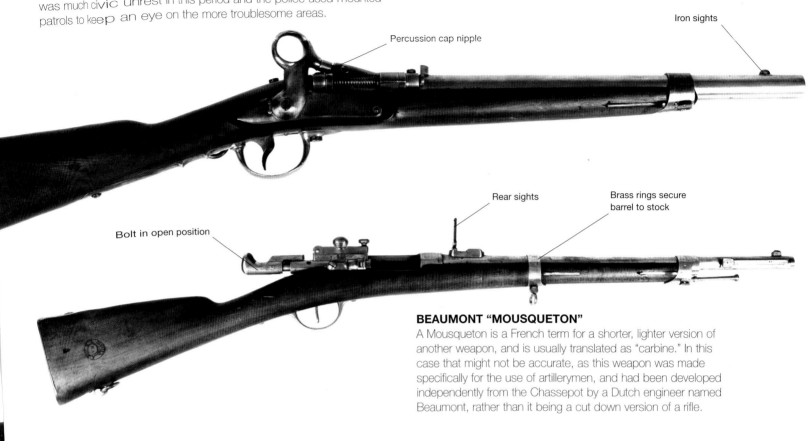

Iron sights

Percussion cap nipple

Rear sights

Brass rings secure barrel to stock

Bolt in open position

BEAUMONT "MOUSQUETON"

A Mousqueton is a French term for a shorter, lighter version of another weapon, and is usually translated as "carbine." In this case that might not be accurate, as this weapon was made specifically for the use of artillerymen, and had been developed independently from the Chassepot by a Dutch engineer named Beaumont, rather than it being a cut down version of a rifle.

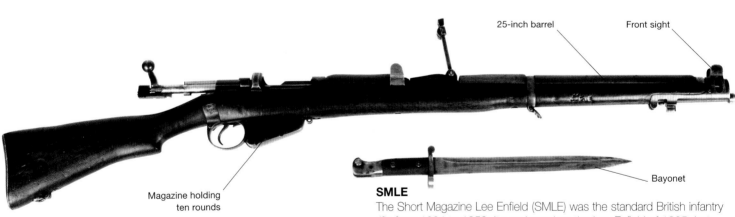

25-inch barrel

Front sight

Bayonet

Magazine holding ten rounds

SMLE

The Short Magazine Lee Enfield (SMLE) was the standard British infantry rifle from 1904 to 1950. It was based on the Lee Enfield of 1895, but had a 25-inch barrel instead of a 30-inch barrel. The shorter barrel was introduced to make the gun lighter and easier to handle.

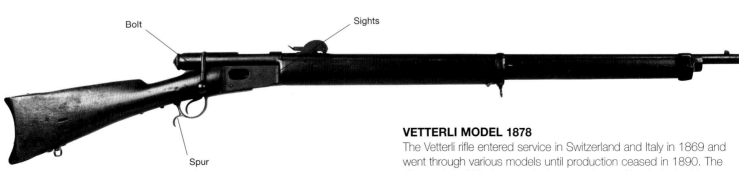

Bolt

Sights

Spur

VETTERLI MODEL 1878

The Vetterli rifle entered service in Switzerland and Italy in 1869 and went through various models until production ceased in 1890. The rifle used the Winchester tubular magazine and had a bolt with two opposed rear locking lugs, considered a major advance at the time. This example is the 1878 model, which had a spur on the trigger guard and improved sights.

THE SEMIAUTOMATIC PISTOL

Unlike the revolver, which utilized a design first produced for cap and ball weapons, the semiautomatic was developed to use metal-jacketed cartridges. The weapon has a single barrel and single firing chamber, with cartridges stored in a magazine that has a spring to push the cartridges into position beside the breech. The first cartridge has to be loaded into the firing chamber by hand, usually by pulling back and releasing a slide mechanism. When a shot is fired, the mechanism is powered by the shot to eject the used cartridge and load the next cartridge into the firing chamber. This may be achieved by a recoil, blowback, or gas operation. Each time the trigger is pulled a single shot is fired.

5.5-inch barrel

BROOMHANDLE MAUSER
The Mauser C96 was widely known as the "broomhandle pistol" due to the shape of the wooden grip. The magazine was positioned in front of the trigger, giving this weapon a unique profile. The gun came in a wooden holster that doubled as a shoulder stock to give added stability when aiming. Mauser itself made over a million of these guns, and thousands more were made under license abroad.

Magazine holding ten rounds

Wooden handle

6.5-inch barrel

The bulky rear bulge of this pistol housed the spring-loaded two-piece arm that rose and flexed as the gun was fired.

BORCHARDT C93
The Borchardt C93 pistol was designed by Hugo Borchardt for Ludwig Loewe & Company of Berlin, Germany. It went into production in 1893, hence its designation of Construktion 93. It was the first Semiautomatic pistol to go into mass production, but its hefty recoil and cumbersome shape meant that it failed to become popular and production stopped after 3,000 had been made. Among the potential customers to test the pistol was the U.S. Army, which turned the gun down on grounds of cost and difficulty of maintenance in the field.

Magazine holding eight rounds

BERGMANN 1896

As different gunsmiths experimented with different mechanisms to automatically reload a cartridge after the previous one was fired, Louis Schmeisser of Germany tried using the hot gas created by the discharge of the cartridge. The pistols he designed were sold by Theodor Bergmann and marketed under Bergmann's name. This example is the 1896 pattern, which proved to be prone to jamming. The cartridges had no grooves or rims and relied on the pointed nose of the bullet to guide them into the breech. The Schmeisser-Bergmann collaboration continued under Schmeisser's son Hugo, and would ultimately produce some of Germany's finest gun designs of the early twentieth century.

Magazine

Trigger

Wooden grip

Metal side plate pivots down to allow reloading of magazine from a metal clip of five cartridges.

4-inch barrel

LUGER P08

After the failure of the Borchardt C93 to win any lucrative military contracts, Borchardt turned to a junior designer named Georg Luger to try to improve the design. By 1900 Luger had produced a toggle-lock that was the basis of a whole family of enormously popular pistols. When a shot is fired the barrel and toggle move back together for half an inch. The barrel then strikes a block and stops, while the toggle continues back, extracting the spent cartridge and compressing a spring. The spring then pushes the toggle forward, loading the next cartridge into the barrel. The cartridge is then pushed forward again and locked into position, ready to fire. The Swiss Army adopted the Luger in 1900, followed by the German Army in 1908 with the famous P08 model. It remained in production in Germany until 1942, and unlicensed versions were made after World War II in other countries up to the present day.

Magazine holding eight rounds

THE SEMIAUTOMATIC PISTOL

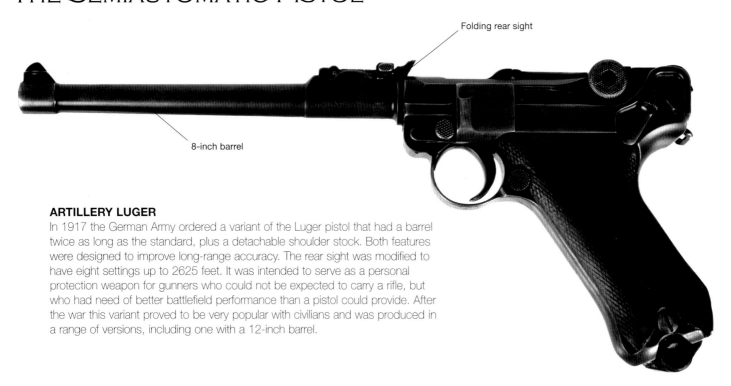

Folding rear sight

8-inch barrel

ARTILLERY LUGER

In 1917 the German Army ordered a variant of the Luger pistol that had a barrel twice as long as the standard, plus a detachable shoulder stock. Both features were designed to improve long-range accuracy. The rear sight was modified to have eight settings up to 2625 feet. It was intended to serve as a personal protection weapon for gunners who could not be expected to carry a rifle, but who had need of better battlefield performance than a pistol could provide. After the war this variant proved to be very popular with civilians and was produced in a range of versions, including one with a 12-inch barrel.

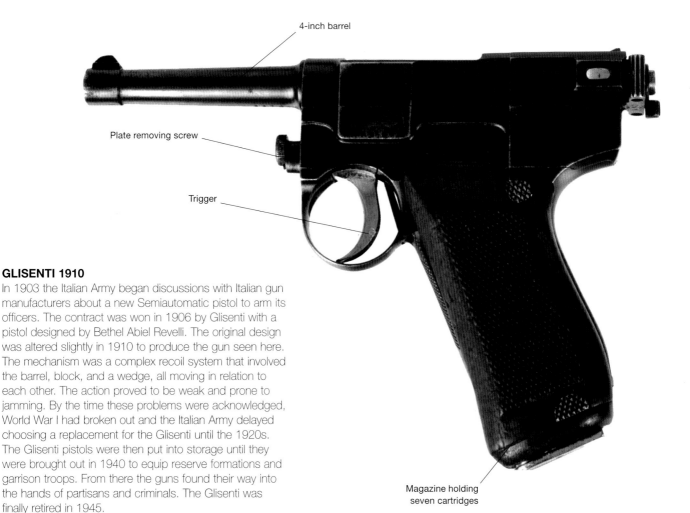

4-inch barrel

Plate removing screw

Trigger

Magazine holding seven cartridges

GLISENTI 1910

In 1903 the Italian Army began discussions with Italian gun manufacturers about a new Semiautomatic pistol to arm its officers. The contract was won in 1906 by Glisenti with a pistol designed by Bethel Abiel Revelli. The original design was altered slightly in 1910 to produce the gun seen here. The mechanism was a complex recoil system that involved the barrel, block, and a wedge, all moving in relation to each other. The action proved to be weak and prone to jamming. By the time these problems were acknowledged, World War I had broken out and the Italian Army delayed choosing a replacement for the Glisenti until the 1920s. The Glisenti pistols were then put into storage until they were brought out in 1940 to equip reserve formations and garrison troops. From there the guns found their way into the hands of partisans and criminals. The Glisenti was finally retired in 1945.

Extractor port

Front sight

Trigger

Grip containing magazine

BROWNING PATENT PISTOL

American gun designer John Browning spent most of his life developing guns for the Winchester company, but in 1898 he fell out with them over a fee for his new Auto-5 Shotgun. Having already made contact with Fabrique Nationale de Herstal (FN) in Belgium, Browning moved there. Browning was already working on a Semiautomatic pistol, and at FN he produced a number of designs of which this is one. Browning was still working on the pistol design when he died in 1926. The work was taken over by Dieudonne Saive and finally emerged as the massively successful Browning Hi-Power. This earlier model has some key features, including the side ejection window, but is clearly inferior to the finished product.

Grip safety. The lever at the rear of the grip is a spring-loaded safety catch that is in the off position when a hand holds the grip, but which springs out to the safety on position when the gun is put down.

Extractor port

5-inch barrel

Spring-loaded safety catch

Magazine contains seven rounds

COLT .45

The Colt M1911 .45 Semiautomatic originated in 1911 and has never been out of production. It is a recoil-operated pistol that is chambered for the .45 Automatic Colt Pistol (ACP) cartridge, which had been designed by John Browning for an earlier project that was aborted. The pistol was adopted by the U.S. Army for its rugged reliability. Its heavy weight of 2.5 pounds was considered a minor drawback. About 2.7 million pistols were purchased by the military, and perhaps another 300,000 by private buyers. It was phased out by the U.S. military in the mid-1990s, although some officers continue to carry it and it remains in production for civilian customers.

THE SEMIAUTOMATIC PISTOL

Ring hammer

Trigger

Lanyard ring

BROWNING HI-POWER

The name of the Browning Hi-Power is rather misleading on two counts. First, it was not designed by John Browning, who died ten years before it was launched in 1936, though it was based on his work. Second, it is no more powerful than other contemporary pistols—the reference is to the magazine holding thirteen rounds when other Semiautomatics held five or six. At first, the pistol came with a detachable shoulder stock, but this was discontinued in 1946. Over the decades since the pistol was first produced it has undergone a number of modifications. The extractor, sights, and hammer have all been changed and it has appeared in a wide number of variants.

SMITH & WESSON MODEL 1913

This pistol was the first Semiautomatic produced by Smith & Wesson. It entered production in 1913 and was manufactured for eight years, during which time over 8,000 were made. It had an unusual safety catch that was located under the trigger guard and was operated by the middle finger of the firing hand. Unlike many Semiautomatics, it had a smooth wooden grip.

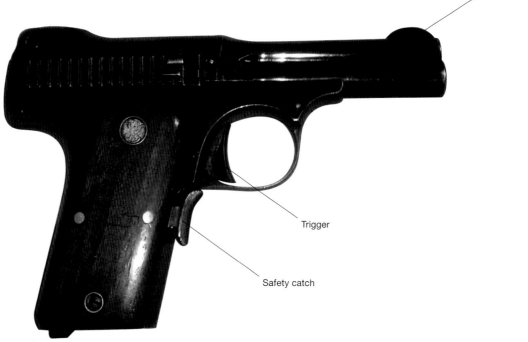

Front sight

Trigger

Safety catch

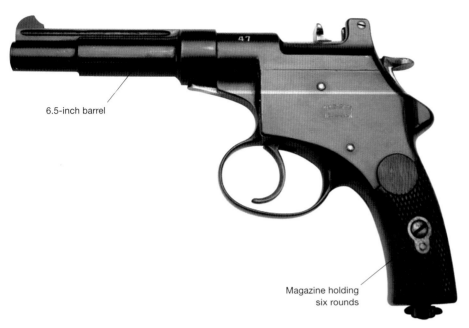

6.5-inch barrel

Magazine holding
six rounds

STEYR MANNLICHER M1894

When the M1894 was first produced it introduced an entirely new concept of Semiautomatic operation that became known as the "blow-forward" mechanism. When the bullet is fired, it travels up the barrel, dragging the barrel forward with it. A spur on the side of the barrel forces a spring to contract as the barrel goes forward. The breech block, meanwhile, remains stationary and the recoil gasses of the discharge hold the cartridge case firmly against it. As the back edge of the barrel clears the front side of the cartridge, the extractor flips the empty cartridge out of the way. The spring in the magazine then pushes a new cartridge into position. The barrel is then pushed back again by the spring acting on the spur until it returns to its original position, with a new cartridge in place ready to be fired. The pistol failed to find many customers, mostly due to the effort needed to reload and cock the gun. It went out of production in 1897, though the basic action was later improved and used in other guns.

5.1-inch barrel

ROTH-STEYR M1907

The M1907 was produced in Budapest, when that city was part of the Austro-Hungarian Empire ruled by the Hapsburgs. It was designed for the Imperial cavalry, being adopted in 1909, and thus has the distinction of being the first Semiautomatic pistol to be used by any army. A few hundred guns were sold on the private market, but the bulk of the 99,000 guns made to this design went to the Hapsburg military. After the Hapsburg Empire collapsed in 1918 these pistols passed to the armies of successor states such as Yugoslavia and Hungary, as well as to neighboring states, including Poland and Italy.

Heavy trigger pull for
added safety when
used by cavalry

Magazine holding
ten rounds

Cylinder holds eight cartridges

RAST-GASSER M1898

The M1898 entered service with the army of the Hapsburg Austro-Hungarian Empire in 1898 and remained the sole official pistol until 1909 when the Roth-Steyr M1907 began to replace it for use by the cavalry. The outbreak of World War I forced the Hapsburgs to bring their M1898 pistols out of storage to be used by the flood of new troops conscripted for the war. Although the design was rather old fashioned, even in 1898, its robust construction and famed reliability meant that it remained in service with the Italian Army and Yugoslav partisans until 1945.

Lanyard ring

PERSONAL DEFENSE WEAPONS

As the nineteenth century progressed, the enforcement of law and order in most countries passed out of the hands of private individuals and local magistrates and into formal agencies of national governments. In France, a team of detectives, the Surete, was founded in 1812. In Britain, the Metropolitan Police began patrolling the streets of London in 1829, and

similar bodies followed in New York in 1845, Berlin in 1848, New South Wales in 1862, and other areas soon after. Law enforcement was patchy in the beginning and many individuals still felt the need to protect themselves against robbery and attack. The weapons shown here were designed for this purpose, though some ended up being used for less respectable causes.

MUFF GUN

This functional little weapon was made in France around the middle of the nineteenth century. It has a small stud trigger and a hammer with an elegantly curved spur that allowed it to be cocked by the thumb of the hand holding the gun. It uses a percussion cap firing system, and was loaded from the muzzle of the octagonal barrel.

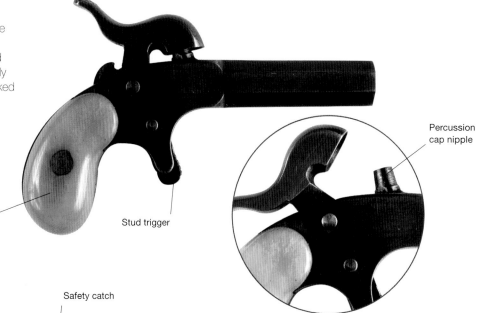

Percussion cap nipple

Ivory grip

Stud trigger

Barrels

Safety catch

HARMONICA GUN

This late nineteenth century pistol was made in France. Each barrel is loaded with a cartridge, then the four-barrel assembly is pushed down into the body of the pistol. As the trigger is pulled, the barrels are pushed up to bring a barrel into line with the hammer, which then falls and discharges the gun. Each time the trigger is pulled, a new barrel is pushed up.

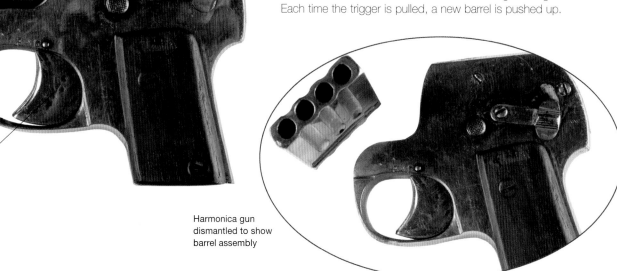

Trigger

Harmonica gun dismantled to show barrel assembly

GAULOIS GUN

This small gun was manufactured in France from 1894 to 1912. The name is deliberately archaic, adopted for marketing purposes. It refers to a person or thing from Gaul, the name used in Roman times for the lands now occupied by France. In the later nineteenth century the French revived interest in their Gallic heritage, in part because Gaul, unlike contemporary France, had extended to the west bank of the Rhine.

Safety catch

Squeeze trigger

Cartridge disk

Leaf spring

Trigger

PROTECTOR PALM PISTOL

This curious little gun was patented by French gunsmith Jacques Turblaux in 1882. The disk held either ten 6mm rounds, or seven 8mm rounds. The lever to the right serves as the trigger. When it is squeezed, the disk rotates to bring a cartridge into line with the short barrel and fires. The leaf spring then pushes the trigger back to its original position ready to be fired again.

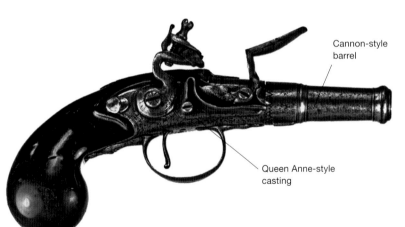

Cannon-style barrel

Queen Anne-style casting

QUEEN ANNE MUFF PISTOL

The Queen Anne style of pistol first became popular in England during the reign of Queen Anne (1702–1714). These guns had the lockplate, trigger plate and breech all cast in one solid block, not as separate pieces as was more common. The vast majority of these weapons had a round barrel that was shaped to mimic that of a contemporary cannon. This example was made later in the eighteenth century, and is small enough to be classed as a muff pistol.

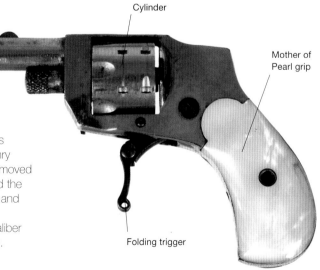

Cylinder

Mother of Pearl grip

Folding trigger

BABY REVOLVER

This little pistol with its elegant mother of pearl handle was made in Philadelphia by German immigrant gunsmith Henry Kolb. Kolb had been born in Württeumberg in 1861 and moved to the United States in 1895. Two years later, he acquired the machines of the bankrupt Columbian Firearms Company and began manufacturing pistols identical to those of the old company. This "Baby Hammerless" model held six .22 caliber cartridges in its cylinder, and was less than 3 inches long.

CONCEALED WEAPONS

People have all sorts of reasons why they might want to carry a concealed weapon. Criminals will want to hide weapons they intend to use to waylay wealthy individuals, or that they are carrying on their way to a planned robbery. Innocent people may prefer to be armed in a discrete manner as it can be difficult to carry on everyday activities with an obvious weapon strapped to your body. The practice of having a hidden weapon, often termed "concealed carry," is taken to an extreme when the weapon is disguised as a generally harmless object.

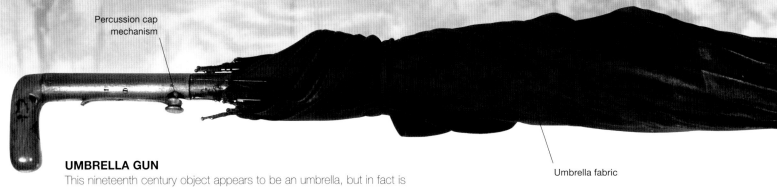

Percussion cap mechanism

Umbrella fabric

UMBRELLA GUN

This nineteenth century object appears to be an umbrella, but in fact is a rifle. The stick of the umbrella is the gun barrel, with the muzzle at the tip. The trigger consists of a small protrusion at the handle end, which operates a percussion cap firing mechanism.

WALKING STICK GUN

The idea of a single-shot gun hidden inside a walking stick was developed by English gunsmith John Day in the 1820s. He marketed the weapon as being suitable for landowners, farmers, and rural workers who wanted to have a walking stick for all the usual reasons, but also wanted to be able to take a shot at passing rabbits or vermin. This example is a percussion cap weapon from the mid-nineteenth century.

Hammer

Barrel / Shank

Trigger

KEY PISTOL

This weapon is something of an oddity. Earlier key pistols seem to have been both functioning keys and functioning guns. They were given to doorkeepers so that they were armed when going about their business. This weapon was made in Central Europe around the year 1840, and seems to have been first and foremost a gun. The item shows no sign of having been used as a key to operate a lock.

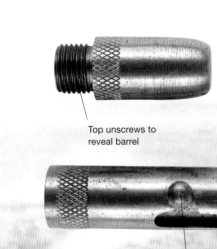

ZIP GUN

A zip gun is a weapon that is improvised from non-firearms materials to fire a cartridge. The barrels of such weapons are usually made out of a hollow metal tube originally used for another purpose. The .22 caliber is commonly used for such weapons as the bullets are small and the cartridges easy to obtain. This example was made in the 1950s.

Top unscrews to reveal barrel

Trigger

Muzzle

Compartments for coins

POCKETBOOK REVOLVER

This appears to be a pocketbook, and has functioning compartments for coins, bank notes, and other small items. However, hidden inside is a tiny revolver which fires through a hole in the metal frame, and is operated by a small button on the exterior. It was made in France in the late nineteenth century.

Revolver

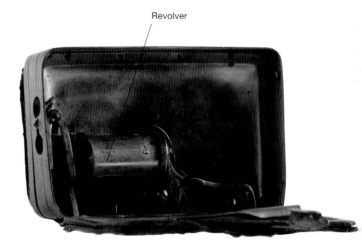

Muzzle

SWORD CANE

This sword has a handle and sheath designed to resemble a stick. It was not a concealed weapon in the true sense of the word, but more a decorative item designed to look like a piece of nature. The blade of the sword is signed by the sixteenth-century Japanese swordsmith Kyushu Higo Do.

Scabbard

Blade

Handle

COMBINATION WEAPONS

The development of reliable revolvers and Semiautomatic pistols solved the perennial problem of the single-shot pistol that was effectively useless once it was fired. Before these improvements came along many gunsmiths sought to ensure that their customers remained armed after having fired their pistol by combining the pistol with another weapon. The earliest efforts saw the pistol handle ending in a large, heavy wooden or metal ball. Once fired, the pistol could be held by the barrel and used as a club. More sophisticated combination weapons saw the pistol combined to a range of other weapons.

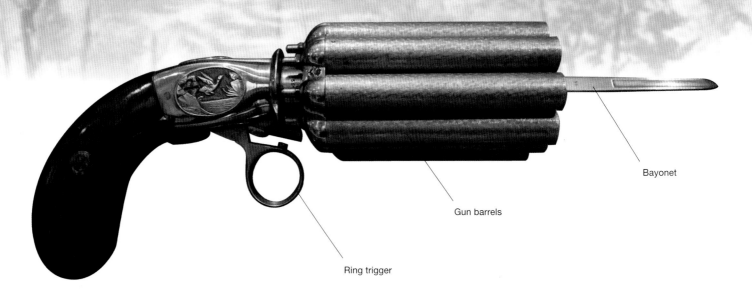

Bayonet

Gun barrels

Ring trigger

PEPPERBOX MARIETTE
This French weapon was made in Saint Étienne in 1855 by a gunsmith named Dessaigne. The gun element of the weapon is an eight-barreled pepperbox that uses the bottom barrel firing system perfected by Gilles Mariette of Liege, Belgium. Should the gun fail or the bullets miss, there was a triangular-bladed bayonet that sprang forward from the central spindle of the pepperbox.

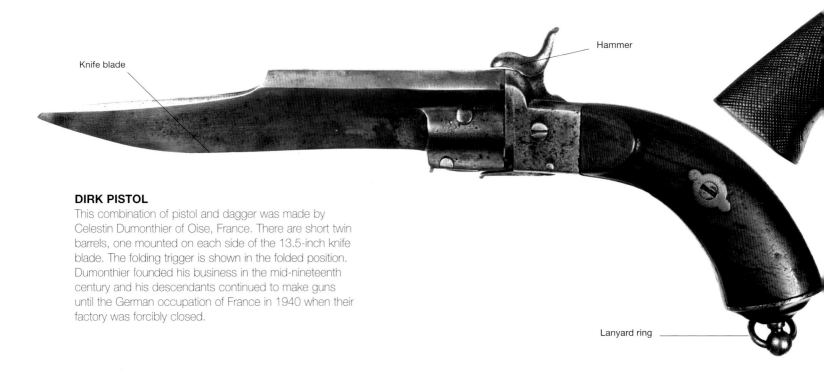

Knife blade

Hammer

DIRK PISTOL
This combination of pistol and dagger was made by Celestin Dumonthier of Oise, France. There are short twin barrels, one mounted on each side of the 13.5-inch knife blade. The folding trigger is shown in the folded position. Dumonthier founded his business in the mid-nineteenth century and his descendants continued to make guns until the German occupation of France in 1940 when their factory was forcibly closed.

Lanyard ring

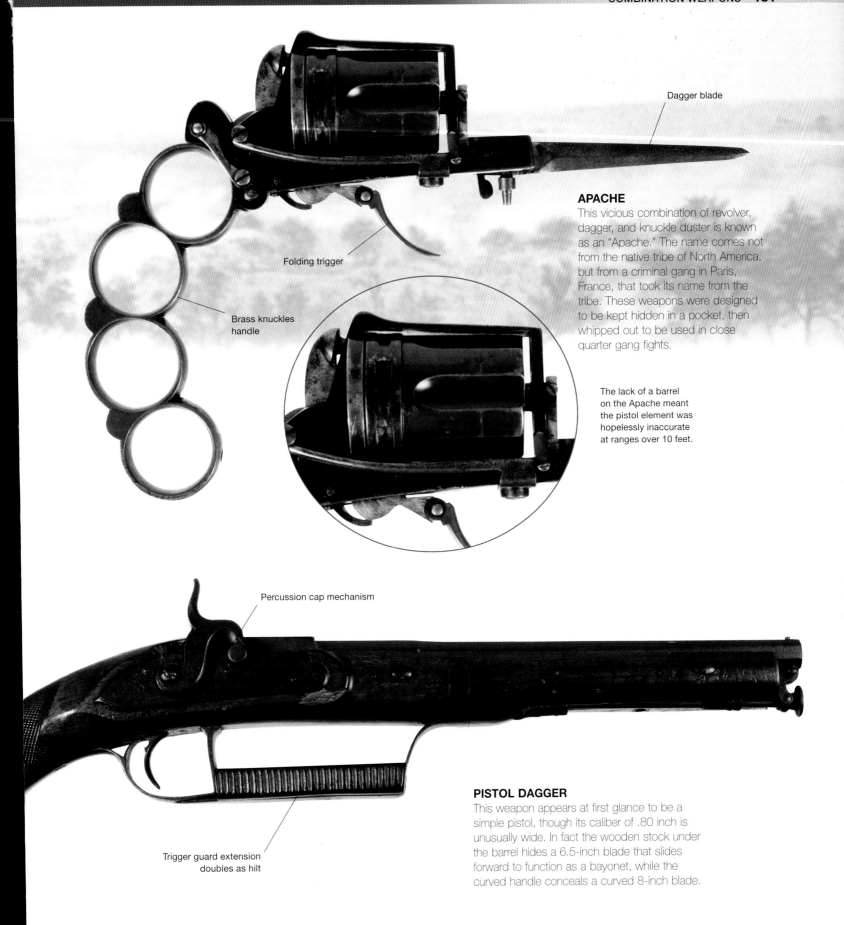

Dagger blade

Folding trigger

Brass knuckles handle

APACHE

This vicious combination of revolver, dagger, and knuckle duster is known as an "Apache." The name comes not from the native tribe of North America, but from a criminal gang in Paris, France, that took its name from the tribe. These weapons were designed to be kept hidden in a pocket, then whipped out to be used in close quarter gang fights.

The lack of a barrel on the Apache meant the pistol element was hopelessly inaccurate at ranges over 10 feet.

Percussion cap mechanism

PISTOL DAGGER

This weapon appears at first glance to be a simple pistol, though its caliber of .80 inch is unusually wide. In fact the wooden stock under the barrel hides a 6.5-inch blade that slides forward to function as a bayonet, while the curved handle conceals a curved 8-inch blade.

Trigger guard extension doubles as hilt

COMBINATION WEAPONS

Macehead

RAIL GUN

This weapon was designed to protect sections of a ship's bulwarks that were vulnerable to boarding. The 66-inch length of timber is studded with ten vertical pistol barrels (three are missing). Each barrel was loaded individually, but they were fired by a single trigger mechanism. When enemy boarders began clambering over the side of the ship the weapon was fired, sending pistol balls upward into the enemy sailors.

Pistol barrel

CENTENAIRE

This murderous little weapon is a steel knuckle duster that has a single-shot .22 pistol incorporated into its handle. It was made in Paris, France, and although it was marketed as a personal protection weapon, it is thought that most ended up in the hands of criminals.

Hammer

Muzzle

Club head

Trigger

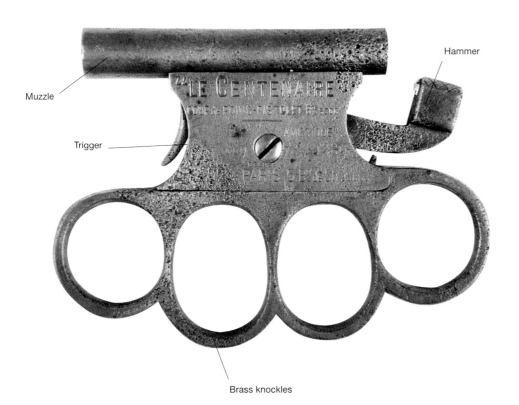

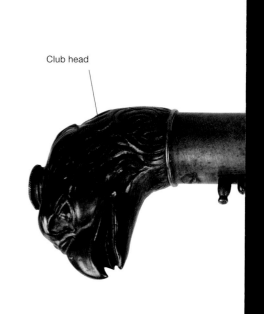

Brass knockles

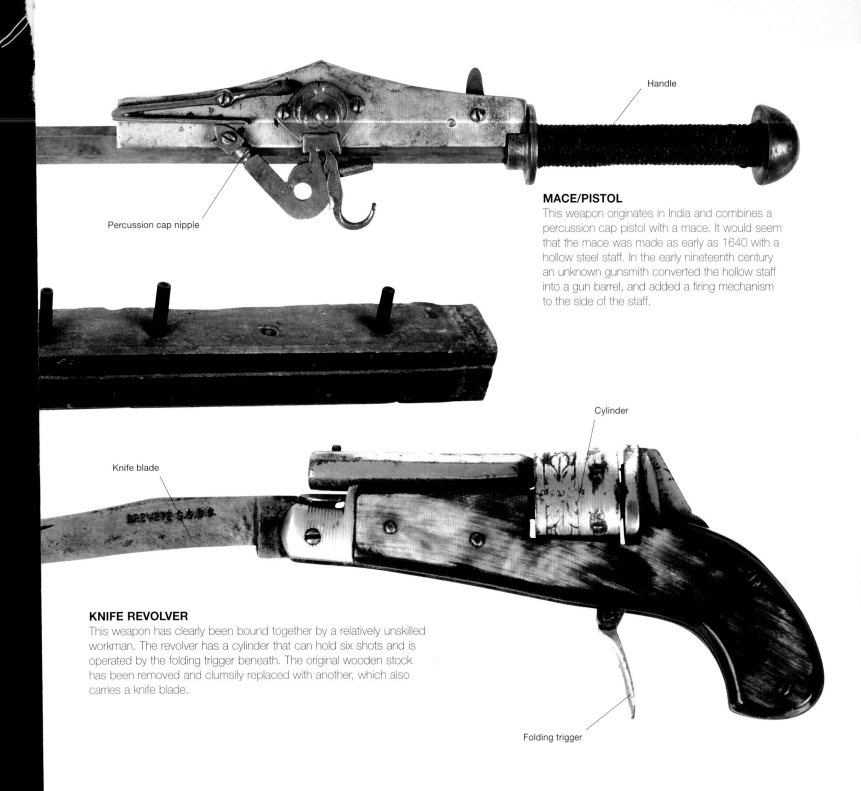

Handle

Percussion cap nipple

MACE/PISTOL

This weapon originates in India and combines a percussion cap pistol with a mace. It would seem that the mace was made as early as 1640 with a hollow steel staff. In the early nineteenth century an unknown gunsmith converted the hollow staff into a gun barrel, and added a firing mechanism to the side of the staff.

Cylinder

Knife blade

BREVETE S.G.D.G.

KNIFE REVOLVER

This weapon has clearly been bound together by a relatively unskilled workman. The revolver has a cylinder that can hold six shots and is operated by the folding trigger beneath. The original wooden stock has been removed and clumsily replaced with another, which also carries a knife blade.

Folding trigger

DAY'S PATENT

Muzzle

Hammer

KNIFE-CLUB-PISTOL

Made in England, perhaps around 1840, this curious brass weapon has a percussion cap pistol firing out of the base of the handle. The top is a heavy metal club shaped to resemble a bird of prey's head. There is also a knife blade hidden behind the bird head. It is marked "Day's Patent" and was made by the company founded by John Day.

THE WORLD WARS
1914–1945

THE TWENTIETH CENTURY WAS DOMINATED BY TWO GREAT WARS THAT ENGULFED MUCH OF THE WORLD IN BLOODSHED ON AN EPIC SCALE. AS MANY AS 17 MILLION PEOPLE MAY HAVE DIED IN WORLD WAR I, AND 60 MILLION IN WORLD WAR II. BOTH WARS SAW TREMENDOUS ADVANCES IN WEAPONS TECHNOLOGY, THE MOST DRAMATIC OF WHICH INCLUDED THE INVENTION AND RAPID DEVELOPMENT OF TANKS AND MILITARY AIRCRAFT. THE IMPROVEMENTS OF SIDEARMS MIGHT APPEAR LESS SPECTACULAR AT FIRST, BUT NEW VERSIONS OF WEAPONS WERE PRODUCED THAT WOULD HAVE AN IMPORTANT IMPACT ON THE WAY BATTLES WERE FOUGHT, AND ON THE OUTCOME OF THE TWO GLOBAL CONFLICTS.

IN THE HEAT OF THE BATTLE
This painting by Canadian artist Richard Jack shows Canadian troops repelling a German assault at the Second Battle of Ypres in April 1915. Note that at this date, the Allied forces still wore soft caps and their German opponents wore the spiked helmet of the pre-war era.

HANDGUNS OF WORLD WAR I

When World War I began, all armies viewed handguns to be distinctly second-rate weapons. Infantrymen were equipped with rifles that could shoot accurately over distances of 600 yards or more, as well as machine guns that were scarcely less accurate. Officers and cavalry were equipped with swords of various kinds that in 1914 remained the mark of a gentleman, and had significant social prestige. Given the experience of combat in the Franco-Prussian War of 1870, sabers and swords were still considered to be effective battlefield weapons. Handguns were viewed largely as weapons for cart drivers and frontline cooks. A few officers carried handguns in preference to swords, but they were in the minority. The reality of twentieth-century warfare would soon show the value of the handgun in combat.

GERMAN ARMY REVOLVER
In 1862 King Wilhelm I of Prussia ordered the construction of the Royal Gun Factory at Erfurt. At this date Erfurt stood on the southern border of Prussia and was a heavily fortified military city with a large garrison of troops. The city grew rapidly as industry expanded and the arms factory continued to produce guns after the foundation of the German Empire in 1871. This pistol was made in Erfurt in 1893.

Cylinder containing six cartridges

Wooden grip

Front sight

Cylinder holding six cartridges

GERMAN REVOLVER
This six-shot revolver was captured from a German cavalryman in the early days of World War I. By this date German troopers should have been armed with the Luger Semiautomatic, but some men preferred to buy their own weapons believing revolvers were more reliable in battlefield conditions.

Lanyard ring

HAPSBURG COMMANDER-IN-CHIEF

The Commander-in-Chief of the Austro-Hungarian armies, Count Conrad von Hotzendorf (right), carried a Steyr handgun strapped to his belt whenever he paid one of his rare visits to frontline units, although he is never known to have used it. His handling of the Hapsburg armies was poor from the start. In August 1914, he launched an attack on Serbia in the belief that the Russian armies would move too slowly to intervene; von Hotzendorf was then taken entirely offguard by a Russian thrust into Galicia. He went on to spend a great amount of time engaged in factional disputes at court, leaving his men to languish with poor supplies and limited ammunition. The Count was finally sacked when the new emperor, Karl I, moved to reform the armed forces.

Short barrel

Folding trigger

SCHEINTOD HAHN GAS REVOLVER
This curious little revolver was made in Germany in the later nineteenth century. It has a very short smoothbore barrel, and a cylinder that can hold five cartridges. Although it could fire shotgun cartridges, the name "scheintod" reveals its original purpose—the word means "fake death" and indicates a gun made to fire blanks.

External hammer

STEYR M1912
The Steyr handgun that saw extensive service with the Austro-Hungarian armed forces in World War I was officially the M1912, but it was widely known as the "hahn," or "hammer," due to its external hammer action. After the end of the war, Steyr continued to manufacture this pistol for civilian customers. The gun was still in production in 1938 when Germany annexed Austria, whereupon the German Army placed an order for 60,000 of these handguns. The pistols made for the German Army were identical to earlier guns, but were stamped with the German eagle carrying a swastika.

Internal magazine holds eight cartridges

Handguns of World War I

Mauser-style hammer action

CHINESE PISTOL

This early twentieth-century Chinese weapon was based on various models of Mauser and other European Semiautomatics brought into the country. These locally made pistols were of varying quality—some were almost as good as the originals, and others were almost as dangerous to the person using them as to the potential target.

Grip

Mauser-style "ring hammer," a spurless hammer with a circular hole through the projecting end.

BERGMANN-BAYARD M1910

The Danish gunmaker Theodore Bergmann designed the M1910 to be the official handgun of the Danish armed forces. It was manufactured by Bayard in Belgium, but deliveries of the gun to Denmark halted in 1914 when Germany overran Belgium; production of this pistol was then diverted to German use.

Magazine holds six or ten cartridges

Sliding trigger

BROWNING M1911A1

An update of the Browning M1911, this pistol was introduced after 1924 and incorporated a number of modifications driven by experience in the trenches of World War I. Some of the revisions were superficial, such as a change from a double-diamond pattern to a cross-hatched pattern on the grip. Others were more important, including a redesign of the hammer to stop it from accidentally cutting open the flesh beside the thumb of users with smaller hands.

5-inch barrel

Magazine holds seven cartridges

The ribbed metal on the rear of the slide helped those with dirty or sweaty fingers to pull the slide back and load the first cartridge.

CHINA IN WORLD WAR I

In October 1911, an uprising organized by business and military interests began in China. By March 1912, the Qing Dynasty had been overthrown and replaced with a provisional Republic of China. The new President, General Yuan Shikai, won a power struggle with the revolutionary democrat Sun Yat Sen (right), and in 1915 declared himself to be Emperor. After Shikai died the following year, China was plunged into civil war as subordinate generals attempted to make themselves independent rulers of local provinces while professing loyalty to the restored Republic. China thus played no official part in World War I, and for this reason was denied any of the spoils of victory. In 1919, German possessions along the Chinese coast were given not to China but to Japan, a source of tension that would contribute to the outbreak of war between the two nations almost two decades later.

Barrel available in six
lengths from 2 to 6 inches

Ejector rod

SMITH & WESSON MODEL 10

This robust and popular pistol has been in continuous production since 1899. It has gone by a variety of names such as the Smith & Wesson .38 Hand Ejector Model of 1899, the Smith & Wesson Military & Police, or the Smith & Wesson Victory Model. The 1904 model was the first weapon in the world to introduce what became known as "service sights." These were larger and marginally less accurate than normal sights, but were intended to allow a soldier to take aim more quickly in a combat situation. This example is a Victory Model, so called as the serial number was prefixed by a V.

Hammer

Cylinder holds
six cartridges

Front sight

JAPANESE-MADE TYPE 26

In keeping with standard Japanese nomenclature, this revolver was named the Type 26 because it was introduced in the twenty-sixth year of the reign of Emperor Meiji (1894). It was developed at the Koishikawa Arsenal under great secrecy, but it is now thought to have been pieced together from several different American and French designs that had been taken apart by experts at Koishikawa. Production stopped in 1923 when the arsenal was destroyed by an earthquake, but the pistol remained in use until 1945.

HANDGUNS OF WORLD WAR I

Front sight

LUGER P08

The P08 was the designation given by the Imperial German Army to the military version of the Luger pistol. It was bought by the army in 1908 with a 100mm barrel and chambered for the 9x19mm parabellum cartridge. The pistol remained in production until 1942. The P08 became popular with collectors, which prompted its manufacturer, Deutsche Waffen und Munitionsfabriken (DWM), to make a limited run of 200 units in 1999. Each was priced at $17,545, compared to the cost in 1908 of $13.

Magazine holds eight cartridges

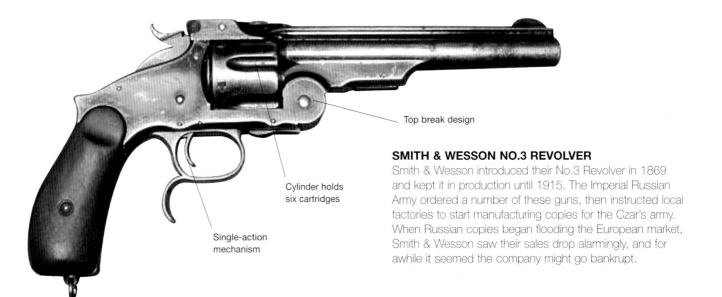

Top break design

Cylinder holds six cartridges

Single-action mechanism

SMITH & WESSON NO.3 REVOLVER

Smith & Wesson introduced their No.3 Revolver in 1869 and kept it in production until 1915. The Imperial Russian Army ordered a number of these guns, then instructed local factories to start manufacturing copies for the Czar's army. When Russian copies began flooding the European market, Smith & Wesson saw their sales drop alarmingly, and for awhile it seemed the company might go bankrupt.

Spiral groove

MAUSER ZIG-ZAG

The Zig-Zag takes its name from the distinctive spiraled groove engraved around the cylinder. It was developed in 1878 for the German military, becoming the first German pistol to use modern metal cartridges. Shown here is the 1886 model with a hinged frame that took a 9mm cartridge; the first models had been chambered for 6mm rounds. The better-known "broomhandle" pistol began replacing it in 1896, but many Zig-Zags remained in use by reservists during World War I.

Ring lug to unlock frame hinge

Iron sights

BROWNING FN M1910

The Browning M1910 was designed by U.S. gunsmith John Browning and manufactured by the Belgian company FN Herstal. The pistol began production in 1910 and could fire either .32 or .38 caliber ammunition. It acquired instant notoriety in June 1914 when Serb terrorist Gavrilo Princip used an M1910 chambered for .38 ammunition to kill Austrian Archduke Franz Ferdinand and his wife, thus precipitating the Austrian-Serb dispute that led directly to the outbreak of World War I six weeks later.

The spent cartridge was expelled through the side port by a claw extractor.

Magazine holds six .38 cartridges

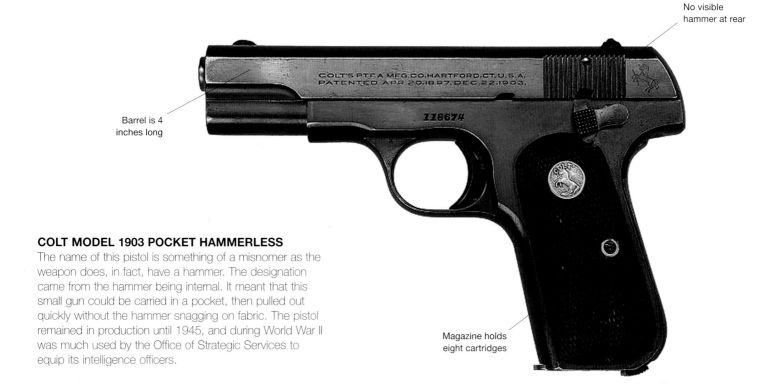

No visible hammer at rear

Barrel is 4 inches long

COLT MODEL 1903 POCKET HAMMERLESS

The name of this pistol is something of a misnomer as the weapon does, in fact, have a hammer. The designation came from the hammer being internal. It meant that this small gun could be carried in a pocket, then pulled out quickly without the hammer snagging on fabric. The pistol remained in production until 1945, and during World War II was much used by the Office of Strategic Services to equip its intelligence officers.

Magazine holds eight cartridges

INFANTRY RIFLES OF WORLD WAR I

During the late nineteenth century, armies of the world had placed emphasis on long-range accuracy in the design of infantry rifles. It was believed that wars would be fought between mobile bodies of men in open countryside, with minimal amounts of combat taking place in urban areas. In this type of fighting, the ability to fire accurately over a long range would be crucial. Some armies, including the British, placed much emphasis on the speed of fire. Experience in the trenches would show that long-range accuracy was less important than had originally been thought. Instead, rate of fire and weapons such as grenades and shotguns—which were able to produce widespread carnage at short range—became more significant.

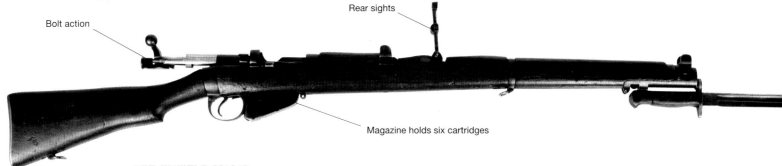

Bolt action

Rear sights

Magazine holds six cartridges

LEE-ENFIELD M1917

When World War I broke out, the British placed orders with American factories to produce large numbers of Enfield rifles. In 1917, it became clear that the United States was about to join the war, so the U.S. Army decided to use the British design to upgrade its own Springfield M1903. The British design was altered to take the Springfield .30-60 cartridge and a few other minor changes were made before it was put into production as the M1917. More than 2.1 million of these rifles were produced. When the U.S. entered World War II, the M1917 was issued to troops operating at the rear.

Rear sights folded down

The bolt of the Moisin-Nagant differed from contemporary designs in that it had a recessed head that allowed the spring-loaded extractor to snap shut over the cartridge as the bolt was closed.

MOSIN-NAGANT M91

When Russia entered the war in 1914, the standard infantry rifle was the Mosin-Nagant M91. The Russian Army was rapidly mobilized, but it was soon clear that there was a drastic shortage of Mosin-Nagants. It resulted in orders for 3.3 million rifles being placed with American companies, which was in addition to orders with Russian factories. Even so, there was still a shortage of weapons— some men were issued wooden sticks and bayonets, and ordered to arm themselves with rifles from dead or wounded comrades.

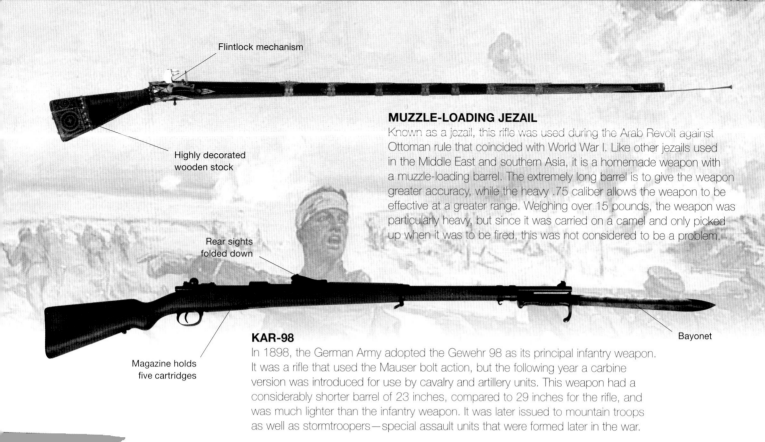

Flintlock mechanism

Highly decorated
wooden stock

Rear sights
folded down

Magazine holds
five cartridges

Bayonet

MUZZLE-LOADING JEZAIL

Known as a jezail, this rifle was used during the Arab Revolt against
Ottoman rule that coincided with World War I. Like other jezails used
in the Middle East and southern Asia, it is a homemade weapon with
a muzzle-loading barrel. The extremely long barrel is to give the weapon
greater accuracy, while the heavy .75 caliber allows the weapon to be
effective at a greater range. Weighing over 15 pounds, the weapon was
particularly heavy, but since it was carried on a camel and only picked
up when it was to be fired, this was not considered to be a problem.

KAR-98

In 1898, the German Army adopted the Gewehr 98 as its principal infantry weapon.
It was a rifle that used the Mauser bolt action, but the following year a carbine
version was introduced for use by cavalry and artillery units. This weapon had a
considerably shorter barrel of 23 inches, compared to 29 inches for the rifle, and
was much lighter than the infantry weapon. It was later issued to mountain troops
as well as stormtroopers—special assault units that were formed later in the war.

Rear sights in
folded position

Mirror

Magazine enlarged to
hold twenty cartridges

Cleaning rod

PERISCOPE RIFLE

This peculiar-looking weapon was developed by the
British Army late in 1914 as a response to the static
trench warfare that had formed on the Western
Front. The two mirrors allowed the user to aim the
rifle while remaining safely below the trench parapet.
The system of levers allowed the periscope rifle to
be fired when a target was observed.

Linking rod

Mirror

To fire the weapon, the user looked
into the mirror attached to the curved
bottom handle to see a view—reflected
from the top mirror—along the barrel of
the rifle without raising his head above
the trench. When a target came into
sight, the firing lever was squeezed.

Firing lever

INFANTRY RIFLES OF WORLD WAR I

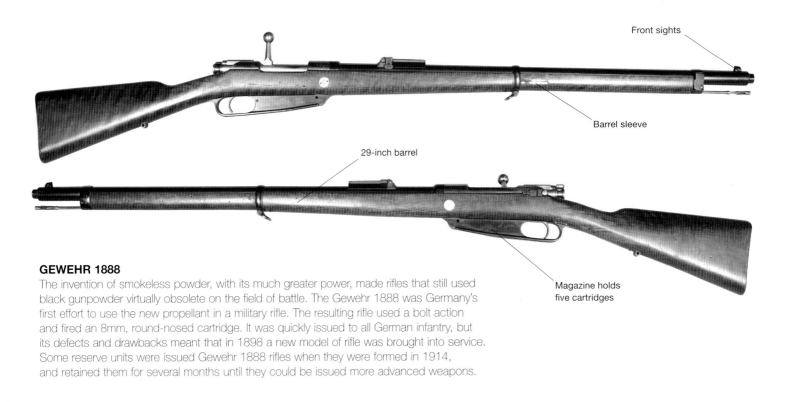

Front sights

Barrel sleeve

29-inch barrel

Magazine holds
five cartridges

GEWEHR 1888

The invention of smokeless powder, with its much greater power, made rifles that still used black gunpowder virtually obsolete on the field of battle. The Gewehr 1888 was Germany's first effort to use the new propellant in a military rifle. The resulting rifle used a bolt action and fired an 8mm, round-nosed cartridge. It was quickly issued to all German infantry, but its defects and drawbacks meant that in 1898 a new model of rifle was brought into service. Some reserve units were issued Gewehr 1888 rifles when they were formed in 1914, and retained them for several months until they could be issued more advanced weapons.

Bolt action

Magazine
holds three
cartridges

BERTHIER RIFLE

By 1890, the French Army needed a new carbine for its cavalry units to replace the 1874 Gras Carbine that was single shot and used black powder cartridges. The answer came in the form of the Berthier Carbine, which was not only light, but easy to load by a rider on a moving horse. So successful was the Berthier Carbine that a rifle version, shown here, was produced in 1907 and manufactured in vast numbers to equip French infantry in World War I. Some French regiments retained their Berthiers when war returned in 1939.

CARCANO MODEL 1891

The name Carcano is given to a series of rifles that was in service with the Italian Army from 1891 to 1981, and is still in use elsewhere. The example shown here is the original Model 1891 rifle, designed by Salvatore Carcano at the Turin Army Arsenal. The Model 1891 was also produced as a carbine for the cavalry. The weapon is a straightforward bolt-action rifle with a magazine.

Bolt action

21.3-inch barrel

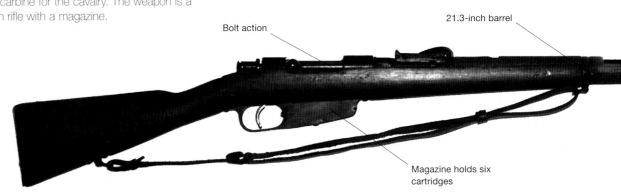

Magazine holds six
cartridges

HITLER ON THE SOMME

Among the many German soldiers to be equipped with the different versions of the official Gewehr in 1914 was a volunteer named Adolf Hitler. Though Hitler was an Austrian citizen, he had volunteered for the Bavarian Army as he was living in Bavaria when war broke out. He joined the Bavarian Reserve Infantry Regiment No.16, and was soon fighting the British in the frontline at the First Battle of Ypres. He was decorated for bravery with the Iron Cross, Second Class.

In 1916, he fought on the Somme, where he was wounded, and then at Arras and Passchendaele in 1917. Hitler's main task was to act as a dispatch runner, a job that brought him into contact with senior officers. It is thought that this military experience gave him a lifelong distrust of senior German officers as well as a strong belief in his own military skills. Both were to have important repercussions in World War II.

Gas-operated, cylinder-and-pistol semiautomatic mechanism

22.7-inch barrel

Gunstock

Magazine holds eight cartridges, and could be replaced with a 30-round drum magazine

MONDRAGÓN RIFLE

In 1908, the Mexican Army became the first in the world to adopt a semiautomatic rifle while everyone else was still using repeating, bolt-action rifles. The weapon had been designed by veteran rifle designer Manuel Mondragón and was made by SIG (Schweizerische Industrie Gesellschaft) in Germany. When World War I broke out, the German government impounded the 3,000 rifles in storage at SIG and issued them to its own army. The weapon initially performed well, but was soon discarded when it proved susceptible to jamming when fouled by mud in the trenches.

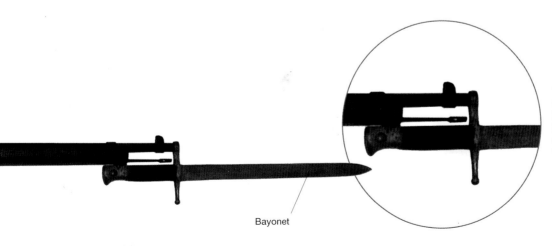

The bayonet fitted to this Carcano is a fully detachable knife bayonet, with a tapering point and single cutting edge. After 1931, a folding bayonet was introduced.

Bayonet

Infantry Rifles of World War I

Bolt action

31.5-inch barrel

Tubular
magazine holds
eight cartridges

LEBEL MODEL 1886

The French Lebel 1886 was the first military rifle to use cartridges holding smokeless powder and it revolutionized infantry warfare. The new propellant and the equally novel full metal jacket bullet made the Lebel 1886 accurate enough to reliably hit a man-sized target at 450 yards, and gave it a maximum range of a mile. Other armies scrambled to catch up with the French and within a dozen years the Lebel had been superseded by more modern designs. Nevertheless, nearly 3 million Lebel rifles were made and they remained in service with the French Army to 1940.

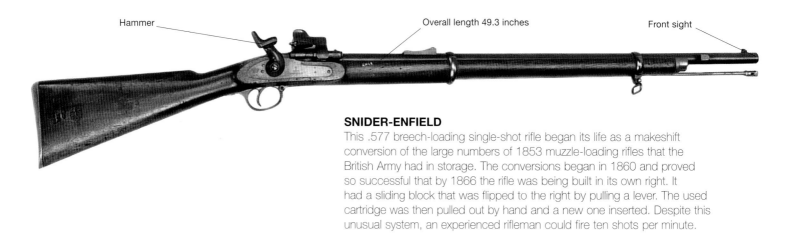

Hammer

Overall length 49.3 inches

Front sight

SNIDER-ENFIELD

This .577 breech-loading single-shot rifle began its life as a makeshift conversion of the large numbers of 1853 muzzle-loading rifles that the British Army had in storage. The conversions began in 1860 and proved so successful that by 1866 the rifle was being built in its own right. It had a sliding block that was flipped to the right by pulling a lever. The used cartridge was then pulled out by hand and a new one inserted. Despite this unusual system, an experienced rifleman could fire ten shots per minute.

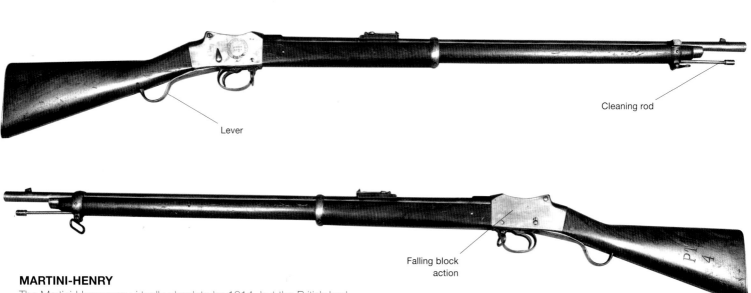

Lever

Cleaning rod

Falling block
action

MARTINI-HENRY

The Martini-Henry was virtually obsolete by 1914, but the British had so many of them in storage that they were brought out and assigned to auxiliary troops in the colonies. The rifle had been introduced in 1871 and had a single-shot lever action, firing .577 black powder cartridges. It was relatively accurate and fast to load compared to contemporary rifles, though its use of black powder soon made it obsolete.

24-inch barrel

Bipod

Detachable
magazine holds
twenty cartridges

M1918 BROWNING AUTOMATIC RIFLE

Known by its users as the BAR, the Browning Automatic Rifle was
designed to lay down a high quantity of fire in front of advancing
infantry. The idea was that the weapon would be held at the hip,
supported by the shoulder strap, and fired continuously as you
walked forward—a concept dubbed "walking fire." Bitter experience
in World War I showed that it was better for attackers to run forward
as fast as possible, not walk while firing. The BAR was, in fact, used
mostly as a light machine gun fired from a bipod mount.

Metal sights

Bolt action

32.2-inch barrel

FUSIL GRAS MODEL 1874

In the 1870s, colonial rivalries led to the French expecting to fight a future
war against Britain. When the British introduced the metal Boxer cartridge,
the French rushed to find an answer. In 1874 Colonel Basile Gras produced
an 11x59mm metal cartridge together with the Fusil Gras to fire it. It proved
to be an accurate and relatively fast-firing rifle, but was soon superseded by
the Lebel. In 1914, about 146,000 Fusil Gras were brought out of storage to
equip hastily raised reserve formations, but by 1915 they had been discarded.

VINTAGE GUNS

The Martini-Henry is a famously robust, reliable,
and long-lasting weapon. It was used by the
British Army in a number of Imperial conflicts,
including the Zulu War of 1879 (pictured right is
the Battle of Rourke's Drift, with Martini-Henry
rifles being used by men of the 24th Regiment)
and the Second Afghan War of 1880. It was
replaced as a frontline weapon in 1888, but was
first passed to rear echelon troops, then to native
troops, and finally put into storage. It was used
in World War I to equip colonial troops, and then
the remaining weapons were sold off to the police
in the British colonies. The rifle continued to be
used by civilians in many areas. In April 2011,
U.S. Marines in Paktika, Afghanistan, found
a local fighter still using one to good effect.

MACHINE GUNS OF WORLD WAR I

When World War I began, the machine gun was not a highly rated weapon. It was expected to be used to support infantry by laying down heavy covering fire, but its relative immobility was thought to be a major problem. Senior commanders expected the war to be fought primarily as a war of movement, in the style of the Franco-Prussian War of 1870 and the Boer War of 1900. It was thought that armies would march across the continent seeking to outflank each other, cut off each other's supply lines, and engage in dramatic contests of charge and counter-charge. In fact, the war soon became a static slogging match. The cumbersome nature of machine guns was a moot point when the frontline did not move for months on end. In such circumstances, machine guns came to dominate the battlefield.

26.5-inch barrel

Magazine holds forty-seven rounds; a 97-round magazine was also available

Aluminum shroud aids cooling of the barrel

LEWIS LIGHT MACHINE GUN
The Lewis gun was developed by U.S. Army Colonel Isaac Lewis in 1911, but was used most by the British. The gun featured gas operation to maintain continuous fire—when a cartridge was fired, a part of the expanding gasses rushing up the barrel behind the bullet was siphoned off to operate a piston backward against a spring. The piston disengaged the bolt and pushed it back to eject the spent cartridge. The spring then pushed the piston forward again, taking the bolt with it to engage the next cartridge and push it into place ready to be fired. The Lewis could fire at a rate of 600 rounds per minute.

Watercooled barrel

SPANDAU 15
The Spandau 15 was a development of the standard German machine gun of World War I, the Spandau Maxim, which was itself a version of the American Maxim machine gun. The 15 was designed to be both lighter and smaller than the standard Spandau Maxim so that the four-man crew could operate it while they were lying prone on the ground. The changes proved to be successful, although the new gun was noticeably less accurate than the standard model. By 1918, it was the principal machine gun in use by the German Army.

Low-slung stock to allow firing when prone

Bipod support

BARBED WIRE

An unexpected feature of World War I was barbed wire. It had been invented in the 1860s to make cheap, easily erected, stockproof fences on farms. Its use by the military was limited to being placed around camps and buildings. Soon after the trenches were first dug in 1914, barbed wire fencing was erected in front of them to slow down any attack. Barbed wire was so effective that considerable effort was put into designing how the wire should be set out. By 1916, both sides were building impenetrable barbed wire entanglements that stood over six feet tall, up to 20 feet deep. Efforts were made before an attack to destroy the wire with artillery, but this was never entirely effective. Shown here are British infantry advancing with barbed wire and metal wiring posts.

Magazine holds twenty rounds

Pistol grip

Shoulder stock

FRENCH CHAUCHAT

The Chauchat was a mold-breaking weapon when it first appeared on battlefields in 1916, but its drawbacks would lead to it being dubbed the worst machine gun of the war. The Chauchat was light enough to be carried by a single soldier, unlike other machine guns of the time that required crews of four or six men. It had a selective fire mechanism allowing single shots, bursts, or continuous fire, a pistol grip, and an inline shoulder stock—all of these were radical innovations. However, it was generally poorly made and suffered more jams and breakdowns than any other weapon of the war.

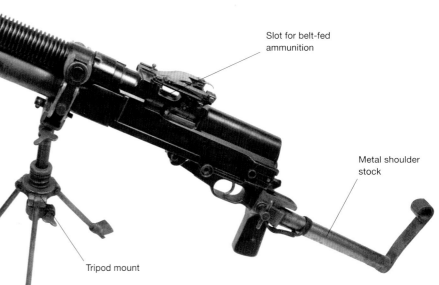

Slot for belt-fed ammunition

HOTCHKISS PORTABLE MACHINE GUN

In 1875, American gunsmith Benjamin Hotchkiss moved to France hoping that the recent French defeat by Prussia would give him a market for his innovative designs. His company produced the Hotchkiss M1909 light machine gun for the French Army just in time for the outbreak of World War I. The gun was designed to be light enough to be carried by cavalry units. The crew would dismount to fire the weapon from cover. Once the war settled down to trench combat, the Hotchkiss saw little active service. This example was used by British cavalry in the Middle East.

Metal shoulder stock

Tripod mount

MACHINE GUNS OF WORLD WAR I

Sights

Plug

Grip

Trigger

In action, this plug was removed and a hose screwed into the top of the water-filled brass jacket. As the water boiled, steam was taken through the hose to a metal can, where it recondensed into water. This water would be poured back down the hose to refill the jacket.

BROWNING M1917

The M1917 was a reliable and effective machine gun, though its massive size and water-cooling jacket made it heavy and cumbersome in action. The fully assembled gun with tripod, spare ammunition, and water weighed over 100 pounds and required a six-man crew to carry it. It was therefore used mostly in static defensive positions. The gun did not enter service until the summer of 1918, but remained in use through World War II to the Korean and Vietnam Wars.

23.5-inch barrel

Pistol grip

Bipod support

HOTCHKISS M1922

The lessons of World War I were learned by Hotchkiss and put into practice with their M1922 light machine gun. This weapon could fire at a rate of 450 rounds per minute, using either a twenty-round overhead box magazine, or a thirty-round stripper feed. It was tough and reliable, used not only by the French Army, but also by the British, Greek, Spanish, and Chinese forces. It was still in use by Vietnamese forces in the early stages of the Vietnam War in the 1950s.

Water-filled cooling jacket
for barrel

Slot for belt-fed
ammunition

COLT VICKERS

By 1913, the U.S. Army had a number of different automatic
weapons in service, acquired piecemeal for different reasons. It
was decided to standardize a single machine gun and a search
began for the best one to use. After a series of tests, the Army
opted for the Vickers machine gun. The gun was made under
license by the Colt Manufacturing Company and a first order of
4,000 was placed for delivery in 1916. Colt had problems with
the manufacturing process, so deliveries did not actually begin
until some weeks after American troops entered combat in 1917.

Sights

Detachable barrel

Long rear arm of
tripod could support
seat for gunner

MARLIN MACHINE GUN

Although this gun was manufactured by Marlin Rockwell Corporation, it was
virtually identical to the Colt M1895 machine gun. In 1917, Colt decided to
concentrate on producing their version of the Vickers, and sold the machinery
for making the M1895 to Marlin Rockwell, along with the rights to complete
the still-active orders for the gun from the Russian and Italian militaries. Marlin
introduced a number of improvements, including a detachable barrel so that
barrels could be swapped out when they became hot after continuous fire.
The guns sent to Italy saw service in World War II as defensive weapons at
rear echelon sites, while those stored by the U.S. Army were sent to Britain
in 1940 to be used by the Home Guard.

WEAPONS OF ESPIONAGE

The men and women who engaged in espionage had very specific needs for their weapons. They needed to be small and easily hidden, but reliable and effective in a sudden crisis. However, they did not generally need to be accurate at a great range, nor did they need to be easy to reload; the ability to continuously fire was even less necessary. These weapons were often used at close quarters and for specific purposes. They might have been used for assassinations, but more likely they were intended to wound and incapacitate an enemy to give the spy enough time to flee from any danger of arrest and subsequent execution.

Weapon is fired by pulling lid fully back

ZIPPO LIGHTER PISTOL

The Zippo lighter first went on the market in 1933 and within months had become the favored lighter of the American military. The fact that the integral windshield allowed the Zippo to stay alight in windy conditions made it especially useful to those who spent a lot of time outdoors—including service personnel. The ubiquitous nature of the Zippo meant that it did not attract attention and so could be used to hide a weapon. This small pistol is fired by pulling the top of the lighter back so it is flush to the side. It was a single-shot weapon firing a tiny-caliber bullet.

Barrel

AMERICAN MACHINE-GUN SHELL

This appears to be a normal .50 caliber machine gun bullet of the type used extensively by U.S. aircrew in World War II and beyond. In fact, it comes apart to reveal a single-shot .22 caliber gun. It is not clear when or by whom the weapon was made.

Fixing lug

SPRING GUN

This small metal item seems quite innocuous, but when the brass finial is pulled out, it arms the .22 caliber gun hidden inside. It is then fired by pushing the finial back into position.

Brass finial

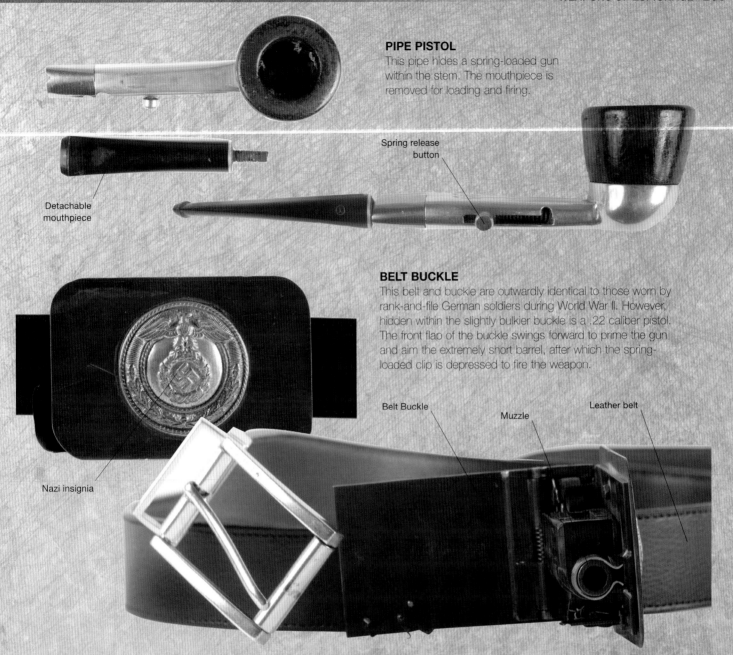

PIPE PISTOL

This pipe hides a spring-loaded gun within the stem. The mouthpiece is removed for loading and firing.

Detachable mouthpiece

Spring release button

BELT BUCKLE

This belt and buckle are outwardly identical to those worn by rank-and-file German soldiers during World War II. However, hidden within the slightly bulkier buckle is a .22 caliber pistol. The front flap of the buckle swings forward to prime the gun and aim the extremely short barrel, after which the spring-loaded clip is depressed to fire the weapon.

Belt Buckle

Muzzle

Leather belt

Nazi insignia

THE ABWEHR

The military intelligence organization of Nazi Germany was the Abwehr, a deliberately vague name that means simply "defense." It was founded in 1921, then thoroughly reorganized in 1938 under its chief Wilhelm Canaris (right) as war loomed. Before the war, Abwehr operatives usually worked at German embassies, given a fake job to explain their presence. Once the war began, the Abwehr concentrated on recruiting undercover agents and enjoyed much success. By 1941, every large U.S. armaments company had an Abwehr agent working within it, as did several British companies, while the Abwehr also infiltrated resistance movements in the Netherlands and France. However, by late 1941, British codebreakers were able to read some Abwehr radio traffic and many operations were unmasked. In February 1944, the SS (Schutzstaffel) discovered Canaris was friends with several notable anti-Nazis. Hitler fired Canaris and closed down the Abwehr, transferring all its responsibilities to the SS.

WEAPONS BETWEEN THE WARS

When World War I ended, many people declared it to have been "the war to end all wars." It was widely assumed that the carnage had been so horrific that no modern, technologically advanced states would ever again go to war with another as the costs would outweigh the potential gains. Weapons designers and manufacturers therefore concentrated on producing weapons for different purposes. Weapons for personal protection and hunting dominated small arms, while manufacturers of aircraft and artillery concentrated on weapons that would be useful in colonial conflicts fought over difficult terrain against technologically inferior opponents.

Cylinder

MITRAILLEUSE
This personal defense weapon was a remote-controlled rifle that had a twenty-four-cartridge magazine in the form of a wide cylinder. The weapon could be screwed to a wooden object and was fired by pulling a string or wire attached to the ring trigger. Each pull fired one bullet, then advanced the cylinder to bring the next cartridge into line with the barrel. In the 1920s, weapons of this type were used by gangster Al Capone on boats carrying illegal alcohol across the Great Lakes to Chicago.

Ring trigger

Blowback mechanism

10.5-inch barrel

THOMPSON SUBMACHINE GUN
In 1915, U.S. General John Thompson came up with the idea of a weapon capable of short bursts of automatic fire that was light enough to be used by one man. The lightness resulted in accuracy limited to 60 yards, but a rate of fire of 700 rounds per minute. Thompson envisaged the weapon being used to clear trenches of enemy soldiers, but by the time it entered production the war was over. Instead, the gun was marketed as a military and police weapon. Its high price put off most civilian customers, but gangsters quickly appreciated its murderous qualities in confined spaces. By 1930, it was synonymous with gangsters and gangster movies, and had earned the nickname "Tommy Gun."

Box magazine holds thirty rounds; also available with 100-round drum magazine

PROHIBITION AND GANGSTER WARS

One of the great social experiments of the twentieth century was the prohibition of alcohol in the United States between 1920 and 1933. It was intended to combat the social and criminal problems caused by drunkeness and alcoholism. However, a large part of the population did not support Prohibition and many people wanted to continue drinking alcohol. As a result, a massive illegal trade in making, importing, and selling alcohol sprang up. In some areas the illegal drinks trade was small scale and local; elsewhere the trade was on a huge scale and was controlled by violent, organized crime gangs. Nowhere were the gangs bigger or more brutal than in Chicago. The gang headed by Al Capone (right) had an income running to the tens of millions of dollars and acquired effective immunity by bribing or intimidating local politicians and law enforcement agencies. On February 14th, 1929, Capone settled scores with the rival North Side Gang by having seven gangsters executed using Thompson guns and shotguns. The St. Valentine's Day Massacre, as the incident became known, was a turning point. Public revulsion at the gangsters' methods hit an all-time high, resulting in the police being given better inside information. Capone himself was jailed for tax evasion in 1932.

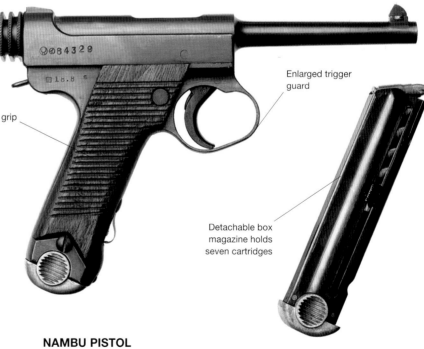

Wooden grip

Enlarged trigger guard

Detachable box magazine holds seven cartridges

NAMBU PISTOL

The Nambu was a family of pistols produced in Japan between 1906 and 1945. Shown here is a Type 14 produced in 1925, but there were several other variants. The Type 14 was a later version that was adapted to make it easier to produce, with more stamped components, although this resulted in a less robust weapon. It was intended for issue to NCOs (non-commissioned officers) in the Japanese Army, although officers were permitted to purchase one if they wished. This example has an enlarged trigger guard, introduced after men serving in Manchuria reported that their gloved fingers had trouble accessing the trigger.

WEAPONS BETWEEN THE WARS

Hammer spur

Cylinder contains six cartridges

Lanyard ring

ENFIELD NO.2 MK1 REVOLVER

The Enfield No.2 was one of a trio of revolvers used by the British Army that were all chambered to take the same .380 Revolver Mk1 cartridge. In the 1920s, it was decided that the World War I Webley .55 pistol was too heavy for use on long colonial patrols, so a new pistol was required. The .38 cartridge fired an elongated lead bullet that was heavy for its caliber, and so had the stopping power of the .55 while being fired from a .38 weapon. This made it popular with colonial officials, who would sometimes be faced by dangerous wild animals.

Blowback mechanism

BERETTA M1934

In 1934, Italian gun manufacturer Beretta learned that the Italian Army was testing the German Walther PP pistol. Determined not to lose a valuable customer, Beretta hurriedly produced the M1934, which secured the contract with the Army. The pistol is famously robust and durable, though the 9mm Corto cartridge that it featured was less powerful than that used by most contemporary pistols.

Magazine holds seven cartridges

MAB 38

Officially known as the Moschetto Automatico Beretta Modello 1938, the MAB 38 was the official submachine gun of the Italian Army throughout World War II, and also saw service with German and Romanian forces. The weapon had an effective firing range of about 280 yards, which was impressive for its time, and it could fire at rates of up to 600 rounds per minute. Due to problems of manufacture, it was initially available only in small numbers, so it went to paratroopers, tank crews, and military police. It was more widely issued after 1943.

Shoulder stock

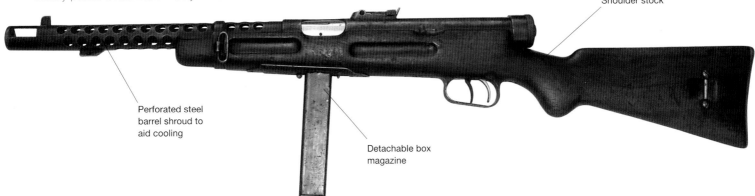

Perforated steel barrel shroud to aid cooling

Detachable box magazine

TANK CREWS

During the 1930s, it was realized that tank crews needed to have sidearms that they could turn to if their tanks were knocked out, or for fighting if their units were overrun—something that would become a particular hazard in the highly mobile desert warfare of North Africa. The Webley Mk IV and Enfield Mk I pistols were the standard tank crew weapons going into World War II. It was quickly discovered that in the confined space inside a tank the long, curved spur on the hammer of these weapons was almost purpose-made to snag on clothing and pieces of equipment, and the tank crews complained. As a result, new models of the pistols were produced without the spur. This meant that they operated in double action only, resulting in less accuracy and a slower rate of fire. That suited tank crews, but infantry officers then found that they were outgunned by German officers. Pictured right is a British-made Churchill tank.

Adjustable rear sight

24-inch barrel

Magazine holds eight cartridges

Winged front sight

M1 GARAND

The M1 Garand became the standard infantry rifle of the U.S. Army in 1936, and retained that status throughout World War II. It was the first semiautomatic rifle to go into service with the American military and was highly prized as its faster rate of fire gave U.S. infantrymen an advantage over German and Japanese troops armed with bolt-action rifles. It began to be replaced in 1957, but was still in use with some units until 1976.

WEAPONS BETWEEN THE WARS

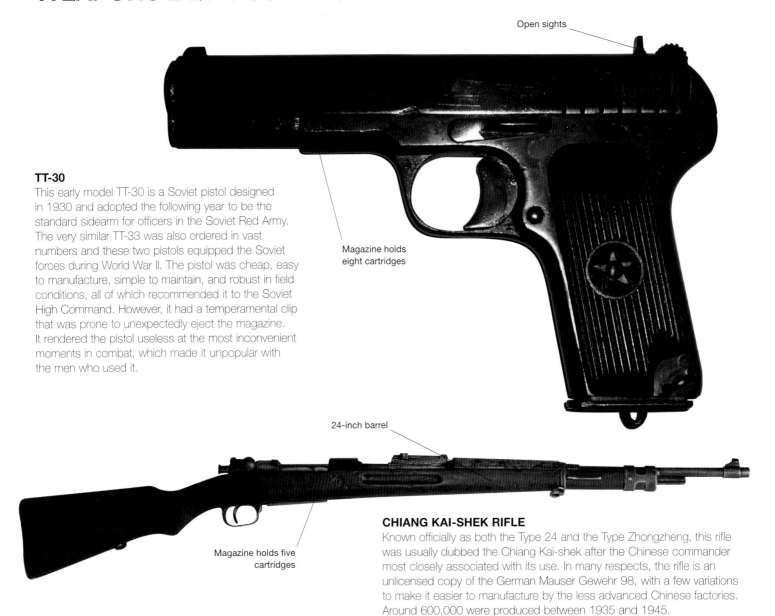

Open sights

TT-30

This early model TT-30 is a Soviet pistol designed in 1930 and adopted the following year to be the standard sidearm for officers in the Soviet Red Army. The very similar TT-33 was also ordered in vast numbers and these two pistols equipped the Soviet forces during World War II. The pistol was cheap, easy to manufacture, simple to maintain, and robust in field conditions, all of which recommended it to the Soviet High Command. However, it had a temperamental clip that was prone to unexpectedly eject the magazine. It rendered the pistol useless at the most inconvenient moments in combat, which made it unpopular with the men who used it.

Magazine holds eight cartridges

24-inch barrel

Magazine holds five cartridges

CHIANG KAI-SHEK RIFLE

Known officially as both the Type 24 and the Type Zhongzheng, this rifle was usually dubbed the Chiang Kai-shek after the Chinese commander most closely associated with its use. In many respects, the rifle is an unlicensed copy of the German Mauser Gewehr 98, with a few variations to make it easier to manufacture by the less advanced Chinese factories. Around 600,000 were produced between 1935 and 1945.

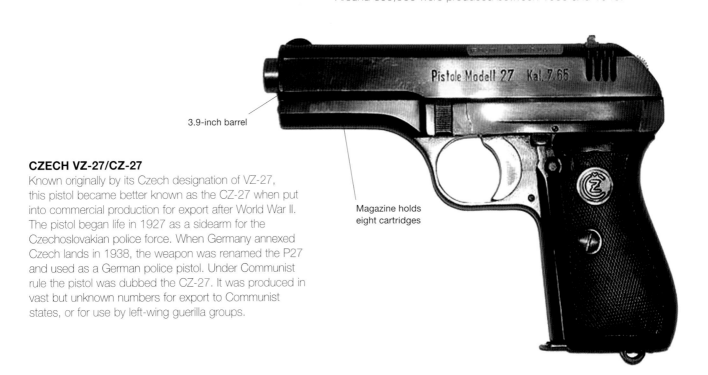

Pistole Modell 27   Kal. 7.65

3.9-inch barrel

CZECH VZ-27/CZ-27

Known originally by its Czech designation of VZ-27, this pistol became better known as the CZ-27 when put into commercial production for export after World War II. The pistol began life in 1927 as a sidearm for the Czechoslovakian police force. When Germany annexed Czech lands in 1938, the weapon was renamed the P27 and used as a German police pistol. Under Communist rule the pistol was dubbed the CZ-27. It was produced in vast but unknown numbers for export to Communist states, or for use by left-wing guerilla groups.

Magazine holds eight cartridges

Blowback mechanism

BALLESTER-MOLINA

Production of this Argentine pistol began in 1938 to provide the police with a cheap, locally produced weapon that was easy to use and quick to fire. It was later adopted by the military and remained in production until 1953. The Argentine armed forces continued to be equipped with this pistol as a sidearm well into the 1980s. This particular example is a training pistol that has been rechambered to take a .22 cartridge instead of the more powerful .45 of the service model. The much lower recoil allows recruits to get used to handling the gun before progressing to the .45.

Like all Ballester-Molina weapons, this example is stamped "HAFDASA," the initials of the manufacturing company that produced the pistols— Hispano Argentina Fábrica de Automotores SA.

Magazine—service model holds seven .45 cartridges

RED ARMY OFFICER CORPS

From the earliest days of Communist rule in Russia, the Red Army was the leading armed force of the Soviet state. Such a powerful organization had to be politically loyal to the state, but there was a latent suspicion among top Communists that army officers might harbor elitist and unreliable attitudes. To counter this, every unit from company to division had a political commissar whose job was to educate the men in Communist theory and to keep an eye on the commanding officer for signs of non-Communist views. Every officer had to be careful what he said or did, which tended to hamper operational effectiveness. In 1934, Soviet leader Josef Stalin (right) began a purge of army officers. The aim was to remove from command positions anyone who did not slavishly follow the lead set by Stalin and his clique of senior Communists. Tens of thousands of officers were removed from the army and sent to menial civilian jobs, while thousands were executed without trial by the NKVD secret police. Exactly how many officers were killed is not known, but up to 10 percent of officers lost their jobs. The impact on the operational efficiency of the Red Army was immense.

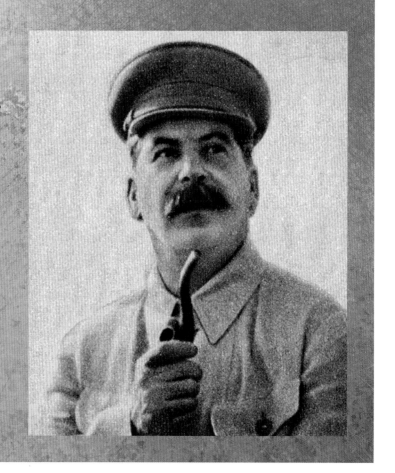

SPECIALIZED WEAPONS

World War I was fought between large armies in which equipment was more or less homogenous—one infantry regiment had weapons broadly similar to those of the next. World War II saw a more diverse selection of weapons being taken to combat. In large part this was due to the diversification of troop types away from the infantry-artillery-cavalry trio that had dominated battlefields for centuries. By 1939, there were tank crews, motorized infantry, bicycle troops, and a host of other new varieties of fighting forces, all of which needed equipment specialized for their newly developed roles.

GERMAN WHIP

This whip was used by German guards at prisoner of war and concentration camps. The Germans usually respected the Geneva Convention when it came to treatment of western prisoners, but as the Soviet Union had never ratified the Convention, the Germans felt justified in delivering appalling treatment to captives from the east. Around 3.5 million of the 8.75 million Russian prisoners taken by the Germans died in captivity.

Handle

Leather thongs

BOOBY TRAP PISTOL

Developed by the British, this weapon was designed to be left behind by retreating troops. It was buried in the ground so that the barrel pointed upward. The weapon discharged when stepped on, shooting a bullet vertically upward through the foot and perhaps into the body of the unfortunate victim.

Barrel   Shaft

ITALIAN FASCIST PARTY KNIFE

This official blackshirt knife is a 1937 model with the eagle's beak facing the back of the blade. The fasces, which was the insignia of Mussolini's Fascist Party, is set into the handle. Both this and the eagle were borrowed from Ancient Rome, the glories of which Mussolini hoped to emulate.

Eagle head

Fasces

Cheek rest

GERMAN SNIPER RIFLE

The gunsmiths of Germany had a long tradition of making rifles for hunting boar, deer, and other game. These weapons often featured decorated metal parts and a broad cheek rest on the shoulder stock. This example was made for Nazi leader Heinrich Himmler, who, as head of the SS, played a leading role in the Holocaust.

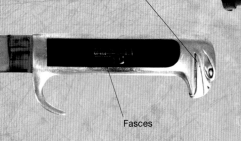

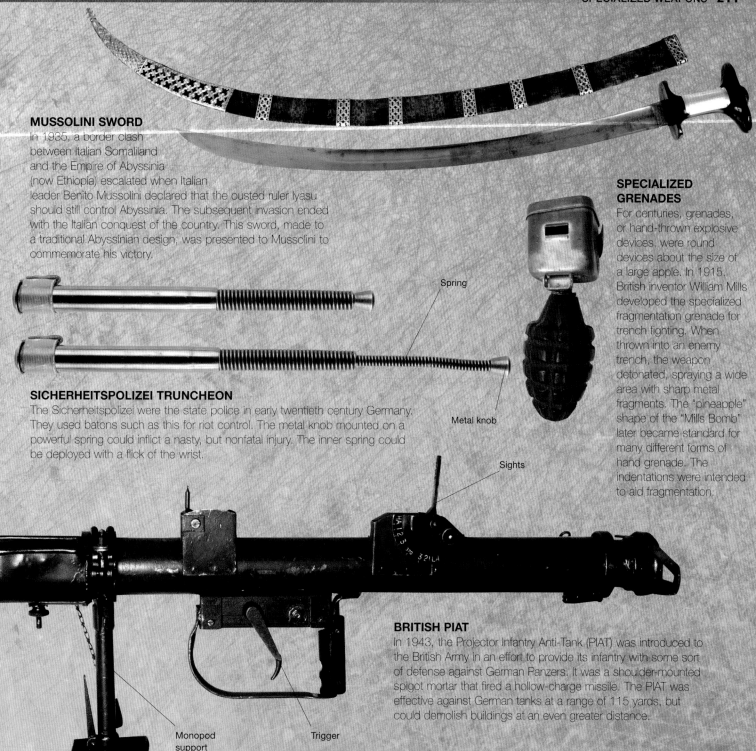

MUSSOLINI SWORD

In 1935, a border clash between Italian Somaliland and the Empire of Abyssinia (now Ethiopia) escalated when Italian leader Benito Mussolini declared that the ousted ruler Iyasu should still control Abyssinia. The subsequent invasion ended with the Italian conquest of the country. This sword, made to a traditional Abyssinian design, was presented to Mussolini to commemorate his victory.

Spring

Metal knob

SICHERHEITSPOLIZEI TRUNCHEON

The Sicherheitspolizei were the state police in early twentieth century Germany. They used batons such as this for riot control. The metal knob mounted on a powerful spring could inflict a nasty, but nonfatal injury. The inner spring could be deployed with a flick of the wrist.

SPECIALIZED GRENADES

For centuries, grenades, or hand-thrown explosive devices, were round devices about the size of a large apple. In 1915, British inventor William Mills developed the specialized fragmentation grenade for trench fighting. When thrown into an enemy trench, the weapon detonated, spraying a wide area with sharp metal fragments. The "pineapple" shape of the "Mills Bomb" later became standard for many different forms of hand grenade. The indentations were intended to aid fragmentation.

Sights

BRITISH PIAT

In 1943, the Projector Infantry Anti-Tank (PIAT) was introduced to the British Army in an effort to provide its infantry with some sort of defense against German Panzers. It was a shoulder-mounted spigot mortar that fired a hollow-charge missile. The PIAT was effective against German tanks at a range of 115 yards, but could demolish buildings at an even greater distance.

Monopod support

Trigger

RIFLE GRENADES

The idea of firing a grenade from a rifle originated in the early twentieth century. The British had a grenade mounted on a rod that was launched using a blank cartridge as early as 1907, but production problems meant it saw little service in World War I. By World War II, a wide variety of projectiles (some shown here) were available to infantry of all nations to discharge from their rifles using either blank charges or attachments.

Front sight

AXIS PISTOLS OF WORLD WAR II

World War II could be better described as two major conflicts fought between loosely linked alliances. In the Pacific, a war was fought between Japan on one side against China, Australia, the United States, Britain, and New Zealand. In Europe, the hostilities pitted Germany and its allies of Italy, Romania, Slovakia, Croatia, Albania, Hungary, and Bulgaria against France, Britain, Denmark, Belgium, the Netherlands, Norway, Poland, Russia, the United States and a host of smaller nations. The Axis was a loose grouping of Japan with Germany and her allies, but was never a formal military alliance with shared strategic aims and practical cooperation. Other than the fact that Germany and her allies faced some of the same enemies as Japan, the Axis had little real operational meaning.

ARTILLERY LUGER

The Luger pistol of the German Army was a popular civilian pistol in the interwar years. During World War I, a version for artillery officers had been produced with an elongated 7.8-inch barrel and detachable wooden shoulder stock. After the war ended this was marketed as a carbine-pistol combination and enjoyed good sales. In 1930, a new version with a 12-inch barrel was produced, having adjustable rear sights calibrated up to 2,625 feet. This example is shown without the wooden shoulder stock that came with all such weapons.

Adjustable rear sights

12-inch barrel

Magazine holds eight cartridges

5.3-inch barrel

SPANISH ASTRA 600 PISTOL

The Spanish company Astra-Unceta produced a range of pistols in the 1920s, 1930s, and 1940s that were based on a blowback mechanism and the 9mm Largo cartridge. Although available in various models, the Astra series were all fairly heavy handguns, which were mass produced to be rugged and reliable rather than complex or accurate. This example is an Astra 600, which was made in 1943 for export to Germany to be used by the police.

Magazine holds eight cartridges

3.8-inch barrel

NAMBU TYPE 94

The Type 94 grew out of a requirement by the Japanese Army for a small, light pistol to be used by tank and aircraft crews. Work began in 1924, but it was not until 1935 that the weapon entered production. Despite this surprisingly long design process, the pistol was not particularly good and suffered from problems such as accidental firing and a complex cleaning procedure.

Box magazine holds six cartridges

3.4-inch barrel

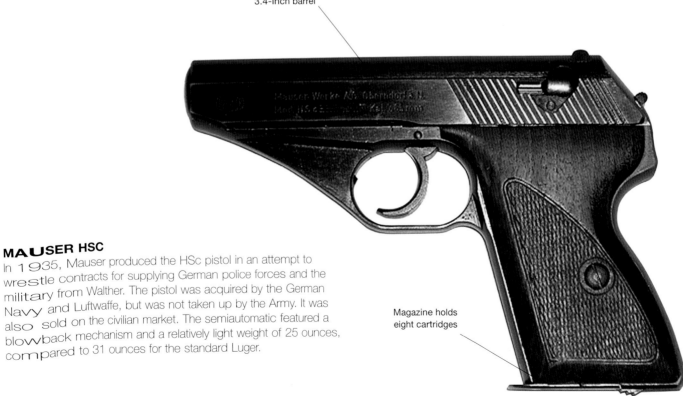

MAUSER HSC

In 1935, Mauser produced the HSc pistol in an attempt to wrestle contracts for supplying German police forces and the military from Walther. The pistol was acquired by the German Navy and Luftwaffe, but was not taken up by the Army. It was also sold on the civilian market. The semiautomatic featured a blowback mechanism and a relatively light weight of 25 ounces, compared to 31 ounces for the standard Luger.

Magazine holds eight cartridges

WORLD WAR II RIFLES

When World War II began, opinions were divided among military experts as to the best role of the rifle on the battlefield. Experience of trench warfare had shown that long-range accuracy was no longer necessary, while an ability to still function when exposed to mud and damp was more important than ever. The successes of tanks and aircraft in the later stages of World War I had convinced some that trench warfare was a thing of the past. However, if war was again to be fought in a fluid and mobile fashion, long-range rifle fire could return to being a vital component in battle. This thinking fed into rifle design for some armed forces. Nevertheless, many nations chose to retain their rifles as they were, with some simply upgrading them to include modern manufacturing techniques.

20-inch barrel

Cleaning rod

RUSSIAN M1944 CARBINE

The Mosin-Nagant design was already 50 years old when World War II began, but the Russians continued to manufacture and refine it. The M1944 Carbine version shown here was designed for use by rear echelon and noncombat troops. It had a considerably shorter barrel than other Mosin-Nagants and featured a permanently affixed bayonet that was stored alongside the wooden stock—the blade could be swung forwards and locked into place for use.

Bolt action

19.2-inch barrel

JAPANESE TYPE 38

When Japan went into World War II it was still using the Type 38 rifle that had entered service in 1906, although it had been refined and upgraded. The Japanese Army was, however, in the process of introducing a new weapon, as the Type 38 used the underpowered 6.5x50mm Arisaka cartridge, and was not considered to be a match for U.S. weapons. Shown here is the carbine version.

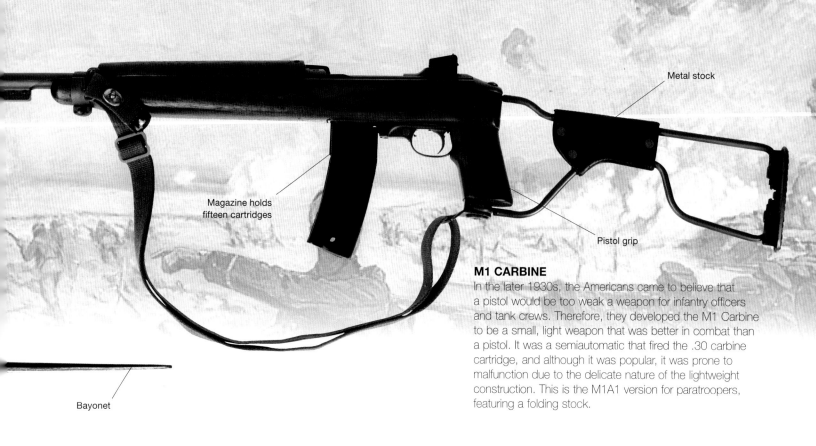

Metal stock

Magazine holds
fifteen cartridges

Pistol grip

Bayonet

M1 CARBINE

In the later 1930s, the Americans came to believe that
a pistol would be too weak a weapon for infantry officers
and tank crews. Therefore, they developed the M1 Carbine
to be a small, light weapon that was better in combat than
a pistol. It was a semiautomatic that fired the .30 carbine
cartridge, and although it was popular, it was prone to
malfunction due to the delicate nature of the lightweight
construction. This is the M1A1 version for paratroopers,
featuring a folding stock.

25.8-inch barrel

Magazine holds
five cartridges

JAPANESE TYPE 99

Designed in 1939, the Type 99 was starting to replace the
Type 38 when Japan attacked Pearl Harbor in December
1941. This example is shown with the wire monopod and
anti-aircraft sights that came with some early versions. After
being supported on the monopod, the soldier would adjust
the sights while aiming at an enemy aircraft.

Grip

PHILIPPINE HUCK GUN

This basic, makeshift gun was made by Richardson Industries
of Connecticut for use by the anti-Japanese guerrillas active in
the Philippines. The simple mechanism was designed to be
cheap to produce and easy to maintain. There were minimum
working parts, so the gun is fired by jerking back on the forward
grip to ram the cartridge against the firing pin.

Wooden stock

WORLD WAR II RIFLES

23-inch barrel

Iron sights

Magazine holds
five cartridges

CZECH VZ.24

As part of the Treaty of Versailles in 1918, Germany was not allowed
to manufacture rifles, though carbines were permitted. Production of
the famous Mauser rifles was moved outside Germany, with a slightly
redesigned Gewehr 98 reappearing as the Czech-made vz.24. The
rifle was sold to the Bolivian, Lithuanian, and Spanish armies, and
became a valuable export for Czechoslovakia.

Bolt action

Cleaning rod

HANYANG 88

First produced in 1897, the Chinese Hanyang 88 continued in production until 1947,
by which time more than a million had been made. The rifle was commissioned by the
Qing Dynasty from its Hanyang armory, and was based on the German Gewehr 88—
hence its name. It was accurate to 550 yards and could reach well over a mile.

Magazine holds
five cartridges

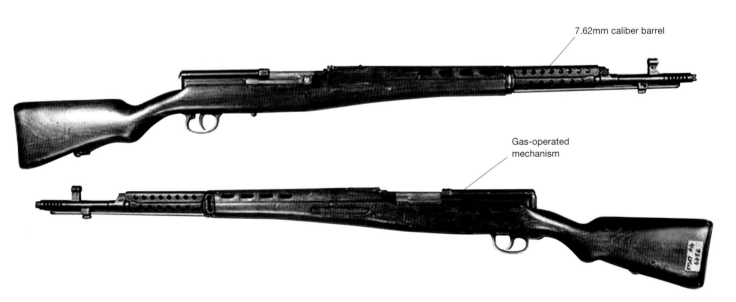

7.62mm caliber barrel

Gas-operated
mechanism

SOVIET SVT-40

In the summer of 1941, the Soviet Red Army planned to replace the aging Mosin-Nagant infantry
rifle with a new semiautomatic weapon featuring a ten-round magazine—the SVT-40. However,
the sudden German offensive that year, and the damage to industrial plants, forced the move to
be delayed. More than a million SVT-40s were made, but in combat the rifle was found to be
inaccurate and often jammed due to dirt getting in the mechanism. The Red Army ordered
production to cease and reverted to the Mosin-Nagant design.

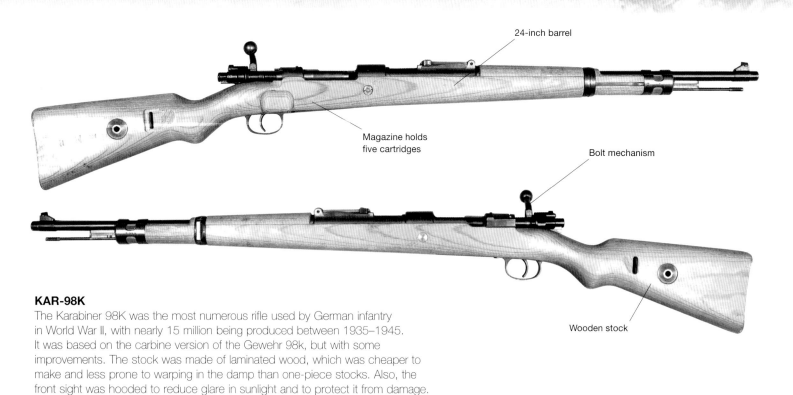

24-inch barrel

Magazine holds
five cartridges

Bolt mechanism

Wooden stock

KAR-98K

The Karabiner 98K was the most numerous rifle used by German infantry
in World War II, with nearly 15 million being produced between 1935–1945.
It was based on the carbine version of the Gewehr 98k, but with some
improvements. The stock was made of laminated wood, which was cheaper to
make and less prone to warping in the damp than one-piece stocks. Also, the
front sight was hooded to reduce glare in sunlight and to protect it from damage.

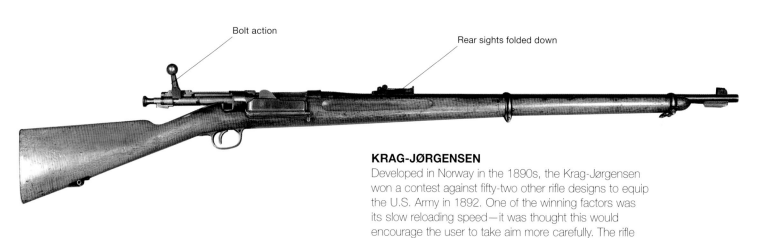

Bolt action

Rear sights folded down

KRAG-JØRGENSEN

Developed in Norway in the 1890s, the Krag-Jørgensen
won a contest against fifty-two other rifle designs to equip
the U.S. Army in 1892. One of the winning factors was
its slow reloading speed—it was thought this would
encourage the user to take aim more carefully. The rifle
was produced in several variants for the U.S. Army,
including a rifle with a 30-inch barrel, a carbine with a
22-inch barrel and a sniper rifle with telescopic sights.
The gun shown here is the original 1892 rifle variant.

PLAUSIBLE DENIABILITY

In 1959, the North Vietnamese Communist Party
(known as the Viet Cong, its flag pictured right)
launched an armed struggle against the South
Vietnamese government. The Soviet Union was keen
to help the Viet Cong, but did not want to be actively
seen doing so. The answer came in the vast stocks of
KAR-98K rifles that the Red Army had captured at
the end of World War II. These were brought out of
storage, refurbished, and in many cases their identifying
marks were filed off. They were then sent to North
Vietnam for the Viet Cong. The Soviets denied that
they had sent the weapons and, given the lack of
identifying marks, this denial was superficially plausible.

WORLD WAR II RIFLES

Gas-operated mechanism

21.5-inch barrel

GEWEHR 43

After the failure of the Gewehr 41 to cope with the rigors of battle, Walther modified its design—it took elements of the Russian SVT-40 to produce the superior Gewehr 43. A new ten-round detachable magazine greatly speeded up the reloading process compared to the fixed five-round magazine of the previous model. About 400,000 entered combat before the end of the war.

Rear sights at rear of receiver

Chambered for the .30-06 Springfield cartridge

M1917 ENFIELD

Sometimes called the P1917, the M1917 was an American version of the British Enfield No.3 Rifle that was manufactured in vast numbers late in World War I, and that remained in use until the Vietnam War. When the United States entered World War II, it brought the M1917 out of storage to equip artillerymen and troops at the rear. Large quantities had been shipped to the Philippines in the 1930s, and these were captured—and then used—by the Japanese.

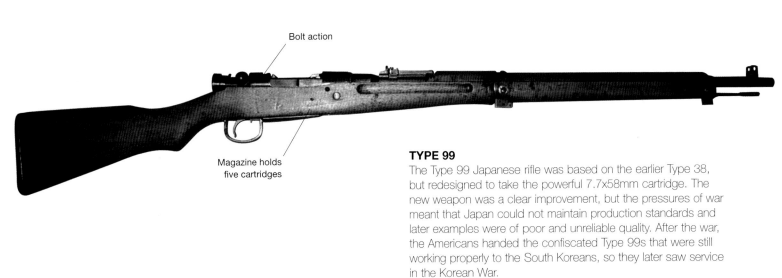

Bolt action

Magazine holds five cartridges

TYPE 99

The Type 99 Japanese rifle was based on the earlier Type 38, but redesigned to take the powerful 7.7x58mm cartridge. The new weapon was a clear improvement, but the pressures of war meant that Japan could not maintain production standards and later examples were of poor and unreliable quality. After the war, the Americans handed the confiscated Type 99s that were still working properly to the South Koreans, so they later saw service in the Korean War.

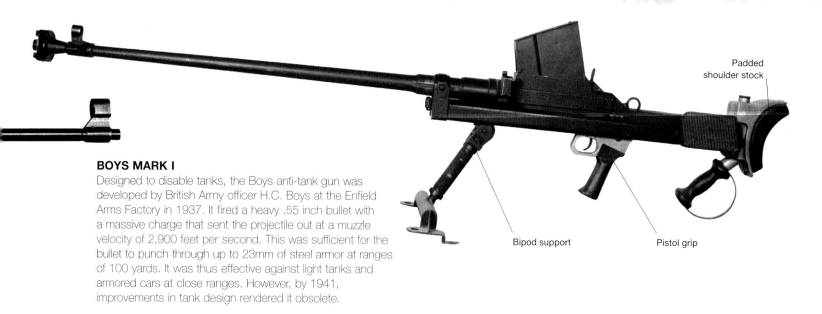

Padded shoulder stock

BOYS MARK I

Designed to disable tanks, the Boys anti-tank gun was developed by British Army officer H.C. Boys at the Enfield Arms Factory in 1937. It fired a heavy .55 inch bullet with a massive charge that sent the projectile out at a muzzle velocity of 2,900 feet per second. This was sufficient for the bullet to punch through up to 23mm of steel armor at ranges of 100 yards. It was thus effective against light tanks and armored cars at close ranges. However, by 1941, improvements in tank design rendered it obsolete.

Bipod support

Pistol grip

Bolt action

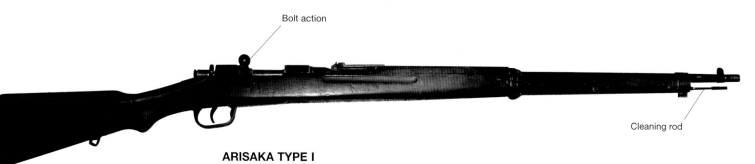

Cleaning rod

ARISAKA TYPE I

In the late 1930s, the Japanese were looking to replace their Type 38 Rifle that had been in production since 1905. The Type I was a minor upgrade that was contracted out to Italy for production. The outbreak of war came when only a few had been delivered; the rest were stranded in Italy. The few that had been shipped to Japan were given to Japanese marines.

A CASE OF MISTAKEN IDENTITY

During the retreat to Dunkirk in 1940, some British soldiers using the Boys anti-tank rifle reported that they had knocked out Panzer IIIs. This convinced the British that German tank design was not particularly advanced and saw them keep the Boys in frontline use. In fact, the Panzers that had been destroyed were Panzer IIs, which had only 20mm of armor, while the Panzer III had 30mm of armor and could not be penetrated by the Boys or similar weapons. It was a simple case of mistaken identity in the heat of battle, but one that caused British troops to remain equipped with obsolete anti-tank weapons for far longer than was sensible. Pictured is a preserved Panzer II in simulated action during a re-enactment in Poland.

WORLD WAR II RIFLES

Chambered for standard
8.50mm Lebel ammunition

Magazine holds
five cartridges

RSC M1917

The Fusil Automatique Modele 1917 was a semiautomatic rifle that entered service with the French Army in the closing months of World War I and saw limited use in World War II. The rifle was accurate, fast firing, and easy to use. However, it was removed from service after 1923 because the automatic reloading system was prone to foul after about 100 firings, and was difficult to take apart for cleaning.

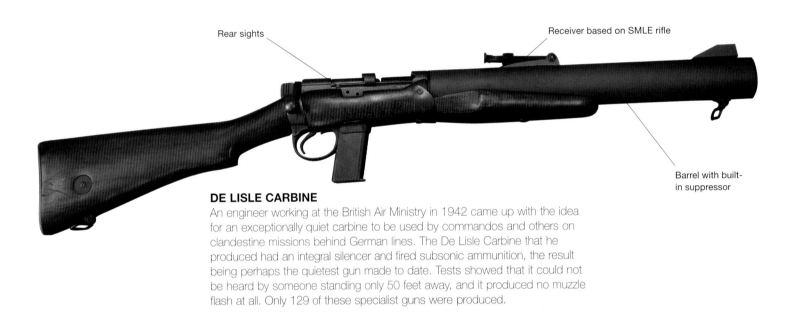

Rear sights

Receiver based on SMLE rifle

Barrel with built-in suppressor

DE LISLE CARBINE

An engineer working at the British Air Ministry in 1942 came up with the idea for an exceptionally quiet carbine to be used by commandos and others on clandestine missions behind German lines. The De Lisle Carbine that he produced had an integral silencer and fired subsonic ammunition, the result being perhaps the quietest gun made to date. Tests showed that it could not be heard by someone standing only 50 feet away, and it produced no muzzle flash at all. Only 129 of these specialist guns were produced.

Short 18-inch barrel

Muzzle shroud

JUNGLE CARBINE

The official name of the British Jungle Carbine was the Rifle No.5 Mk I. It was based on the paratroop carbine version of the basic British Lee-Enfield rifle, and entered production in 1944. It had a shorter barrel than normal and the wooden stock and various metal components were reduced in size to make the gun lighter. This made the gun effective in confined spaces and quick to use, but also made it considerably less accurate than the rifle on which it was based. About 250,000 were made and it remained in use into the 1960s.

THE COMMANDOS

In June 1940, France surrendered and Britain stood alone against Germany. Prime Minister Winston Churchill demanded that a force should be set up to launch raids against German-occupied Europe. His aim was both to stop the Germans from relaxing their guard, and to provide a morale boost for the beleaguered British public. The result was the Commandos, a force that was trained in amphibious assault, parachute drops, and clandestine operations. The first raid took place on the French coast at Le Touquet on June 23, 1940, with two Germans killed and no British losses. The first major raid came in December 1941 when 300 men landed on the Lofoten Islands to destroy German ships, radio stations, and meteorology facilities. Between 1940 and 1944, nearly one hundred commando raids were carried out, involving anywhere from 2 to 2,000 men. It has been estimated that the Germans deployed an extra 100,000 troops on coastguard duties to counter the Commando threat. After the war, most Commando units were disbanded, although the Royal Marines Commando and No.2 Commando (now the Parachute Regiment) were retained. Pictured right is the Commando Monument, which overlooks the British Commandos' World War II training ground near Achnacarry Castle, Scotland.

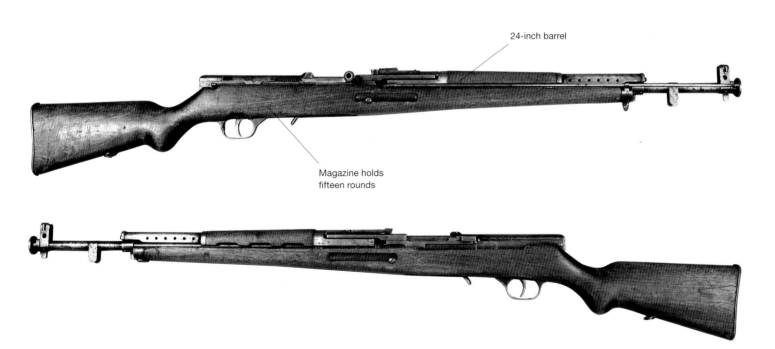

24-inch barrel

Magazine holds
fifteen rounds

AVS-36

The Avtomaticheskaya Vintovka Simonova 1936 model, or AVS-36, was the first attempt by the Soviet Union to produce a semiautomatic rifle for the Red Army. It was developed by Sergei Simonov in the early 1930s and went into production in 1936. Only a few thousand were made before production was stopped in 1938. Tests in the field had shown that dirt entered the rifle easily and caused it to jam, and the weapon was almost uncontrollable when the continuous fire option was selected.

WORLD WAR II RIFLES

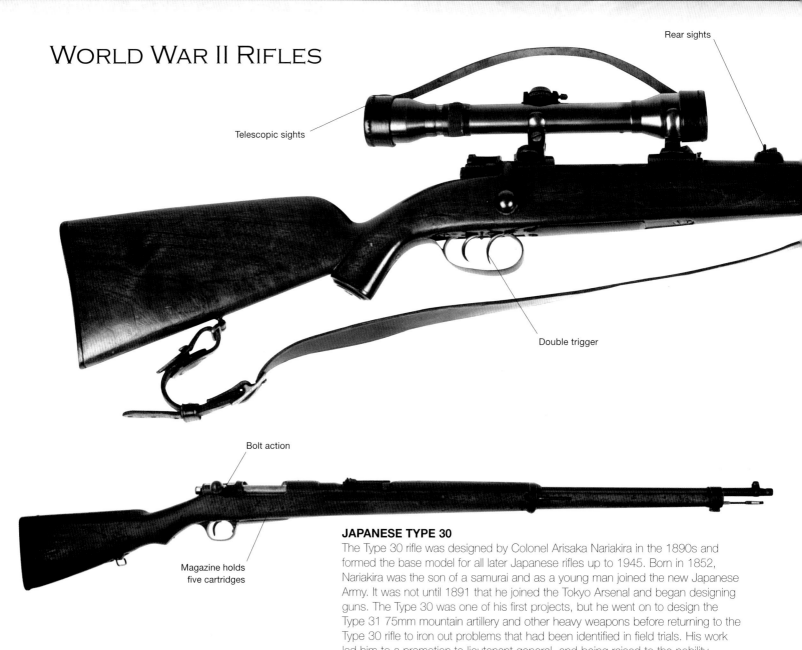

Rear sights

Telescopic sights

Double trigger

Bolt action

Magazine holds
five cartridges

JAPANESE TYPE 30

The Type 30 rifle was designed by Colonel Arisaka Nariakira in the 1890s and formed the base model for all later Japanese rifles up to 1945. Born in 1852, Nariakira was the son of a samurai and as a young man joined the new Japanese Army. It was not until 1891 that he joined the Tokyo Arsenal and began designing guns. The Type 30 was one of his first projects, but he went on to design the Type 31 75mm mountain artillery and other heavy weapons before returning to the Type 30 rifle to iron out problems that had been identified in field trials. His work led him to a promotion to lieutenant general, and being raised to the nobility.

Iron sights

Open-sided magazine
holds twenty cartridges

The Breda PG's unusual magazine had open sides that allowed the user to check how many cartridges remained. Unfortunately, it allowed dirt in, which caused an unacceptable level of jamming.

BREDA PG AUTOMATIC RIFLE

The Italian engineering company Breda Meccanica Bresciana was founded by Ernesto Breda in 1886 to make railway equipment, but during World War I it made gun parts for Fiat. After the war, the company began making weapons on its own, and it was soon experimenting with semiautomatic and automatic weapons. The PG Automatic Rifle was produced in 1935 and is best known for being the first weapon to have a selector switch so the user could chose to fire a single shot, a burst of four shots, or to use continuous fire. Although innovative, the weapon was not particularly successful and only 300 were ever made.

Front sight

GERMAN SNIPER RIFLE

This rifle was taken from a German sniper by an American officer during the Battle of the Bulge late in 1944. It is a prewar 7.92mm Mauser civilian hunting rifle that has been fitted with a Hensoldt Dialytan 4x telescopic sight. The Germans used civilian rifles for sniping because the standard KAR-98K infantry rifle could not easily mount a telescopic sight. The bolt handle traveled high over the breech when it was lifted and pulled back; civilian rifles had a lower movement on the bolt handle. The shoulder stock was fitted with a rubber buttplate to stop the weapon from slipping when in action.

The Hensoldt Dialytan 4x telescopic sight was usually set to an elevation of 300 meters by the sniper, who would then aim lower or higher to take account of shorter or greater distances.

EMERGENCY FIREPOWER

In June 1940, France surrendered to Germany and Britain was alone to fight. The government formed a local militia, the Home Guard (right), composed of older men, teenage boys, and those not yet called up. At first, they brought their own weapons—shotguns, pistols, and carving knives tied to broom handles. Then, the U.S. sent stocks of M1917 rifles (below) used in World War I that had been brought out of storage to be reconditioned for use. The metal parts were sandblasted to remove the rust patina that many had acquired; they were then parkerized, a process that involved coating the metal in zinc phosphate to prevent corrosion. Many weapons required new stocks and some needed new parts. More than 700,000 reconditioned M1917 rifles were sent to Britain for use by the Home Guard and rear echelon units. After the war, they were passed on to Denmark and Norway as temporary weapons until their reformed armies could be re-equipped. By the mid-1950s, the weapon had been taken out of service.

MORTARS OF WORLD WAR II

The modern mortar was developed during World War I, originating with a design by retired engineer Wilfred Stokes in 1915. The weapon consists of a light metal tube that can be set at an angle of 45 or 85 degrees, supported by two or three legs. At the bottom of the tube is a firing pin. When a mortar bomb is dropped down the tube, the pin sets off a charge on the base of the bomb. This propels the bomb back up the tube, firing it at a high angle to then descend almost vertically onto its target. The mortar can fire high–explosive bombs, star shells, or incendiary ammunition. Its mobility, high firepower, and ability to shoot over intervening obstacles have made it a popular infantry support weapon ever since it was originally developed to fire from one trench into another.

BRIXIA MODEL 35

This Italian mortar was designed to be a quick-firing weapon, propelling small bombs at the enemy with bewildering speed. Every Italian infantry battalion had nine of these weapons, plus a healthy supply of shells. The men operating the Brixia underwent intense training so that they could fire ten bombs per minute with great accuracy over ranges of up to 500 yards.

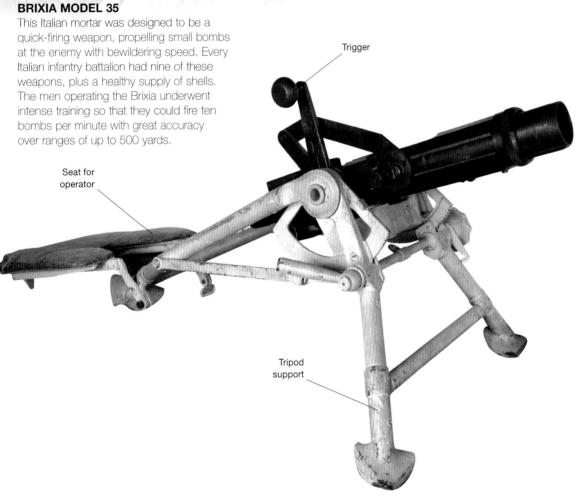

Trigger

Seat for operator

Tripod support

Shortened barrel

Base plate

AIRBORNE MORTAR

In 1940, the British were deeply impressed by the success of German paratroops and glider-borne troops during the invasion of France and the Low Countries. Prime Minister Churchill ordered the British Army to form a 5,000-strong airborne brigade, and the new unit was ready for action by February 1942. One problem that had to be solved was the lack of artillery that could be carried by glider. The answer came in the form of a new variant of the standard infantry 2-inch mortar—the Mk VIII pictured here. The barrel was reduced in length and made of thinner metal, while the supports were discarded in favor of handles so an operator could hold it in position while it was fired.

MODEL 89 GRENADE LAUNCHER

The Japanese Type 89 was designed to launch a standard infantry grenade at the enemy. When used in this way, the grenade was first fitted with a propellant base that detonated when dropped down the barrel and projected the grenade through the air. As the grenade was launched, its time fuse was set off so that it would explode within two seconds of landing. The weapon made a distinctive popping sound, and Allied troops soon learned to dive for cover when they heard the noise.

Rifled barrel

Base plate

FINNISH MORTAR

This Finnish 47 KRH 41 mortar was a trial weapon—only 50 were made. It saw service during the Winter War against Russia in 1939, but was never put into full-scale production. The lightweight weapon was designed to be slung over the shoulder by one man, while a second man carried the boxes holding ten shells each on shoulder straps. The 47 KRH 41 was reliable and easy to use, but the small 47mm shells proved to be relatively ineffective.

Base spike

Bipod supports

Traversing wheel

Base plate

M2 MORTAR

The American M2 Mortar was produced in high quantities from 1940 and saw extensive service throughout World War II and the Korean War. Based on a French design, it had a caliber of 60mm and could fire high-explosive, smoke, or illumination rounds. The M2 had a maximum range of 2,000 yards, considerably greater than most contemporary mortars, and could traverse 7 degrees without needing to be repositioned. These factors combined to make the weapon more effective as an infantry support weapon than its specifications might have suggested.

Bipod supports

Elevation screw

MACHINE GUNS OF WORLD WAR II

The dominant machine guns of World War I had been heavy, water–cooled weapons that were able to fire thousands of rounds over extended periods of time without malfunction, but they were cumbersome and heavy to move. In the static conditions of trench warfare, these weapons proved to be ideal. However, between the wars most armies expected future combat to be more mobile than in World War I, so machine guns that needed crews of six or eight men to carry them were deemed unsuitable except for defending permanent bases and buildings. Instead, most armies were keen for machine guns that were light enough to be carried by one man, usually with a second person to carry the ammunition. This would ensure that the weapon could keep up with a marching infantry regiment.

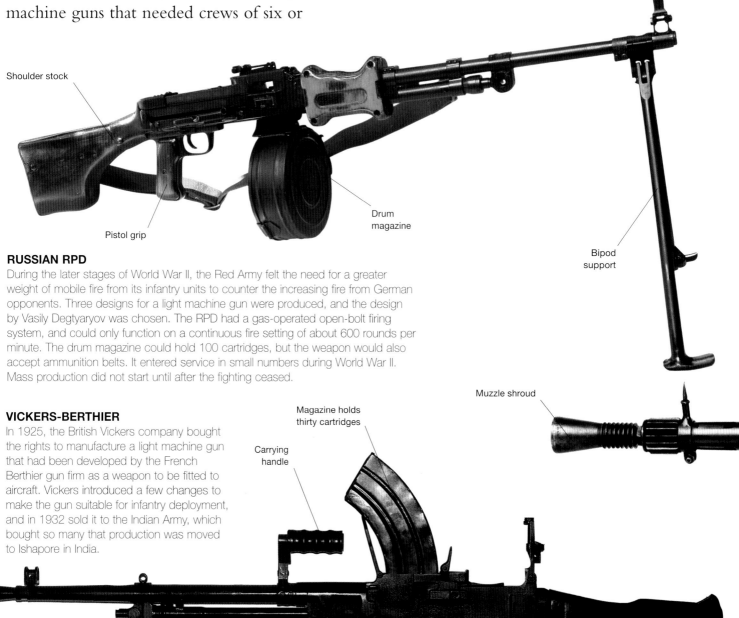

Shoulder stock

Pistol grip

Drum magazine

Bipod support

Muzzle shroud

RUSSIAN RPD

During the later stages of World War II, the Red Army felt the need for a greater weight of mobile fire from its infantry units to counter the increasing fire from German opponents. Three designs for a light machine gun were produced, and the design by Vasily Degtyaryov was chosen. The RPD had a gas-operated open-bolt firing system, and could only function on a continuous fire setting of about 600 rounds per minute. The drum magazine could hold 100 cartridges, but the weapon would also accept ammunition belts. It entered service in small numbers during World War II. Mass production did not start until after the fighting ceased.

VICKERS-BERTHIER

In 1925, the British Vickers company bought the rights to manufacture a light machine gun that had been developed by the French Berthier gun firm as a weapon to be fitted to aircraft. Vickers introduced a few changes to make the gun suitable for infantry deployment, and in 1932 sold it to the Indian Army, which bought so many that production was moved to Ishapore in India.

Magazine holds thirty cartridges

Carrying handle

Bipod support

INDIAN ARMY

During British rule in India, there was an Indian Army that was quite distinct from the British Army. At first, the Indian Army was controlled by the East India Company and formed into three separate forces, each located on one of the company's main bases at Madras, Bengal, and Bombay. When the company was disbanded and the British government took over, the three armies continued until 1895 when they were unified into a single Indian Army. There were also twenty-one Princely States that each had its own military force. Though the Indian Army was staffed mostly by British officers, it was a separate entity and bought its own weapons. Several British manufacturers specialized in supplying the Indian Army, which required weapons that would work in hot, dusty conditions quite unlike the cold, muddy environment in Europe. Given the mountainous terrain of India's north and northwest where many troops were based, the Indian Army also tended to favor smaller, lightweight weapons, and chose artillery that could be easily dismantled and transported on mules. Pictured below is the Delhi Durbar of 1911, where King George V was presented as Emperor of India.

BROWNING M1919

The M1919 was a medium machine gun introduced after World War I to provide support to U.S. infantry, but it was also used on aircraft and mounted on vehicles. Browning marketed the gun as requiring only a two-man crew— one to carry and fire the gun, the other to carry the ammunition and feed it into the weapon. However, in practice it was soon found that four men were needed as the gun was so heavy that two men soon grew tired and were unable to keep up with marching infantry.

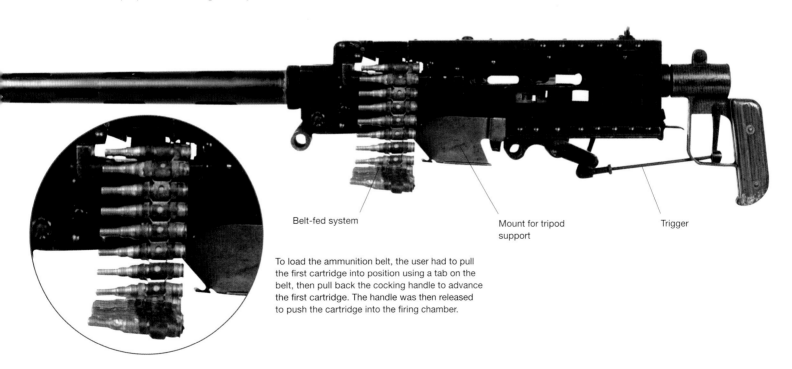

Belt-fed system

Mount for tripod support

Trigger

To load the ammunition belt, the user had to pull the first cartridge into position using a tab on the belt, then pull back the cocking handle to advance the first cartridge. The handle was then released to push the cartridge into the firing chamber.

MACHINE GUNS OF WORLD WAR II

Bipod support folded
forward for carrying

Shoulder stock

Pistol grip

KG M/40

This Swedish light machine gun was rushed into production in 1940 when the
Swedish Army found its usual sources of weaponry cut off by the outbreak of World
War II. The design was a collaboration between German Hans Lauf and two Swedes,
Ivar Staeck and Torsten Lindfors—Lauf secured the patent in Germany, with the two
others acquiring the Swedish patent. The gun was gas operated and could fire at
a rate of 480 rounds per minute from a side-mounted twenty-cartridge magazine.

Carrying handle

Magazine holds thirty
cartridges; also available
with twenty or 100 cartridges

BREN GUN

The Bren gun was the British machine gun that saw most
action during World War II. Each infantry platoon had six
Brens, with three platoons to a company, and five or six
companies to a battalion. The role of the Bren was to lay
down additional firepower to support the rifle-armed infantry.
The Bren required a crew of two men: the gunner, who
carried the gun and fired it, plus the loader, who carried the
ammunition, spare barrel, and maintenance kit. However,
everyone was expected to play his role, so each man was
given two magazines to carry. British soldiers were trained
to fire the gun while lying down, while Australians fired it
from the hip with the gun slung from a shoulder strap.

Pistol grip

Barrel

Drum magazine

Trigger

REIBEL MACHINE GUN

The Reibel was a heavy machine gun adopted by the French for use against tanks or in fixed defensive positions. It had a side-mounted drum magazine holding 150 7.5x54mm cartridges that could be fired at a rate of 750 rounds per minute. It fired in continuous mode only, and was gas operated with an open-bolt firing mechanism. The Reibel is perhaps best known as the weapon positioned in the Maginot Line on France's border with Germany to repel enemy infantry. Each position in the Maginot Line was surrounded by an area 800 yards wide—all bushes, trees, and other cover was removed to provide a clear zone across which carefully sited Reibels would sweep.

Bipod
support

1937 PATTERN WEBBING

In 1937, the British Army introduced a new style of infantry webbing to specifically match the Bren gun. The webbing was made of cotton-woven straps that were waterproofed, dyed khaki, and featured fixtures made of stamped brass. The basic layout was a waist belt plus two shoulder straps, with cross belts to keep the main straps in position. To the webbing were attached a water bottle, bayonet sheath, rifle and Bren gun ammunition pouches, grenade clips, and a general-purpose pouch. The large pack could be carried on the back, as could an entrenching tool, though these were more usually transported on a truck. This style of webbing remained in use by British and Empire troops throughout World War II. Here, a museum model wears the standard World War II webbing.

Machine Guns of World War II

DEGTYARYOV MACHINE GUN

When Vasily Degtyaryov was designing this machine gun for the Soviet Red Army in 1928, he had in mind its ease and cost of manufacture, and robustness in action. The manufacturing aims were achieved by the weapon having only 80 parts—most of them able to be stamped rather than machined—while wide tolerances of component design made it durable. To test if the gun would be reliable in the dirty, difficult conditions of campaign, Degtyaryov buried the prototype in mud overnight, then dug it up and pulled the trigger—it fired perfectly the first time.

Sights

Pan magazine holds sixty cartridges

In World War II, Red Army soldiers found that the swivel joint between the bipod mount and the gun was fragile and broke easily—during the Battle of Stalingrad, nearly all Degtyaryovs lost their bipods.

CHE GUEVARA

The South American Marxist revolutionary Ernesto "Che" Guevara habitually used the M1941 Johnson machine gun in combat. Born in Argentina in 1928, Guevara initially intended to become a doctor, but he abandoned his studies for radical politics. After meeting Fidel Castro in Mexico, Guevara agreed to join their bid to start a Marxist Revolution in Cuba. During a two-year campaign, Guevara emerged as a courageous soldier, skilled tactician, and thoughtful commander. Before long, he was recognized as second only to Castro when it came to leading the Marxist struggle. After Castro took power in Cuba, Guevara was placed in command of the new Cuban Army. He also spearheaded a literacy campaign and oversaw agrarian land reform. In 1965, he left Cuba to try to initiate Marxist revolutions elsewhere around the world. After his first effort in the Republic of Congo failed, he moved to Bolivia, where he was captured and then killed by government troops.

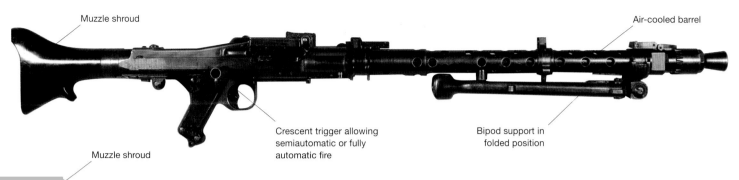

Muzzle shroud

Air-cooled barrel

Muzzle shroud

Crescent trigger allowing
semiautomatic or fully
automatic fire

Bipod support in
folded position

GERMAN MG34

The Maschinengewehr 34 was the most important German machine gun of World War II and, at the time it entered service, probably the most advanced weapon of its kind in the world. It combined a high rate of fire—900 rounds per minute—with a light weight of 26 pounds so that it could be carried by one man, though others were needed to carry the ammunition. The tactical use of the MG34 played an important role in the early German victories of World War II. One MG34 would lay down heavy fire while another pushed forward with rifle-armed infantry. Once the second gun was in position and laying down fire, the first one would be brought forwards. In this leap-frogging motion German infantry were able to rapidly outflank, outgun, and overwhelm opposing infantry in defensive positions.

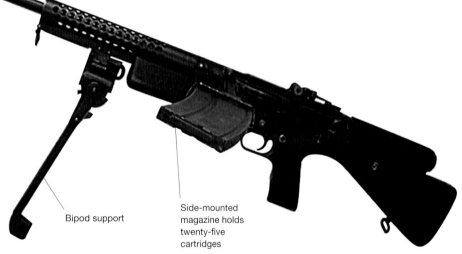

Front sight

M1941 JOHNSON

The M1941 light machine gun designed by Melvin Johnson weighed less and was more compact than other machine guns used by the U.S. military. This made it popular with the Marines and special forces, although its complex design meant that it was not acquired for the general U.S. Army. The curiously high front sight was made necessary by the layout of the gun, which had the barrel in-line with the shoulder stock—this allowed the recoil force to be transmitted straight back to the shoulder of the user, keeping the gun on target as it was fired.

Bipod support

Side-mounted
magazine holds
twenty-five
cartridges

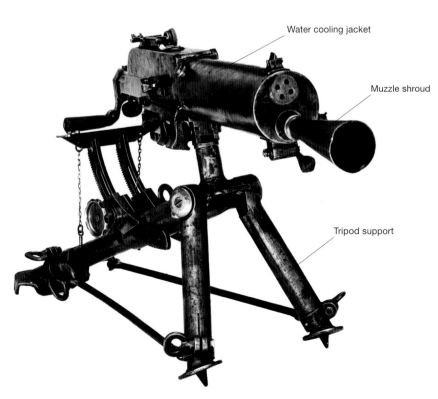

Water cooling jacket

Muzzle shroud

Tripod support

GERMAN MG08

The German MG08 was the standard machine gun used by the Kaiser's army during World War I. In German service the MG08 was generally mounted on a sled, but when used by Ottoman forces it was usually given a tripod mounting as seen here. After the war, the gun continued to be produced as the Type 24 for export to China. When World War II broke out, the Germans considered the MG08 to be obsolete, but as it existed in large numbers it was used as a static defensive gun at barracks, Luftwaffe bases, and other permanent military installations.

MACHINE GUNS OF WORLD WAR II

Water outlet valve

Slot for
ammuntion

Water cooling
jacket

Twin
handles

Elevation
screw

Tripod mounting

VICKERS MACHINE GUN

During World War I, the Vickers machine gun was initially issued to infantry
units, but it was found to be heavy and cumbersome to carry. When the
conflict stagnated into trench warfare, the Vickers was removed from infantry
units and passed to the specialist Machine Gun Corps, which had three
companies attached to each infantry division. This new arrangement allowed
the machine guns to be concentrated where they were needed rather than
being dispersed along the line. In 1922, the Corps was disbanded and the
Vickers returned to infantry units, where it remained during World War II.

Carrying handle

Shroud

Pan magazine
holds ninety-
seven cartridges

swivel mounts
for leather
carrying strap

LEWIS GUN

The most distinctive feature of the Lewis Gun was a huge
aluminum shroud that ran the entire length of the barrel and
was open at both ends. The idea was that the muzzle blast
would suck air forward through the shroud, creating a draft
that would ensure a constant flow of cool air over the barrel
and prevent it from overheating. From 1940 onward, old
aircraft guns—which lacked the shrouds—were issued
to the British Home Guard and were found to work
perfectly well. It brought into question whether the shroud
on the Lewis gun had any effect at all.

GERMAN MG13

The German MG13 was introduced in 1930 and was always something of a stopgap weapon. It was essentially an old Dreyse 18 from World War I that was stripped of its water cooling jacket and adapted to air cooling. In 1934, it was superseded as an infantry light machine gun by the MG34. Thereafter, it was mounted in pairs on the Panzer I tank and as the rear defensive armament on the Stuka dive bomber. Those surplus to requirement were sold to Portugal, where they remained in service until around 1950.

Anti-aircraft sights

Carrying handle

Padded shoulder stock

Bipod support

Pilstol grip

Ring sight

Ribbed barrel to aid cooling

Drum magazine

Swivel mount

ANTI-AIRCRAFT NAVAL MACHINE GUN

During the 1930s, it became increasingly obvious that aircraft armed with bombs would be a major threat to ships operating in coastal waters. The full scale of the threat was not accepted until 1941, but efforts were made to increase the effectiveness of naval anti-aircraft fire by installing heavy .50 machine guns on swivel mounts. These weapons proved to be ineffective against Japanese aircraft, and by the end of 1942 had been generally replaced by either 20mm Oerlikon or 40mm Bofors cannon.

Deck mounting

SUBMACHINE GUNS OF WORLD WAR II

A submachine gun is a weapon that has the automatic firing capability of a machine gun combined with a carbine-length barrel, and it also fires pistol ammunition. The weapons have a number of advantages. Their high rate of fire is advantageous in close-quarter combat, while the use of pistol rounds means that the recoil is light and the weapon can be held steady even in continuous fire mode. In addition, the carbine-length barrel offers improved accuracy. These factors made it an ideal weapon for the type of urban warfare that became such a feature of World War II. What's more, the decreased weight and small proportions of the submachine gun made it a viable alternative to the pistol for officers and NCOs.

GERMAN MP18

The MP18 was introduced in spectacular fashion when it was used in large numbers by the Sturmtruppen (Stormtroopers) who spearheaded the last major German offensive of 1918. The weapon was so effective on the field of battle that the Treaty of Versailles specifically banned the Germans from making any more. The MP18s that remained were handed to the police to use in close combat in urban areas. It was reasoned that the less-powerful ammunition of the MP18 would mean fewer innocent passersby falling victim to shootouts. Lack of spare parts meant that the number of functioning MP18s declined, and by 1939 they were restricted to the Sicherheitspolizei, the security arm of the SS, who used them in diminishing numbers until 1945.

Drum magazine holds thirty-two cartridges

Barrel sleeve to aid cooling

Cocking handle

FRENCH MAS

The 7.65mm MAS-38 was the standard French submachine gun of World War II. It was an expensive weapon to produce because nearly all the parts had to be machined. The weapon was very compact as the bolt mechanism recoiled into a tube set within the shoulder stock. This meant that the bolt had to meet the barrel at an angle—something achieved by a clever, if complex, internal design. The trigger had an unusual combination safety catch; the trigger was pushed forward to engage the safety.

Bulge housing bolt recoil tube

Detachable magazine holds thirty-two cartridges

Pistol grip

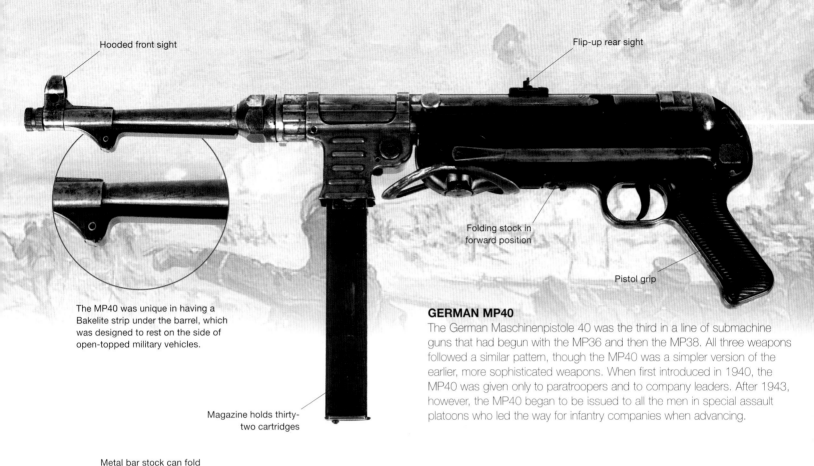

Hooded front sight

Flip-up rear sight

Folding stock in forward position

Pistol grip

The MP40 was unique in having a Bakelite strip under the barrel, which was designed to rest on the side of open-topped military vehicles.

Magazine holds thirty-two cartridges

GERMAN MP40

The German Maschinenpistole 40 was the third in a line of submachine guns that had begun with the MP36 and then the MP38. All three weapons followed a similar pattern, though the MP40 was a simpler version of the earlier, more sophisticated weapons. When first introduced in 1940, the MP40 was given only to paratroopers and to company leaders. After 1943, however, the MP40 began to be issued to all the men in special assault platoons who led the way for infantry companies when advancing.

Metal bar stock can fold up over the top of gun

Air-cooled barrel

Magazine holds thirty-five cartridges

RUSSIAN PPS

The Russian PPS was designed to be a cheap but reliable short-range weapon issued to vehicle crews, rear echelon troops, and support service personnel. Around two million of these guns were made in a number of variants between 1942 and 1946. The PPS was born in the desperate days when German forces were driving deep into Russia, overwhelming large numbers of factories, and capturing or killing the skilled workforces employed at pre-war Soviet arms factories. Alexei Sudayev designed this gun so that it could be produced by unskilled workers using the minimum of metal. Monthly output of submachine guns went up from 135,000 to 350,000 when the PPS was introduced. However, the weapon achieved a rate of fire of only 100 rounds per minute, and was hopelessly inaccurate except at close range.

Submachine Guns of World War II

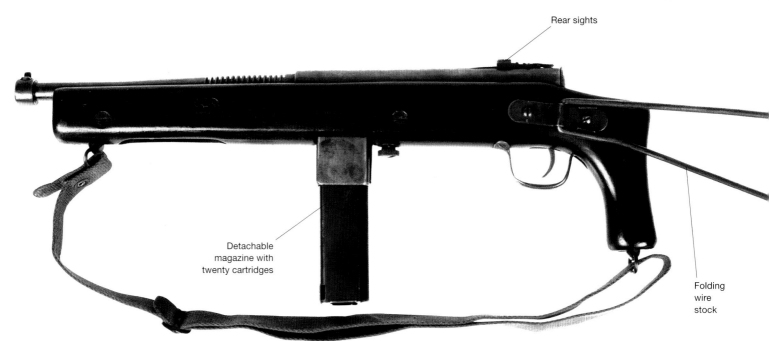

Rear sights

Detachable
magazine with
twenty cartridges

Folding
wire
stock

M55 REISING

When the United States entered World War II, the military found themselves in sudden
need of large quantities of submachine guns. There were only two U.S.-produced
models suitable for military use—the Thompson and the Reising. The Thompson
cost $200, while the Reising cost only $62, so the latter was chosen and went into
mass production with Richardson Arms of Worcester, Massachusetts. The Reising was
light, accurate, and had a high rate of fire, so it seemed ideal for the job. Unfortunately,
it tended to jam if dirt got into the workings, and it needed constant cleaning in damp
conditions. This made it all but useless in campaign conditions, so orders were
cancelled and by 1944 it was no longer in use. This version is the M55 with folding
wire stock; the solid wooden stock version was the M50.

Chambered for
7.65x17mm cartridge

Ring to clip
weapon to
webbing

Magazine
holds thirty-two
cartridges

FRENCH MAS-38

MAS (Manufacture d'Armes de Saint-Étienne) developed the MAS-38 submachine
gun for the French Army in the mid-1930s. However, the Ministry of War did not
approve the design until 1938, and did not order any until the eve of war in the
summer of 1939. The reason for the delay in ordering a very effective weapon was
that the Ministry was short of money, having spent a large part of its budget on the
static defenses of the Maginot Line. As a result, only about 2,000 were produced
before France was overrun by the Germans in 1940, after which the bulk of the
production run went straight to the German war effort.

Wooden stock

Slot for insertion of detachable magazine

Front grip

GERMAN MP41

Produced in small numbers, the German Maschinenpistole 41 was basically an MP40 model with a wooden rather than metal stock. The model was produced for the Romanian Army. In 1940, Hitler was in talks with Romania's leader, Ion Antonescu, about an invasion of Russia. Though Antonescu was keen to regain lands annexed by Russia, he was hostile to Hitler, whose motives he deeply mistrusted. Providing the Romanian Army with quantities of modern weaponry at knock-down prices was a part of Hitler's wooing of Antonescu. It proved to be successful, and Romanian troops took part in the invasion of Russia that summer.

Fixed sights set at 100 yards

8-inch barrel

M3 GREASE GUN

Officially known as the United States Submachine Gun, Cal. .45, M3, this weapon quickly acquired its nickname due to its visual similarity to a workman's grease gun. The weapon was designed in 1943 to replace the aging Thompson Gun, and was lighter, cheaper, and more accurate than its predecessor. The M3 was so cheap to make—with stamped parts and riveted joints— that it was decided that a soldier should simply throw it away when it malfunctioned, and no spare parts or repair kits were made. However, complaints soon flooded in about the weak stock, frequent jams, and inaccurate sights. Production was stopped until design changes could be made. As a result, very few of these guns actually saw service in World War II.

Magazine holds thirty cartridges

.45 ACP cartridges

Rear sight

Front sight

Slot for magazine holding thirty-two cartridges

Pierced muzzle sleeve to aid cooling

LANCHESTER SMG

War is no time for legal niceties, so the British Sterling Armaments Co. felt no qualms in 1941 about manufacturing a direct copy of the German MP28. They called it the "Lanchester" after George Lanchester, who had supposedly designed it. In fact, Lanchester's role was restricted to rechambering the design to take British ammunition and adding a fixture for the British 1907 Pattern Bayonet. Around 100,000 Lanchesters were made during the war. They were issued to the RAF, Navy, and police who were guarding bases and other strategic targets within the UK and abroad. They continued in use until the 1970s.

WORLD WAR II WEAPONS OF ESPIONAGE

During World War II, espionage was an increasingly professional and difficult enterprise. Many of the loopholes and lapses that had allowed spies to flourish in earlier conflicts had been tightened up, and even civilians were more on the alert for the presence of spies and saboteurs than they had previously been. As the role of an agent became more dangerous and less productive, enormous efforts were poured into other ways of gaining intelligence. All sides sought to make use of aerial photographs to find out what the enemy forces were up to, while efforts to crack the secret codes used in radio transmissions were expanded as radio became increasingly used. Even so, there was often no substitute for having a person on the ground to see what was going on and making contacts with people. These agents led a dangerous life and needed weapons that could be easily hidden about their person.

LOZENGE CASE GUN

Neutral countries such as Portugal, Switzerland, and Spain were places where diplomats, businessmen, and travelers could move about relatively freely, and carry on as if there were no war going on. Several of these people were, in fact, secret agents seeking to pass on information, gather intelligence, or murder each other. This apparently innocuous tin of lozenges actually hides a tiny pistol, which is fired by opening the tin and pushing on one of the lozenges. It was used by an Italian assassin to kill an American spy in Switzerland.

Concealed trigger

Concealed barrel

TIRE GAUGE

Appearing to be an example of a popular pre-war bicycle tire pressure gauge, this object is, in fact, a single shot .22 caliber pistol.

Dummy gauge

Muzzle

SCREWDRIVER

This fully functioning screwdriver can be used to tighten or loosen screws to deflect suspicion from the user. But removing the blade head reveals the muzzle of a single shot .22 pistol. The knob on the side is lulled back and swiveled sideways to cock the weapon, then flicked forward to fire the gun.

Cocking knob

Screwdriver head

Plunger

GAS GUN

This little weapon was made legally in 1932 by the Lake Erie Chemical Corporation of Ohio. The company specialized in making tear gas and nauseating gas for police departments both in the United States and, far more profitably, in South America. Most tear gas canisters were fairly large and were fired from small mortar-like devices to help break up crowds. This item was sold as a personal defense weapon. It could be clipped to a pocket like a pen, but when the plunger was pressed a small quantity of tear gas was sprayed into the face of an aggressor. It was bought by the Office of Strategic Services to equip its agents.

Clip to fix to pocket

Chamber

Muzzle

PEN GUN

This deadly weapon was used by German security forces from around 1937. It is designed to look like a pen and can be clipped into a jacket pocket. Secreted in the shaft is a .22 caliber cartridge. The knob on the side is pulled back to cock the weapon, then pressed so that it springs forward to drive the firing pin into the cartridge, and so fire the weapon.

Cocking knob

Muzzle

Trigger disguised as key

Functional keys

FLUTE GUN

This flute is fully functional as a musical instrument and can be played to allay suspicions. However, it has an extra key that, instead of operating a hole cover on the flute, is the trigger for a concealed single-shot .22 pistol. It is not known if it was ever actually used.

WORLD WAR II WEAPONS OF ESPIONAGE

DART AND DAGGER

These two weapons were issued by the OSS (Office of Strategic Services) during World War II. The upper item is a dart fired from a small crossbow, which was powered by a rubber band. It could be easily dismantled and hidden in a pocket. The lower weapon is a wrist dagger that was flattened so that it could be secured in place through a wristwatch strap and lie flush along the underside of the forearm. When needed, it could be quickly pulled out by the right hand and used to deadly effect.

Crossbow bolt

Stiletto blade

Small stabilizing fins

COFFIN NAIL DAGGER

This little weapon was used by OSS operatives during World War II. It was hollow for lightness and could be stitched into the seams of jackets or other clothing to evade detection. Its name of "coffin nail dagger" comes from its resemblance to a common wood working nail.

Blade

Hollow shaft

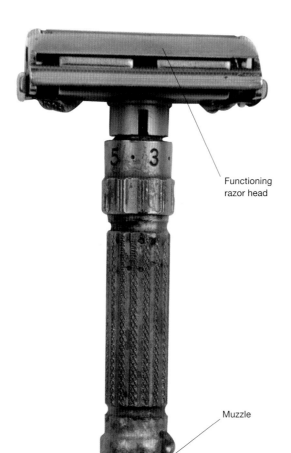

Functioning
razor head

RAZOR PISTOL

The safety razor was developed by a number of inventors over the course of the later nineteenth century. Nevertheless, it was King Camp Gillette of the United States who, in 1904, patented a safety razor that brought together all the different elements into a single successful package. By 1939, tens of millions of these razors were in use by Americans, and it soon spread to Europe and beyond. A safety razor was therefore a perfectly normal item for an American man to carry when traveling abroad. This example, however, conceals a tiny single-shot .22 caliber pistol in its handle.

Muzzle

Muzzle

Detachable base
to reveal pistol

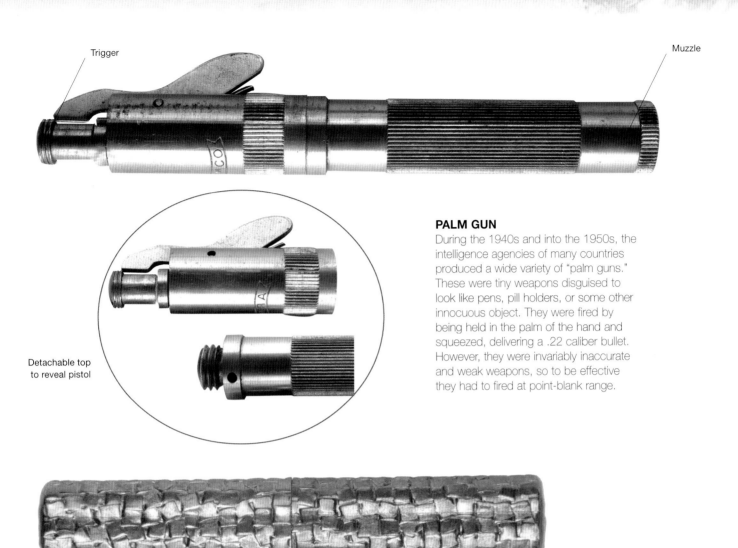

Trigger

Muzzle

Detachable top
to reveal pistol

PALM GUN

During the 1940s and into the 1950s, the intelligence agencies of many countries produced a wide variety of "palm guns." These were tiny weapons disguised to look like pens, pill holders, or some other innocuous object. They were fired by being held in the palm of the hand and squeezed, delivering a .22 caliber bullet. However, they were invariably inaccurate and weak weapons, so to be effective they had to fired at point-blank range.

LIPSTICK GUN

This American device was given to female operatives for self defense. It was not intended to be a particularly effective weapon, but could be used to disable or distract a policeman or enemy agent for long enough to give the agent time to flee. From the outside it looks exactly like a normal lipstick, but inside is a small .22 pistol, which is fired by first removing the top and then twisting the knurled ring.

Knurled ring

Interior gun

POST-WWII WEAPONS
1945–PRESENT

THE WEAPONS THAT CAME OUT OF WORLD WAR II WERE AT THE CUTTING EDGE OF TECHNOLOGY AND SCIENCE. THEY WERE DESIGNED SPECIFICALLY FOR LARGE–SCALE MILITARY CAMPAIGNS BASED AROUND TANKS, AIRCRAFT, AND INFANTRY. SOME OF THE SMALL ARMS WERE SOON ADAPTED FOR USE AS CIVILIAN WEAPONS; OTHERS WERE DEEMED SO EFFECTIVE THAT MANY GOVERNMENTS FELT THEY SHOULD BE RESTRICTED TO THE MILITARY. THE RESULT WAS THAT A LARGE AMOUNT OF GUN LEGISLATION FOLLOWED. MEANWHILE, THE MILITARY FOUND ITSELF FORCED TO CONFRONT NEW STYLES OF INSURGENT WARFARE AND LOW–LEVEL COMBAT IN URBAN AREAS, OFTEN POPULATED BY NONCOMBATANTS. NEW WEAPONS WERE NEEDED FOR THESE SITUATIONS, SO OVER THE PAST FEW DECADES WEAPONRY, AND SMALL ARMS IN PARTICULAR, HAVE UNDERGONE A REVOLUTION IN DESIGN AND CAPABILITY.

FIREFIGHT IN AFGHANISTAN
U.S. troops with 2nd Battalion, 327th Infantry Regiment, 101st Airborne Division return fire during a fight with Taliban forces in Barawala Kalay Valley in Kunar province, Afghanistan, March 31, 2011.

SNIPER RIFLES

The idea of sniping at the enemy is centuries old. In medieval times, more than one nobleman or monarch fell victim to a well-aimed arrow or crossbow bolt, and Admiral Horatio Nelson was famously killed after being hit by a musket ball fired from a French warship during the Battle of Trafalgar in 1805. It was not until World War I that the idea of a sniper claiming a victim out of the blue on an otherwise relatively peaceful day became commonplace. Skilled marksmen were given specialized rifles and, from hidden or camouflaged positions, would shoot to wound or kill from long distances without warning. The modern sniper had been born.

ACCURACY INTERNATIONAL AWM

The AWM entered service in 1996 and ceased production in 2013. For some years it has been the standard sniper rifle of the British Army, seeing service in Afghanistan and Iraq, but has also been used by German, Dutch, Norwegian, and other armed forces. The muzzle brake on this rifle is designed to reduce muzzle flash, as well as to reduce recoil. It has an adjustable bipod support at the front and a monopod support at the rear to help stabilize the weapon.

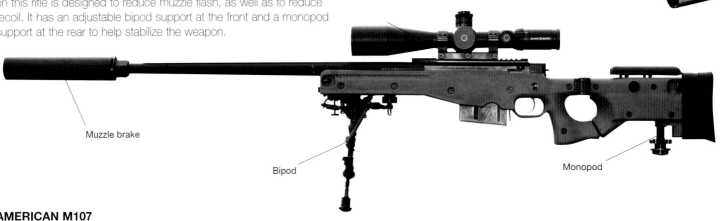

Muzzle brake

Bipod

Monopod

AMERICAN M107

Known to the U.S. military as the M107, the Barrett M82 is an anti-materiel sniper rifle that can knock out soft-skinned vehicles and other targets. The Barrett company was founded in Tennessee in 1982 by gunsmith Ronnie Barrett, who saw the possible market for a semiautomatic rifle chambered for the powerful 12.7x99mm cartridge. The idea was a new one, and Barrett had to fund the development of the weapon himself as nobody would back him. The M82 was his first product, but soon others were on the market and the company continues to flourish. There has been a considerable amount of debate over whether the M82 and its derivatives can be legally used against troops as well as against vehicles. When the U.S. Army Judge Advocate decreed that the gun could be used against humans in combat situations, it seemed that the debate was over. However, this ruling has never been tested in court, so the possible use of this powerful weapon against troops remains controversial.

Muzzle brake

Bipod support

Magazine holds ten cartridges

Pistol grip

M40 RIFLE

Entering service with the U.S. Marine Corps in 1966, the M40 is one of the longest-serving sniper rifles still in use today. The rifle is based on the commercial Remington 700, but each gun is taken into the Marine Corps Armorers workshop for individual adaptation and improvement before it goes into military service. Over the years it has gone through four variants—the current one is the M40A5, which has a stainless steel barrel and a Schmidt & Bender 3–12×50mm Police Marksman II LP scope.

3–12×50mm Police Marksman II LP scope.

24-inch barrel

Bipod rest

24.4-inch barrel

Gas-operated rotating bolt mechanism

Wooden stock

RUSSIAN DRAGUNOV

Soon after the AK-47 assault rifle became the standard infantry weapon of the Red Army, Soviet military strategists became worried that this meant that their infantry had lost their long-range engagement capability. As a result, the SVD was introduced as a squad support weapon. After the collapse of the Soviet Union, the manufacturers, TsKIB SOO, offered the gun to the commercial market as the Dragunov—the name of its designer, Yevgeny Dragunov.

HANDGUNS

Since 1945, the development of handguns has been marked by two main themes. The first is practical, with an attempt to make existing layouts and mechanisms smoother to operate, more reliable, and less prone to jamming or accidental firing. The second is related to politics, since the legal restrictions on handgun ownership vary enormously from one country to the next. Therefore, some gun manufacturers concentrate on making handguns that are legal in a particular country—in Australia, for instance, civilians may not own a gun with a caliber greater than .38.

Cylinder holds
six cartridges

Octagonal barrel

EASTERN EUROPEAN REVOLVER
This revolver was produced in Eastern Europe during the turbulent years after the end of World War II and before imposition of Communist rule that would last for half a century. Although the Soviet Red Army was occupying countries such as Hungary, Romania, and Czechoslovakia, these countries were still operating a free-market economy under generally chaotic conditions. This pistol was one of many weapons— often based on unlicensed designs—that were made in small factories and workshops before being offered for sale in the open market.

Safety catch

4.9-inch barrel

BERETTA M9
In 1990, the Beretta M9 entered service with the U.S. Army as its standard sidearm, although for various reasons some units use other weapons. It is a version of the Beretta 92F, with modifications as requested by the U.S. military. One of the changes was that the trigger guard be given a lip at the front to enable the second finger to be used to support the gun and assist aiming. Another was that the interior of the barrel be lined in chrome to reduce corrosion and increase the working life of the gun.

Magazine holds
fifteen cartridges

Iron sights

Polymer grip

Magazine holds seven,
eight, or nine cartridges

DESERT EAGLE

The Desert Eagle has been manufactured by a number of contractors, but was developed by Magnum Research, Inc. of Minneapolis. The company was founded in 1979 to develop guns able to take magnum cartridges—an enlarged version of a cartridge, usually one that is longer to allow for greater propellant content. The Desert Eagle can be chambered for five different magnum cartridges, including one of the most powerful in the world—the .50 action express.

4-inch barrel

Squared trigger guard

Magazine holds
twelve cartridges

WALTHER P99

The P99 went into production in 1997 after four years of development work by the German company Carl Walther GmbH Sportwaffen. The pistol was designed for the police market, and has been taken up by several forces in Germany as well as by those in Poland and Finland. One of the sales points of the P99 was that it came in a training model that fired paintball or rubber-ball ammunition so it could be used by recruits while they learned shooting techniques. The example shown here is a later model, with the squared trigger guard and a smoother action.

HANDGUNS

Barrel tilts up at full recoil

Locking block

Two stage
trigger

Magazine holding
seventeen cartridges

GLOCK 17

A Glock 17 with the slide pulled back to show how the barrel tilts up slightly at full recoil. This was the first weapon made by Glock, not the 17th as its name might suggest, and made extensive use of polymers and other non-traditional materials. It was designed for an exacting Austrian military specification that demanded less than twenty malfunctions in the first 10,000 shots fired, no accidental discharge when dropped 6.5 feet to a steel plate, and no need for tools when disassembling the gun for maintenance.

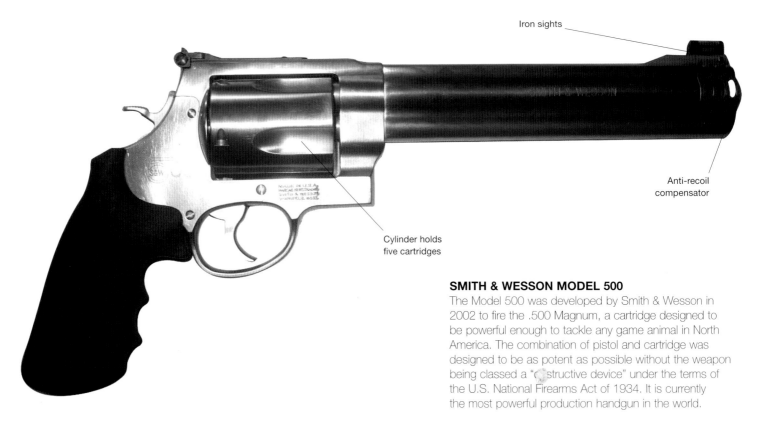

Iron sights

Anti-recoil
compensator

Cylinder holds
five cartridges

SMITH & WESSON MODEL 500

The Model 500 was developed by Smith & Wesson in 2002 to fire the .500 Magnum, a cartridge designed to be powerful enough to tackle any game animal in North America. The combination of pistol and cartridge was designed to be as potent as possible without the weapon being classed a "destructive device" under the terms of the U.S. National Firearms Act of 1934. It is currently the most powerful production handgun in the world.

3.9-inch barrel

Slide stop

Metal sights

Hammer

Safety catch

CZ 75

The CZ 75 has been made by Czech company CZUB in Moravia ever since its introduction in 1975. It is thought that more than 1.1 million of these handguns have been produced; their popularity is based on quality design and a reasonable price. It is an all-metal gun with a hammer-forged barrel, which makes it heavier than comparable modern pistols made using polymers.

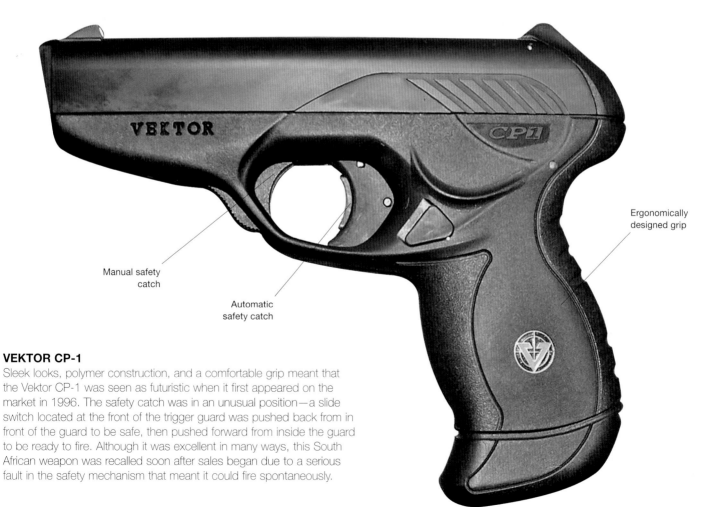

Manual safety catch

Automatic safety catch

Ergonomically designed grip

VEKTOR CP-1

Sleek looks, polymer construction, and a comfortable grip meant that the Vektor CP-1 was seen as futuristic when it first appeared on the market in 1996. The safety catch was in an unusual position—a slide switch located at the front of the trigger guard was pushed back from in front of the guard to be safe, then pushed forward from inside the guard to be ready to fire. Although it was excellent in many ways, this South African weapon was recalled soon after sales began due to a serious fault in the safety mechanism that meant it could fire spontaneously.

HANDGUNS

Metal slide

Polymer case

Slide release lever

Magazine release button

HECKLER & KOCH USP

The USP designation stands for "Universal Self-loading Pistol." It indicates that this weapon was designed for the general market, and that it incorporated design features from a number of other Heckler & Koch handguns. The pistol introduced a new recoil reduction system, which consisted of a heavy-duty coil spring that bufferered the slide and barrel. This not only made the pistol more comfortable to fire, but also reduced the amount of vibration on the components, which extended the weapon's working life.

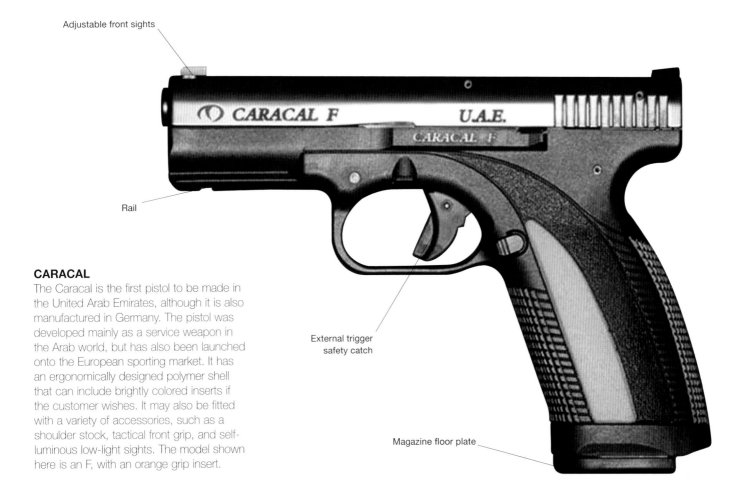

Adjustable front sights

Rail

External trigger safety catch

Magazine floor plate

CARACAL

The Caracal is the first pistol to be made in the United Arab Emirates, although it is also manufactured in Germany. The pistol was developed mainly as a service weapon in the Arab world, but has also been launched onto the European sporting market. It has an ergonomically designed polymer shell that can include brightly colored inserts if the customer wishes. It may also be fitted with a variety of accessories, such as a shoulder stock, tactical front grip, and self-luminous low-light sights. The model shown here is an F, with an orange grip insert.

6.5-inch barrel

Vent rib barrel

Duane Short grip added as custom feature after purchase

Magazine holds seven cartridges

AUTOMAG

The Automag was a high-quality weapon, but it was also a disastrous commercial product that drove its manufacturer into bankruptcy. The pistol sold for $217.50, but once all development and overhead costs were included, each one is estimated to have cost around $1,100 to produce. It is not entirely clear how many of these weapons were sold, but their rarity value and good looks means that collectors must now pay over $4,000 for an example in good condition. Its cult status has led to the pistol being featured in movies such as *Beverly Hills Cop 2*, and computer games including *Grand Theft Auto: The Ballad of Gay Tony*.

3.81-inch barrel

BERETTA CHEETAH

The Cheetah was introduced by Beretta in 1976. Although it is no longer available in the United States, it remains on sale in the European market. It is a conventional blowback-operated semiautomatic pistol that can be chambered for the .32 ACP, .380 ACP, or .22 LR cartridges. The model shown here is an 84F, which had a shorter barrel and a double-stacked magazine.

Magazine holds thirteen cartridges

HANDGUNS

Spent cartridge extractor port

Slide in open position

Safety catch

Barrel tilted up as slide is pulled back

BROWNING BDM

The BDM was designed for the 1991 competition to find a new pistol for the FBI. After it failed to win the contract, it was sold commercially until production ceased in 1998. The pistol had a toggle switch that allowed it to be set to double action only, or to single action/double action firing modes, which explains the BDM (Browning Dual Mode) designation.The pistol was originally produced with ten cartridge magazines but, after changes to U.S. law in 2004, a new fifteen-cartridge magazine was produced to be retrofitted to the gun.

Metal sights

4.4-inch barrel—the P30 variant measured 3.9 inches

Slide release lever

HECKLER & KOCH P30

The P30 is, in effect, an improved version of the older P2000. It was introduced in 2006 as a law enforcement sidearm and was almost immediately ordered in large quantities by the German Federal Police, Norwegian Police, German Customs officers, and other law enforcement organizations. The pistol has an ambidextrous polymer shell and grip, and a cold-forged steel barrel treated to resist saltwater. Pictured here is the P30L variant.

Metal slide

Cartridge extractor port

Rear sights

Rail

Polymer frame

BRAZILIAN PT145

The PT145 was manufactured by Brazil's Taurus Millennium company as a concealed weapon for civilians, and a backup pistol for law enforcement officials. The gun's small size and light weight are important to this market, but an especially appealing feature is its triple safety mechanism.

Integrated trigger safety

Magazine holds eight cartridges

Rail

Checkered trigger guard

GLOCK 38

This .45 GAP variant of the Glock 38 is chambered for the .45 GAP cartridge. This was purpose-built for the weapon by Ernest Durham to combine the power of the .45 GAP with a short length. The wider caliber meant that the rifling on this model was octagonal, rather than hexagonal, to ensure a better gas seal. The Glock 38 is an updated version of the Glock 19, which was a compact version of the original Glock 18.

CARBINES

A carbine was originally a variant of an infantry musket with a shorter barrel to make it easier to use on horseback. The gun barrel was usually of a length so that the stock protruded from a saddle holster, but the muzzle was above the area where the horse's legs moved when at a gallop. During the 1920s and 1930s, carbines were adapted to be used by men driving trucks or other vehicles. In modern parlance, a carbine is a rifle with a barrel measuring 18 inches or shorter. It can fire a variety of ammunition, from bullets designed for pistols up to full rifle rounds. Carbines are generally distinguished from assault rifles by being available in semiautomatic mode only, not with variable functions such as burst fire or fully automatic. However, as there is no universally accepted definition for the weapon, there is a degree of crossover between carbines, rifles, assault rifles, submachine guns, and long-barreled pistols.

Night sight

Telescoping buttstock

Front ring sight

Pistol grip

Front grip

M4
The M4 entered service with the U.S. military in 1994 and is one of the most important weapons used by the U.S. Army. It is a lighter and shorter version of the M16 assault rifle, which was itself derived from the AR15 rifle made by Armalite in the late 1950s. The M4 has a telescopic stock, a selective fire option, and a barrel just 16.5 inches long. It is designed for fast-moving, close-quarter combat of the type found in urban fighting. To further improve its effectiveness in such conditions, it can be fitted with an M203 grenade launcher.

Rear flip sight

Blowback mechanism

Adjustable front post sight

16.6-inch barrel

Extendable rail beneath barrel

BERETTA CX4
The Cx4 Storm is a semiautomatic carbine produced by the Italian company Beretta for the sport and law enforcement sectors. It is chambered to take the same cartridges as Beretta pistols, so a user can be armed with both pistol and carbine without needing to carry two different types of ammunition. The sleek design of the weapon has made it popular, as has the inclusion of a picatinny rail for customization.

Steel tube stock contains bolt

16.1-inch barrel

Adjustable iron sights

Polymer buttstock

Hinge for folding

KEL-TEC SUB-2000

The SUB-2000 semiautomatic carbine is designed for the civilian small-game market. It has a slim shape and is of lightweight construction, but its portability is really improved by its ability to unclip and fold in half around a hinge just in front of the trigger guard. It can be chambered for either the 9 x 19mm or the .40 S&W pistol ammunition.

Suppressor

Raised front sight

Carrying handle

The M4A1 fire selector switch has thee modes: safe, semiautomatic, and fully automatic

Thicker barrel for improved heat dissipation

Telescoping stock

M4A1 CARBINE

The M4A1 variant of the M4 carbine was produced for special operations use. Compared to the M4 it has a heavier barrel, which aids heat dissipation and increases accuracy when the weapon delivers long bursts of automatic fire. The selector can switch between burst and fully automatic modes, with no single-shot option. U.S. Navy Seals and Army Rangers prefer this version to the semiautomatic M4 because the fully automatic option is considered better at dealing with counter-insurgency and counter-terrorist combat conditions.

Fire selector switch

CARBINES

Flash
suppressor

Strap

Detachable magazine

RUGER MINI-14

The Mini-14 was introduced in 1974 by Sturm, Ruger & Co. in an effort to break into the small gamehunter and rancher market. Indeed, early models were called "Rancher Rifles" before the Mini-14 name was adopted to imply this was a version of the U.S. Army's M14 rifle. The weapon has been adopted by some law enforcement agencies as a patrol rifle to fill the gap between pistol and sniper rifle. Shown here is the GB variant that has a flash suppressor and bayonet lug to emphasize its military pedigree.

Detachable magazine
holds thirty cartridges

Magazine
extractor switch

AKS-74U

In 1974, the Red Army sought a design for a lightweight, fully automatic carbine. The weapon was to be used for airborne infantry, support staff, and vehicle crews. The winning design was the AKS-74U, essentially a shortened version of the Kalashnikov AKS-74. It had an 8.3-inch barrel with more tightly twisting rifling to spin the bullets faster, and a new type of sight.

STEYR AUG A3 CARBINE

The hugely successful Steyr AUG can be considered an assault rifle or a carbine, and is available in a wide variety of military and civilian variants. It has a "bullpup" layout, with the action located behind the trigger and alongside the user's face. This allows it to have a longer barrel than other weapons of the same overall length, and reduces weight as a long shoulder stock is not needed. The drawback of this design is that it is more complex to manufacture and makes for a slightly unstable weapon in automatic fire mode.

Bullpup configuration

16-inch barrel

Front grip

Two stage trigger for semiautomatic and fully automatic fire

Box magazine holds up to forty-two cartridges

Muzzle booster

Ventilated front hand guard

8.9-inch barrel

Fire selector switch

Flash suppressor

Pistol grip

SG 552 COMMANDO

The SIG SG 552 is a variant of the SIG SG 550 released in 1998. It has a flash suppressor and ventilated handguards, as well as a very short 8.9-inch barrel. It has rails and can carry a number of accessories. A more recent long-barrel version has a 13.6-inch barrel that can incorporate a bayonet and fire grenades. Shown here is a short-barrel version.

INFANTRY WEAPONS

The lesson that most militaries drew from World War II was that the majority of infantry battles took place at ranges under 400 yards, and that rate of fire was more important than accuracy. Conflicts in Vietnam, Korea, and elsewhere with forested landscapes and urban combat reinforced these views, and armies re-equipped with assault rifles and automatic carbines. More recent combat experience in the mountainous or desert landscapes of Afghanistan and Iraq has called this tactical appraisal into question as the need for longer-range firepower has become more evident. Modern tactics require ground troops to use a variety of armaments, so the concept of equipping all infantry with the same weaponry is fading.

Iron sights

10.2-inch barrel

UZI SUBMACHINE GUN

The Uzi entered service with the Israeli Army in 1954 as a personal protection weapon for officers, tank crew, and rear echelon troops. Before long, it was being used as an assault weapon by elite troops working in urban areas. In the late 1950s, the Uzi was released for sale to other countries, with Germany, the Netherlands, and Ireland being among the first to purchase the weapon. The example pictured here has been fitted with a suppressor.

Iron sights

Shoulder stock

Pistol grip

Magazine holds twenty cartridges

FN FAL

Introduced by the Belgian company FN in 1951, the FAL has proved to be one of the most enduringly popular and successful post-1945 rifles. It has been bought by some ninety countries officially and by many others unofficially, and has seen combat in more than two dozen wars from Suez in 1956 to Libya in 2014. The letters FAL stand for Fusil Automatique Léger (Light Automatic Rifle), though compared to many later weapons it was a distinctly heavy rifle.

Iron sights

Muzzle shroud

Shoulder stock

FN SCAR

The SCAR (Special Combat Assault Rifle) entered service with the U.S. Special Forces in 2009, and is still deployed by units switching to it from the M4 carbine. The weapon comes in four basic variants. The Light (L) version is chambered for the 5.56 x 45mm cartridge, while the Heavy (H) variant fires the 7.62 x 51mm cartridge. Both the Light and Heavy come in long- and short-barreled versions. Pictured here are the SCAR-L (top) and SCAR-H (bottom), both in the long-barreled variant.

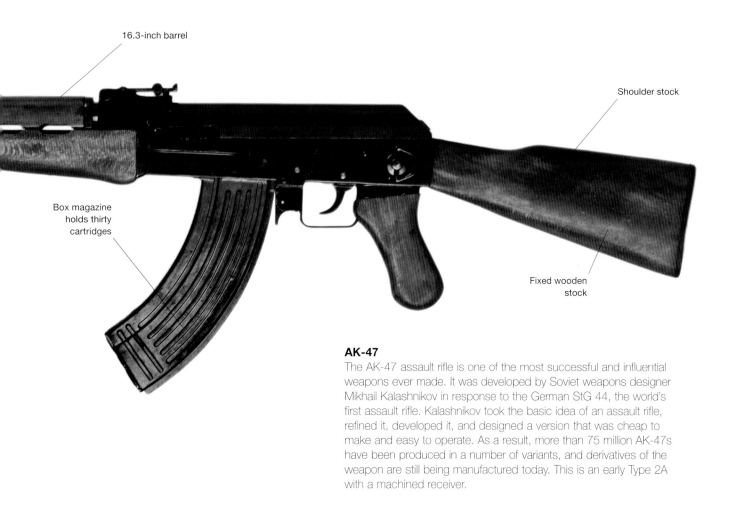

16.3-inch barrel

Shoulder stock

Box magazine holds thirty cartridges

Fixed wooden stock

AK-47

The AK-47 assault rifle is one of the most successful and influential weapons ever made. It was developed by Soviet weapons designer Mikhail Kalashnikov in response to the German StG 44, the world's first assault rifle. Kalashnikov took the basic idea of an assault rifle, refined it, developed it, and designed a version that was cheap to make and easy to operate. As a result, more than 75 million AK-47s have been produced in a number of variants, and derivatives of the weapon are still being manufactured today. This is an early Type 2A with a machined receiver.

INFANTRY WEAPONS

Carrying handle

18-inch barrel

Bipod support

M249

As the need for automatic fire at squad level became clear in the 1980s, the U.S. Army adopted the M249 light machine gun. It provided a high volume of fire that was accurate up to 700 yards, but was portable enough to be carried by a single soldier. The M249 is a version of the Belgian FN Minimi chambered to take the 5.56×45mm NATO cartridge. It has a sustained rate of fire of 100 rounds per minute, but in short bursts can reach 200 rounds per minute.

TYPE 56

In 1956, China began manufacturing a copy of the Soviet AK-47 in the shape of the Type 56. A wide variety of these assault rifles have been produced over the years, with vast numbers exported to China's allies. Since the 1990s, the Type 56 has been increasingly seen in the hands of Islamic militant groups, including the Taliban in Afghanistan, Hamas in Palestine, and Janjaweed in Sudan. Pictured here is the Type 56-1 with a folding metal shoulder stock.

The front sights of the Type 56 are fully hooded, which distinguishes it from all other assault rifles based on the AK-47, which have open or partially open front sights.

Wooden pistol grip

Magazine locking switch

20-inch barrel

Adjustable rear sight with settings to 2,600 feet

M16A2

As a result of combat experience in Vietnam, the U.S. Marines requested a number of changes to the M16 rifle. It resulted in the M16A2, which entered service in the mid-1980s. The changes were extensive and included improvements to the barrel—which was made thicker at the rear to prevent flexing if roughly handled—and improved rifling. The suppressor was no longer open at the bottom, a feature that had been found to kick up dust or snow when the M16 had been fired from a prone position.

Magazine holds twenty cartridges—can be replaced by 100-round drum

Thumb rest

Textured grip

Raised front sight

16.3-inch barrel

GLOCK 17

In the late 1990s, Glock introduced a third generation of Glock 17 pistols. The most important new feature was the Universal Glock Rail fitted to allow the mounting of laser sights, tactical lights, and other accessories. The grip was improved by the addition of ambidextrous thumb rests and modified finger grooves. This new model was also produced in a non-firing version with a bright red polymer frame for training purposes.

GRENADE LAUNCHERS

The idea of throwing an explosive device, or grenade, at the enemy is as old as gunpowder, and may have been used in China as early as 1044. However, it was not until the development of more powerful explosives in the later nineteenth century that the modern fragmentation grenade became feasible. Through the two World Wars, these remained largely hand-thrown devices with a timed fuse—they could be thrown about 30 yards.

Intermittent efforts were made to adapt rifles to launch grenades, but as most designs left the user unable to fire the rifle after it had been adapted, they proved unpopular. It was the modern concept of equipping infantry units with a variety of weapons that saw the development of specialist grenade launchers. These have proved to be a particularly useful assault weapon, and in the twenty-first century have increasingly proved their worth.

Shoulder pad

Laser sights

Magazine holds four grenades

XM25 CDTE "PUNISHER"

The CDTE (Counter Defilade Target Engagement) grenade launcher also goes by the name of "Punisher." As its official designation suggests, the weapon was developed largely to target insurgents in Afghanistan who were in defilade positions—that is, hidden behind rocks, rises in the ground, or other obstructions so that a direct line of sight shot could not be taken. The Punisher was designed to fire grenades that would burst in midair above the target, showering shrapnel downward and circumventing the cover being used by the enemy.

Folding rear sight

Day/night sight

Shoulder pad

Muzzle

M320

In 2009, a five-year quest by the U.S. military for an off-the-shelf grenade launcher able to meet their exacting demands ended when Heckler & Koch's M320 entered service. The weapon can take all 40mm grenades currently in use, but is also configured to accommodate the longer projectiles that are anticipated in the future. A single-shot, breech-loaded device, it can deliver five grenades per minute and is accurate to about 175 yards, with a maximum range of 400 yards.

Folding front grip

RG-6 GRENADE LAUNCHER

Experience in the Chechen Wars showed the Russian Army that there was a need for increased mobile infantry firepower, especially in short-range urban combat. The manufacturer TsKIB SOO responded by producing the RG-6. Firing the same 40mm grenade used by underbarrel launchers, the RG-6 can deliver them accurately over a range of 400 yards, and can fire a burst of two grenades per second from its six-grenade cylinder.

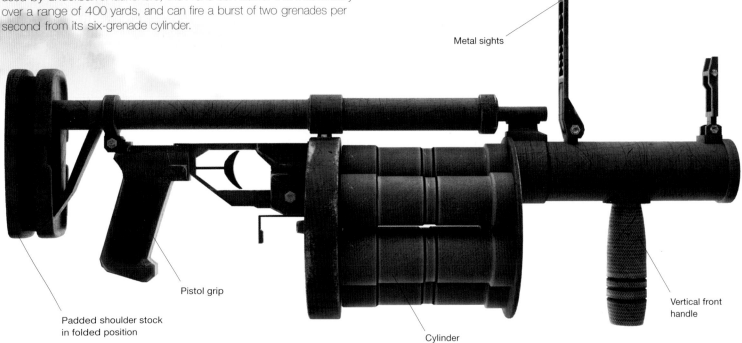

Metal sights

Pistol grip

Padded shoulder stock
in folded position

Cylinder

Vertical front
handle

Rubber pad
on buttstock

Ladder-style rear sight

Iron sights

Swivel mounts
for carrying strap

M-79 "THUMPER"

The M-79 entered service in 1961. Its distinctive sound earned it the name "Thumper" among U.S. troops, while Australian soldiers called it "The Wombat." The M-79 can fire a wide range of 40mm projectiles, including explosive, buckshot, and flachette grenades and flares. It is accurate to about 375 yards, has a maximum range of 450 yards, and in experienced hands can fire six rounds per minute.

ASSAULT WEAPONS

F2000 S

The S designation on this model of the F2000 bullpup assault rifle made by FN in Belgium indicates that it is a model developed specifically for the Slovenian Army. The main difference is that the upper picatinny rail has been raised and adapted so that it doubles as a carrying handle. The Slovenians have 7,300 men under arms with another 1,500 in reserve, plus a pool of militarily trained civilians who can be called up in an emergency.

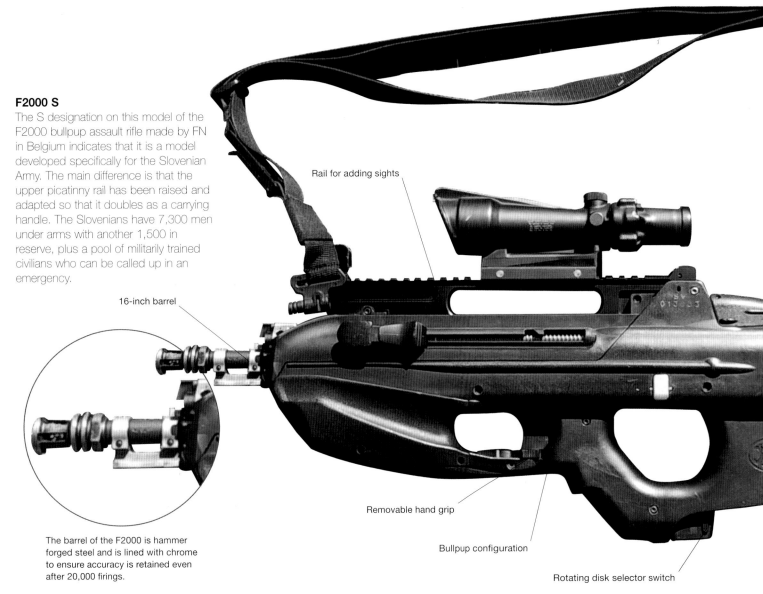

Rail for adding sights

16-inch barrel

The barrel of the F2000 is hammer forged steel and is lined with chrome to ensure accuracy is retained even after 20,000 firings.

Removable hand grip

Bullpup configuration

Rotating disk selector switch

15.9-inch barrel

Iron sights

GP-34 grenade launcher

Magazine holds sixty cartridges

AN-94

The Russian AN-94 was intended to be a replacement for the AK-74, but it has only been adopted in small numbers. This may be due to its high manufacturing costs or its complex design. A key feature of this rifle is that when set to fire a two-shot burst, the second bullet exits the barrel before the recoil of the first shot is felt. This means that both bullets will hit the target very close together to provide a much greater impact, which is particularly useful against a target wearing body armor.

16.4-inch barrel

Suppressor with
bayonet lug

Detachable
magazine holds
thirty cartridges

RK 62

The standard issue weapon for the Finnish Army infantry, the Rk 62
is an assault rifle based on the Polish-licensed version of the Soviet
AK-47. The weapon has a number of unique features, including a
three-pronged flash suppressor that doubles as a mount for a specially
designed bayonet that can also be used as a combat knife. The flash
suppressor was designed to be used as a barbed wire cutter, with the
wire snagged in the suppressor and a round fired to slice through the
wire. Shown here is the M76 version, which made greater use of
stamped steel components to make production cheaper.

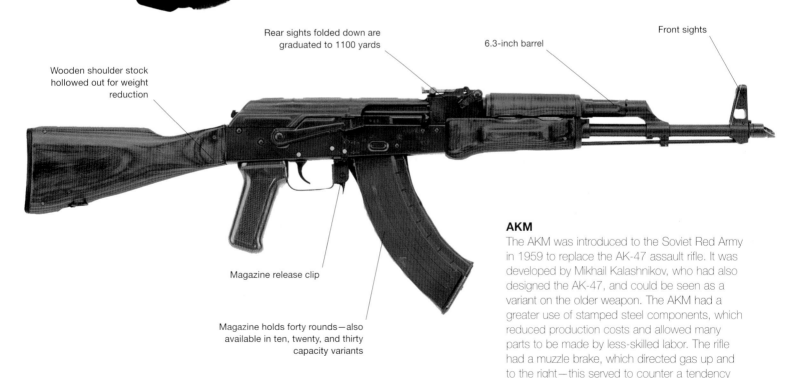

Rear sights folded down are
graduated to 1100 yards

Front sights

6.3-inch barrel

Wooden shoulder stock
hollowed out for weight
reduction

Magazine release clip

Magazine holds forty rounds—also
available in ten, twenty, and thirty
capacity variants

AKM

The AKM was introduced to the Soviet Red Army
in 1959 to replace the AK-47 assault rifle. It was
developed by Mikhail Kalashnikov, who had also
designed the AK-47, and could be seen as a
variant on the older weapon. The AKM had a
greater use of stamped steel components, which
reduced production costs and allowed many
parts to be made by less-skilled labor. The rifle
had a muzzle brake, which directed gas up and
to the right—this served to counter a tendency
of the AK-47 to drift up and right when fired in
automatic mode.

PRECISION TACTICAL RIFLES

In recent years, the term "precision tactical rifle" has come to replace the old designation of "sniper rifle" for several reasons. First, these weapons were increasingly being used by civilians for target shooting and long-range hunting. Second, the origin of the term "sniper rifle"—from snipe hunting—had become obscure. In addition, the military felt a need to distinguish between rifles that targeted personnel and those that were for use against materiel and vehicles. Today, the precision tactical rifle is a weapon that is capable of extreme accuracy at long ranges and can be used against enemy troops or large game.

KALASHNIKOV SNIPER VARIANT

The AK-47 has been produced in a bewildering number of variants, several of which have been tailored for sniping. This modern sniper variant has a purpose-built barrel and telescopic sights fitted over the fixed iron sights, but is otherwise a fairly standard 100 Series AK-47. These weapons are usually issued to the designated marksman in a standard infantry unit rather than to specialist snipers.

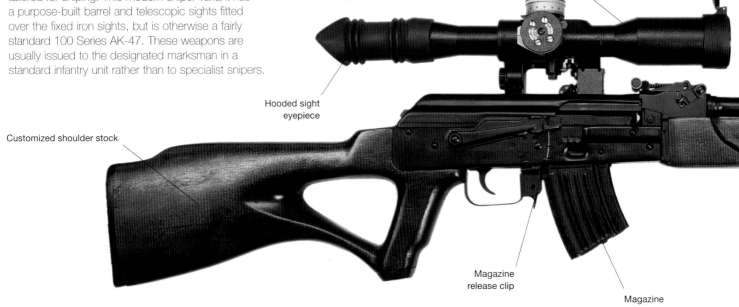

Telescopic sights

Hooded sight eyepiece

Customized shoulder stock

Magazine release clip

Magazine

Computerized sights

Fully adjustable stock

Picatinny rail

24-inch barrel

Folding buttstock

Magazine holds five cartridges

Bipod support

Quick-attach combined suppressor and muzzle brake

XM2010 ENHANCED SNIPER RIFLE

Introduced in 2011, the XM2010 can be fired with high accuracy at ranges of up to 1,300 yards. This was an improvement on the older M24 sniper rifle and it was expected to be especially effective in the desert and mountain conditions of Afghanistan and other combat zones. The cartridge used is the .300 Winchester Magnum. Although this produces increased recoil and reduces the life of the barrel, these are considered to be minor prices to pay for the increased range.

Stock made from polymer foam reinforced with fiberglass, carbon fiber and Kevlar.

Buttstock plate can be extended up to 2 inches

18-inch stainless steel barrel

Swivel bipod support

MK12 SPECIAL PURPOSE RIFLE

This weapon has been in service since 2002 with the U.S. Special Operations Forces. It is based on the M16, but has been modified to achieve much greater accuracy. The concept behind the rifle was a desire for a weapon that combined long-range accuracy with a short overall length to make it ideal for use in urban areas. None of the available rounds offered the desired performance with this weapon, so the Mk 262 Open Tip Match was developed specifically for the Mk12.

Iron sights

Leupold telescopic sight

Barrel made of 416R grade stainless steel

Bipod support

M24

The M24 is the military version of the Remington 700, upgraded for use as a sniper rifle in adverse weather conditions. It fires the 7.62x51mm NATO cartridge from a magazine holding five rounds, with the more recent M24A2 version incorporating a ten-round magazine. It is accurate to around 875 yards using the detachable telescopic sights, and to around 500 yards with the fixed iron sights.

ANTI-MATERIEL RIFLES

Muzzle brake

PGM HÉCATE II

The Hécate II is a sniper rifle used by the French Army. It fires the .50 BMG (12.7x99mm) cartridge in several variants: the incendiary M1, which has a light blue tip for identification purposes, the armor-piercing M2 (with a black tip), and the high-tech HEIAP Mk211 (with a green tip and gray stripe). The last of these has a .30 caliber tungsten penetrator, zirconium powder, and Composition A explosive—it will penetrate lightly armored vehicles and then explode to cause maximum damage.

10x telescopic sights

SCROME LTE J10 F1 10x telescopic sights are fitted as standard. These are made of anodized aluminum and are rigorously tested to be waterproof in most climatic conditions.

Shoulder stock

Muzzle brake

KSVK 12.7

Also known as the Degtyarev Sniper Rifle, the Russian KSVK 12.7 was designed in the 1990s as a counter-sniper weapon. It came out of the realization that many snipers chose to fire from inside buildings or vehicles, where they were difficult to pick out. The KSVK was therefore devised to penetrate brick or concrete walls or metal, to neutralize a sniper hiding inside a room or vehicle. It is thought to be accurate to about 1,600 yards.

Detachable magazine holds five cartridges

Muzzle brake to
reduce recoil

ZASTAVA M93 BLACK ARROW

This Serbian weapon saw action in Kosovo and Macedonia, and
performed well in the region's adverse weather conditions. It uses
a bolt action based on the Mauser system, and fires from a
magazine holding five .50 BMG cartridges. It is accurate to about
1,900 yards and comes with 8x optical sights as standard.

Spring-mounted
shoulder stock

Muzzle brake

TAC-50

The TAC-50 first entered combat with the Canadian Army. In
March 2002, it was used by a five-man sniper team to neutralize
twenty enemy combatants in Afghanistan. A 2,526-yard hit carried
out by Corporal Aaron Perry set a new world record, but only a few
days later that was surpassed by another of 2,657 yards from
Corporal Rob Furlong. The A1-R2 variant pictured here was
introduced in 2012 and features a hydraulic piston in the
shoulder stock to reduce recoil.

Bipod support

Single-shot
bolt action

Muzzle brake
absorbs 60
percent of recoil

NTW-20

Designed and manufactured in South Africa, the
NTW-20 first appeared in 1998. Unlike most other anti-
materiel rifles, the NTW-20 is designed to come apart
into two sections that can then be fitted into backpacks
and carried on foot by its two-man crew. It can fire the
20x110mm Hispano cartridge, more usually associated
with the HS404 anti-aircraft cannon.

ANTI-MATERIEL RIFLES

SR-25

The SR-25 first entered combat with the U.S. SEAL snipers in Somalia in 1993, where its twenty-round magazine proved to be especially useful. The weapon is accurate enough to group shots into 0.5 inches at 100 yards. At the time it was introduced, its free-floating barrel and fiberglass stock were considered to be particularly advanced. The U.S. military are currently in the process of phasing out the SR-25.

24-inch barrel

Suppressor

Bipod support

Magazine holds up to twenty cartridges

Muzzle brake

ZBROJOVKA ZB FALCON

Based in Brno in the Czech Republic, Zbrojovka is perhaps best known for developing the VZ26 that was later modified to create the British Bren gun. The ZB Falcon was designed for use by the Czech special forces and has seen action in Afghanistan, where it performed well in desert conditions. It is produced in two calibers to take both NATO and former Warsaw Pact cartridges.

ZD 10x50 sight

36.5-inch barrel

Carrying handle in folded down position

Adjustable buttstock

Box magazine

Carrying handle

Length adjustable
buttstock

Magazine holds
five cartridges

OSV-96

The Russian OSV-96 was developed to out-range the
majority of sniper rifles issued to the nonspecialist infantry
units of any potential aggressor. It was also designed
to destroy most cover used by snipers. It fired the
12.7 108mm cartridge that was introduced by the
Soviet Union for use in anti-aircraft heavy machine guns.

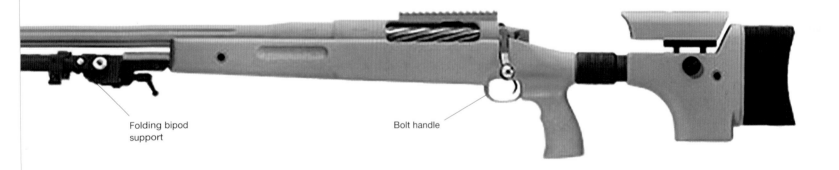

Folding bipod
support

Bolt handle

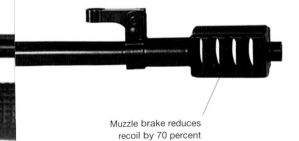

Muzzle brake reduces
recoil by 70 percent

TAC-416

The TAC-416 is the civilian version of the TAC-50. It is chambered
for the .416 Barrett cartridge, a proprietary round made specifically
for Barrett rifles. A key consideration for many purchasers is that
while the guns firing the .50 BMG cartridge are illegal in some
states and countries, the .416 is not. The TAC-416 is a single-
shot weapon; no magazine is commercially available.

RESOURCES

ABOUT THE BERMAN MUSEUM

Since the Berman Museum of World History opened its doors to the public in April of 1996, thousands of visitors have enjoyed its unique and varied collection of art, historical objects, and weapons. Located in the Appalachian foothills in Anniston, Alabama, and next door to the seventy-five-year-old Anniston Museum of Natural History, which is affiliated with the Smithsonian, the Berman Museum's reputation and collection have grown exponentially since its inception. The Berman Museum's holdings number 8,500 objects and it has 3,000 items related to world history exhibited in its galleries. Among the many rare and fascinating objects from around the world, there are items such as an air rifle from Austria, military insignia from German and Italy, a scimitar from the Middle East, and graphically carved kris holders from Indonesia. The Museum attracts both a global and regional audience. All who visit can appreciate the historic significance of the collection and gain greater awareness and respect of other cultures.

Its five galleries—Deadly Beauty, American West, World War I, World War II, and Arts of Asia—exhibit items spanning a period of 3,500 years. A focal point of the Deadly Beauty gallery is the elaborate Royal Persian Scimitar, circa 1550, created for Abbas the Great, King of Persia. The American West gallery covers approximately 200 years (c. 1700–1900), emphasizing the United State's political, economic, social, and cultural structures, and their influences on settling the West.

The World War galleries use objects from the Museum collection to explore the causes and conditions of both wars, the historical significance of the countries involved, and the resulting political, economic, cultural, and social changes brought about by each war. A rare piece of equipment in the World War I gallery is the Tanker's Splinter Goggles, used by tank personnel to protect their eyes and faces from metal splinters from machine-gun fire. Exhibited in the World War II gallery is the M1942 "Liberator" Pistol, as well as a large collection of Adolf Hitler's tea and coffee service, purported to have come from the last bunker that the Führer occupied. The Arts of Asia exhibit features an extensive and ever-growing collection of Asian textiles, ceramics, sculpture, jade, and metal.

The Berman Museum of World History is home to the vast and eclectic collection of Colonel Farley L. Berman and his wife, Germaine. Farley Berman, a lifelong resident of Anniston, Alabama, served in the European theater during World War II, and in the occupation force afterward. There he met Germaine, a French national. They were married and spent the next fifty years traveling the world acquiring historic weapons and artifacts, paintings, bronzes, and other works of art. Berman's self-trained collector's eye recognized the importance of items that were perhaps seen as ordinary, and

he made it his mission to preserve a few. The Bermans established contacts—and a reputation—in numerous auction houses and among antique dealers in Europe and America.

The Bermans freely shared their collection with the public long before the City of Anniston constructed the Museum facility. Hundreds of military dignitaries and others were invited to their home for personal tours of their collection. Colonel Berman could best be described as a colorful storyteller and was notorious for firing blank rounds from his collection of spy weapons when guests least expected. He advised aspiring collectors to purchase good reference books, spend some years reading, and visit a range of museums before acquiring.

During the early 1990s, several large museums expressed interest in receiving the Bermans' collection. They were disappointed when Germaine proposed that the collection remain in Anniston. Colonel and Mrs. Berman's collection stands as the core of Berman Museum. Since the Museum's opening, many have recognized its importance and have contributed their own personal treasures to this impressive collection.

BERMAN MUSEUM OF WORLD HISTORY

www.bermanmuseum.org
840 Museum Drive, Anniston, AL 36206

mail: P.O. Box 2245, Anniston, AL 36202-2245
phone: 256-237-6261

47*br* Tropenmuseum of the Royal Tropical Institute (KIT); 47*br* Apostrophe/Shutterstock; 47*l* Rama; 48-49*t* arindambanerjee/Shutterstock; 48*t* ermess/Shutterstock; 48*ca* Ruben Pinto/Shutterstock; 48*bl* Apostrophe/Shutterstock; 48*bl* Suncan1890/istockphoto; 53*t* ADA_photo/Shutterstock; 53*br* Apostrophe/Shutterstock; 54*b* Samuraiantiqueworld; 55*br* Apostrophe/Shutterstock; 56*t* Rama; 56*bl*, 57*br* Apostrophe/Shutterstock; 58*b* John Buck, Musket Mart; 60*b* Walters Art Museum; 61*br* Apostrophe/Shutterstock; 62*b* Courtesy Rock Island Auction Company; 63*br* Apostrophe/Shutterstock; 63*br* Brian Godwin; 65*c* Courtesy Rock Island Auction Company; 65*br* Apostrophe/Shutterstock; 65*br* MatthiasKabel; 65*br* baku13; 67*ca* Neochichiri11; 66-67 *background*, 68*br* Apostrophe/Shutterstock; 68*br* Sobol2222; 69*br* Apostrophe/Shutterstock; 70*t* Olemac/Shutterstock; 71*b* Jen duMoulin/Shutterstock; 73*cb* Rama; 73*br* Apostrophe/Shutterstock; 75*b* grafnata/Shutterstock; 76*t* Zerbor/Shutterstock; 77*t* Dimedrol68/Shutterstock; 77*c* Zerbor/Shutterstock; 77*b* Apostrophe/Shutterstock; 78*t* Courtesy Rock Island Auction Company; 79*t* Balefire/Shutterstock; 79*c* Olga Popova/Shutterstock; 79*c*, *b* spaxiax/Shutterstock; 81*c* Rama; 81*br* Apostrophe/Shutterstock; 82-83 *background* Apostrophe/Shutterstock; 85*t* Library of Congress, LC-USZC4-4043; 85*t*, 87*tr*, *br* Apostrophe/Shutterstock; 87*tr* Rama; 87*br* Kletr/Shutterstock; 87*c* Olemac/Shutterstock; 89*c* CreativeHQ/Shutterstock; 91*t* Balefire/Shutterstock; 91*br* Library of Congress, LC-DIG-ppmsca-01657; 91*br* Apostrophe/Shutterstock; 93*c* Antiqueweaponstore.com; 93*br*, 95*br* Apostrophe/Shutterstock; 95*br* BasPhoto/Shutterstock; 96*c* Courtesy Rock Island Auction Company; 96*b* Apostrophe/Shutterstock; 96*b* BVA/Shutterstock; 97*ca* Courtesy Rock Island Auction Company; 97*b*, 100*b* Apostrophe/Shutterstock; 101*b* GLYPHstock/Shutterstock; 103*c* Michael Simens' Historical Antiques; 103*cb* Denix; 103*b* MishelVerini/Shutterstock; 105*br* Micha Klootwijk/Shutterstock; 106*b* Olemac/Shutterstock; 107*cb* mj007/Shutterstock; 107*br* Apostrophe/Shutterstock; 109*cb* Olemac/Shutterstock; 109*br* Robert Gebbie Photography/Shutterstock; 110*br* Apostrophe/Shutterstock; 110*br* Furtseff/Shutterstock; 110*br* cosma/Shutterstock; 111*br* Apostrophe/Shutterstock; 111*br*, 112*t* PHGCOM; 112*b* Courtesy Rock Island Auction Company; 113*br* Apostrophe/Shutterstock; 113*br* National Park Service; 115*t* The Cobbs Auctioneers; 115*br* Jeff Banke/Shutterstock; 118-119 Library of Congress, LC-DIG-pga-02102; 120*tl* Hatchetfish; 120-121*b* Apostrophe/Shutterstock; 121*t* Peter Engholm; 121*c* Cordier Auctions and Appraisals; 123*t* Little John's Auction Service; 123*br* Horst Held; 124*t* Tennants Auctioneers; 124*c*, *b* Courtesy Rock Island Auction Company; 124*b* Courtesy Rock Island Auction Company; 125*br* Apostrophe/Shutterstock; 126*t*, 129*t* Courtesy Rock Island Auction Company; 129*b* Apostrophe/Shutterstock; 129*br* Library of Congress, LC-USZC2-1947; 130*b* Heritage Auctions; 131*bl* Courtesy of Cedar Hill Cemetery, Hartford, Connecticut; 131*br* Apostrophe/Shutterstock; 131*br* Library of Congress, LC-USZ62-110403; 132*t* Older Firearms; 132*c*, 133*t* Hmaag; 135*t* Courtesy Rock Island Auction Company; 135*b* Pete Hoffman/Shutterstock; 137*br* Apostrophe/Shutterstock; 141*b* Sailor in Saddle; 143*br* Apostrophe/Shutterstock; 143*br* Library of Congress, LC-USZ62-7622; 146*c* Dave Taylor's Civil War Antiques; 147*br* Apostrophe/Shutterstock; 149*br* Apostrophe/Shutterstock; 149*br* Adam Cuerden; 150*c* Heritage Auctions; 151*br* Apostrophe/Shutterstock; 151*br* Library of Congress, LC-USZ62-40069; 152-153 *background* Apostrophe/Shutterstock; 152*bl* Trekphiler; 152*br* Hmaag; 154*t* adamsguns.com; 154*c* bardbom; 154*t* Apostrophe/Shutterstock; 156*b* James D Julia Inc.; 157*tr* Arthurrh; 157*br* Apostrophe/Shutterstock; 160*b*, 161*t* Armémuseum, Sweden; 161*br* Apostrophe/Shutterstock; 162-163 *background* Apostrophe/Shutterstock; 163*b* Rama; 164 Armémuseum, Sweden; 165*c* Ca.garcia.s; 174*t* Rama; 174*b* Steven.balch; 175*t* Wesley Terrell; 175*c* Atirador; 175*b* Halibutt, cropped and retouched by Atirador; 177*cb* Trulock; 180*t*

Hélène Rival; 187*tr* Apostrophe/Shutterstock; 188*b* M62; 189*t* Apostrophe/Shutterstock; 189*c* Olegvolk; 189*b*, 190*t*, *c*, *b* adamsguns.com; 191*t* Rama; 191*b* adamsguns.com; 194*t* Armémuseum, Sweden; 194*c* adamsguns.com; 194-195*b* Ricce; 195*tr* Apostrophe/Shutterstock; 195*c*, 196*t*, *c* Antique Military Rifles; 196*b* Armémuseum, Sweden; 197*t* Army Heritage Museum; 197*c* PHGCOM; 197*b* Apostrophe/Shutterstock; 199*tr* Apostrophe/Shutterstock; 200*t* U.S. Army Center of Military History; 200*b* Guilmann; 202-203 *background*, 205*tr* Apostrophe/Shutterstock; 205*b* Olegvolk; 206*t*, *c* adamsguns.com; 207*tr* Apostrophe/Shutterstock; 207*tr* Hohum; 207*b* Armémuseum, Sweden; 208*t* SONY at ru.wikipedia; 208*c* Szuyuan huang; 208*b* Ken; 209*t* adamsguns.com; 209*b* Apostrophe/Shutterstock; 210-211 *background* Apostrophe/Shutterstock; 213*br* Morphine; 214*t* Drake00; 214*b*, 215*b*, 216*t* adamsguns.com; 217*b* Hatchetfish; 218*tl*, *c* Rama; 218*b* Mascamon at lb.wikipedia; 219*br* Apostrophe/Shutterstock; 219*br* Moreau.henri; 222*t* Szuyuan huang; 222*c* Antique Military Rifles; 222*b*, 223*t*, *c* Armémuseum, Sweden; 224*t* joelogon/Joe Loong; 225*b*, 226*t*, *c* Armémuseum, Sweden; 226*b* adamsguns.com; 227*br* Apostrophe/Shutterstock; 227*br* Adam Kliczek/Wikipedia, license: CC-BY-SA-3.0; 228*t* Quickload; 228*c* Atirador; 228*b* adamsguns.com; 229*tr* Apostrophe/Shutterstock; 229*tr* Phil Sangwell; 229*b* Armémuseum, Sweden; 230*c* Antique Military Rifles; 231*br* Apostrophe/Shutterstock; 231*br* Imperial War Museum; 231*br*, 232*t* Armémuseum, Sweden; 232*b* Curiosandrelics; 233*tr* Apostrophe/Shutterstock; 233*tr* Bundesarchiv, Bild 101I-219-0595-05/CC-BY-SA; 233*b* Armémuseum, Sweden; 235*b* Curiosandrelics; 236*t* Olemac/Shutterstock; 236*b* Marafona/Shutterstock; 237*t* Apostrophe/Shutterstock; 238*t* Armémuseum, Sweden; 238*b* Olemac/Shutterstock; 239*t* PpPachy; 239*br* Apostrophe/Shutterstock; 239*br* Davric; 240*bl* Apostrophe/Shutterstock; 241*t* Armémuseum, Sweden; 241*b*, 242*b* David Orcea/Shutterstock; 243*t* Olemac/Shutterstock; 243*b* Eugene Sergeev/Shutterstock; 244*c* Quickload; 245*b* Zimand/Shutterstock; 247*c* Curiosandrelics; 252-253 U.S. Army photo by Pfc. Cameron Boyd; 254*t* Defence Imagery; 255*t* U.S. Marine Corps, Gunnery Sgt. Matt Hevezi; 255*b* Zimand/Shutterstock; 256*b* Vartanov Anatoly/Shutterstock; 257*t* Nomad_Soul/Shutterstock; 257*b* MISHELLA/Shutterstock; 258*t* Spectrums; 259*t* Vidiot savant; 260*t* Dybdal/Miroslav Pragl; 260*b* Edmond at en.wikipedia, altered by Francis Flinch; 261*t* Dr.mike; 261*b* Jan Hrdonka; 262*t* Jeanyard; 263*t* Hustvedt; 265*t* DanMP5; 265*b* Steyr Mannlicher; 266*t* S-F/Shutterstock; 266*b* Rama; 267*b* Vartanov Anatoly/Shutterstock; 268*t* Jan Hrdonka; 268*b* The Specialists Ltd; 269*t* Steyr Mannlicher; 270*t* CreativeHQ/Shutterstock; 270*b* Atirador; 271*t* Mark Schierbecker; 272*t* KrisfromGermany; 272*c* Dybdal; 272-273*b* Vartanov Anatoly/Shutterstock; 273*c* The Specialists Ltd; 274*t* Zimand/Shutterstock; 274*b* Vadim Kozlovsky/Shutterstock; 275*t* Armémuseum, Sweden; 275*b* Ken Lunde, http://lundestudio.com; 276*t*, *b* PEO Soldier; 277*t* jnumber9/Shutterstock; 278*t* The Specialists Ltd; 279*b* Outisnn; 280*b* MKFI; 281*t* Apostrophe/Shutterstock; 282*t* Polanksy kolbe; 282*b* Soldatnytt from Oslo, Norway; 283*t* Crochet.david; 283*c* Filip Obr/Shutterstock; 283*b* U.S. Marine Corps, Staff Sgt. Ezekiel Kitandwe; 283*b* Apostrophe/Shutterstock; 284 Zimand/Shutterstock; 286*t* Atirador; 287*t* Forgottenweapons.com; 289*t* Saurabh1212, retouched by Atirador; 290*b* Koalorka at en.wikipedia, Courtesy Concern Izhmash OJSC; 291*t* M62; 291*b* Hombreanos; 292*t* Zimand/Shutterstock; 292*b* PEO Soldier; 293*b* F. ENOT/Shutterstock; 295*b* Pibwl; 296*t* Vitaly V. Kuzmin; 296*b* Koalorka at en.wikipedia; 298*t* Accuracy International; 299*t* Tomketchum; 300*t* Davric; 300*b* Armory TRUTH (http://russianguns.ru/); 301*b* SB2296; 302*t* Zachi Evenor and MathKnight; 303*t* Vitaly V. Kuzmin; 304*t* U.S. Marine Corps; 305*b* Rama; 306*b* Rishal Singh Bajaj; 307*t* Renard98; 307*b* SpetsnazAlpha; 309*b* Olegvolk.